50

12⁰⁰

THE
CLOSING
DOOR

THE
CLOSING
DOOR

Conservative Policy and
Black Opportunity

Gary Orfield and Carole Ashkinaze

With a Foreword by
Andrew Young

The University of Chicago Press
Chicago and London

Gary Orfield, professor of political science and education at the University of Chicago, is the author of numerous books and articles. He has often testified in Congress and in courts on issues of education and race. Carole Ashkinaze, who shared a Pulitzer Prize for investigative reporting at *Newsday*, covered politics and social issues for the *Atlanta Constitution* for thirteen years. She is now a member of the editorial board of the *Chicago Sun-Times*, in which her column regularly appears.

The University of Chicago Press, Chicago 60637
The University of Chicago Press, Ltd., London
© 1991 by The University of Chicago
All rights reserved. Published 1991
Printed in the United States of America
00 99 98 97 96 95 94 93 92 91   5 4 3 2 1

Library of Congress Cataloging-in-Publication Data

Orfield, Gary.
    The closing door: Conservative policy and black opportunity/
Gary Orfield and Carole Ashkinaze; with a foreword by Andrew
Young.
        p. cm.
    Includes bibliographical references and index.
    ISBN 0–226–63272–5 (acid-free paper)
    1. Afro-Americans—Georgia—Atlanta Region—Economic
conditions. 2. Atlanta Region (Ga.)—Economic conditions.
I. Ashkinaze, Carole. II. Title.
F294.A89N45 1991
330.9758'231043'08996073—dc20   90–48542
                                                    CIP

⊗ The paper used in this publication meets the minimum requirements of the American National Standard for Information Sciences—Permanence of Paper for Printed Library Materials, ANSI Z39.48-1984

Contents

Foreword

I get a little discouraged when I hear people say that things are no better, in some respects, than they were twenty-five years ago. It wasn't so long ago that black people did not have the right to eat at a lunch counter or sit in the front of a bus or attend a certain school in Atlanta, and the only thing that denied them those basic rights to public accommodations was the color of their skin. The first time I went to Atlanta, the Klan was marching down Hunter Street, and I was scared to stop there.

Today, blacks make up half of the police force and twenty percent of the force are female. We have more than 1,200 minority contractors involved in everything this city builds, whether it is a new Underground, a domed stadium, or an airport. During my administration, close to forty percent of city business was done with minority contractors—and I signed the checks. That's progress. That's change.

But if it is true that the obvious and outrageous wrongs of segregation—the ironies of African Americans with Ph.D.'s being denied the right to register to vote and the inconsistencies of wealthy black businessmen being sent to the back of the bus—have been righted, it must also be admitted that poverty claimed more victims in the 1980s than it did in the 1960s. It is time we understood what has been happening to these people, even as the brightest and most ambitious completed educations, bought houses, and took their places in the broad middle class. It is time we faced the forces that now threaten these gains, time we took stock and asked why.

The ranks of those with no hope of going to college, buying a home, or supporting their families are increasing even in Atlanta, which has one of the healthiest and fastest-growing economies of any metropolitan area in the entire country. The spoils are not being distributed equally. The schools are not preparing our children to take their place in an economy that desperately needs their labors and their contributions. This educational crisis has frightening implications for businesses, as well as for the young men and women who are dropping out of high school before they learn how to read, who do not even know how to apply for a job.

We are failing our young people and our poor in important ways, even though many of the institutions that once thwarted social progress—the school board, the mayor's office, the city council, the police department—are now headed by blacks. There is deep frustration, and much irony, in this realization; it is far easier to attack white institutions for their failures than it is to admit that local institutions are unable to solve the problems even when they are led by blacks.

But that is sometimes the case, and I think it is critical to social progress—and a sign of our maturity as elected officials and community leaders—that we can now say so, even if it also makes us vulnerable to criticism.

It is important to understand how little a mayor or a school superintendent can do about expanding opportunities to the truly needy in the face of federal cutbacks, taxpayer resistance, and hostile rulings from the Supreme Court. Mayors can change city hiring and contracting policies, but they have no jurisdiction over welfare, college scholarships, or many other social programs (such as Head Start and Chapter 1) that were very slightly funded by Lyndon Johnson but which nevertheless proved that suburbs and cities worldwide for new business investments.

So, while it is gratifying to discover that there are 458 black elected officials in Georgia, the conservative backlash of the last decade that ushered in the Reagan presidency has led to drastically reduced social programs, and that has meant less federal money for states and cities struggling with the awful consequences of hunger, homelessness, drug addiction, and deteriorating schools.

The time has also come, I think, for concerned leaders of every ethnic heritage to be more openly critical of themselves and of each other. There have been missteps and misjudgments on our parts, as on the parts of any elected officials, but we have been reluctant to say so. We must in order to understand where we are and move on.

For example, the civil rights movement was not aimed at ending poverty. It did not focus on economic issues; not because we didn't think economic issues were important, but because we didn't think we could win on economic issues. If you talked too much about class and poverty, you were characterized as a communist, therefore very few wanted to raise economic issues at that time. The primary battle in the 1950s and 1960s was to right the wrongs against a population that was already qualified and middle class, but was still denied the basic right to public accommodations in America. We set out to break down the color barriers for those who were exceptionally well qualified, and we succeeded.

But we always knew we would have to deal with poverty someday, just as the government had to deal with declining opportunity in the years following the Depression and well into World War II. We had a GI bill so that veterans who wanted an education could get an education; once a veteran had an education, he could buy a home at two and one-half or three percent interest. Very few loans, however, were made for new homes purchased by blacks, since the Veterans' Administration opposed financing mortgages in integrated areas. But those critical steps taken to stabilize the economic order were what created America's white middle class, what created our suburbs.

We did not press for economic equity when the pendulum seemed to be swinging our way. And under Ronald Reagan we went back to a kind of economic law of the jungle, in which the federal government withdrew from providing aid or enforcing minority rights while encouraging private industry to play a bigger role.

In an economy with enormous government debt and enormous trade deficits, it is unlikely that there will be money to create low- and moderate-income housing and to fully fund job training, educational, and other social programs (such as Head Start and Chapter 1) that were very slightly funded by Lyndon Johnson but which nevertheless proved that this nation could wipe out poverty if we continued to invest seriously in that goal. Under President Reagan we abandoned the struggle.

How do we get from here to a society where all men, women, and children can share equal justice and opportunity? How can we resolve this continuing dilemma? I'm not sure, but I do have a few ideas.

First, poverty cannot be wiped out as long as a significant portion of a population cannot obtain a quality education. There are no shortcuts to wealth and development. We must again assign top priority to investment in education, target funds for special efforts to help those at greatest risk

of exclusion from a productive life, and hold schools and colleges accountable for the way they serve the disadvantaged.

Second, we've got to give affirmative action a chance to work. We've
learned that in a free market economy, the more people we put into the
economy, the bigger the economy gets. Unfortunately, the conservatives
who have dominated the White House in the 1980s and the Rehnquist
Supreme Court don't understand that. They believe that if we have affirmative action and allow minorities to have a piece of the pie, we will be
depriving some of the majority and it is not so. When minorities use their
talents fully to produce for the economy, the market expands.

We have made economic progress nevertheless, especially in Atlanta.
And yet, as the disturbing picture that emerges in the following chapters
makes clear, the gap between our black citizens and our white citizens
has actually widened. The Reagan Supreme Court has threatened the
future of affirmative action policies that would open the economy to minorities and women. We do have a Congress that may be more responsive
to the people than the Supreme Court, and its task will be to define
affirmative action and discrimination in such a way that it's possible for
mayors, governors, and college presidents and administrators to realize
that including everybody is not only justice, it is good education, good
business, and good politics.

It's more than a southern dilemma now, it's even more than a national
dilemma for the underclass whose problems are so starkly portrayed in
this book. Poor blacks in Chicago, whites in the West Virginia mountains,
Puerto Ricans in New York, Mexican Americans in Los Angeles, and na-
tive Americans in the Dakotas are all suffering similar injuries from the
policies of the conservatives. Their economic needs must be seen as part
of the total struggle for freedom. I am very optimistic because I have seen
what a broad-based movement of well-educated, well-disciplined people
has already accomplished; I never would have believed we would have
come as far as we've come in my lifetime.

Finally, elected officials, white and black, are going to have to be more
accountable. During the first generation of black elected and appointed
leadership in a city, black leaders tend to stick together and to refrain
from criticizing one another. It is, of course, wrong to assume that merely
changing a leader's color will solve fundamental problems, though new
leaders often brought new priorities and understanding. However, all of
us must be willing to openly debate our strategies for serving poor as well
as middle-class constituencies and to learn from each other.

There is a long way to go and the path has become steeper since Reaganism pulled away the helping hand of government and cut hope for those most in need. But I think our goals can be accomplished. If there is a lesson to be learned from *The Closing Door*, it is that minority opportunity has waxed and waned in response to changes in public policy. People must understand the cost that our society has paid because of retrenchment in the areas of education and civil rights, and we must resolve to expand opportunity once more.

Andrew Young
Mayor of Atlanta, 1981–89
November 1989

Preface

The dream of equal opportunity is fading fast for many young blacks in metropolitan Atlanta, in spite of remarkably favorable local economic conditions and strong black political leadership. Many of the basic elements of the American dream—a good job, a decent income, a house, college education for the kids—are less accessible for young blacks than was the case in the mid-1970s.

In some respects, inner-city blacks face a worse situation a generation after Martin Luther King, Jr. set out the goals of the civil rights revolution in his sermons at Atlanta's Ebenezer Baptist Church. Their communities are poorer, more dangerous, and more hopeless. This is true even though one of Dr. King's closest associates, Andrew Young, sat behind the mayor's desk at City Hall in the 1980s, and many of Dr. King's dreams are now inscribed in the U.S. law books and in the decisions of the nation's courts. Even for those blacks who have achieved middle-class status, the opportunities in the area are very different from those available to whites.

The closing of the door of opportunity for young blacks in this booming metropolitan area is directly related to policy changes at several levels of government and to economic decisions made as if race were no longer a serious issue. Civil rights were achieved in the 1960s, the common argument goes, what is needed today is the dollar and the vote. With political power and money, blacks will be able to attain real equality.

Race, however, is still a fundamental issue in metropolitan Atlanta, not in the traditional southern sense, but in much the same way that it is fundamental in Detroit or Chicago. Blacks can vote, they can use hotels and restaurants, there are a few blacks on the white side of the color line within most white institutions and communities, and blacks hold real power in some institutions. Still, however, there is deep racial separation and there are great inequities between the lives of most blacks and most whites.

These problems did not get much attention in the 1980s, in part, because our federal government was dominated by leaders who simply denied their existence and radically cut back the gathering and distribution of relevant data. Much of white society today has neither experience of nor information about conditions in the ghettos. Many believe that civil rights laws have not only removed barriers for blacks but have actually discriminated against whites.

One of the primary goals of this book is to use the best available information, most of it from the vast computer banks of state, federal, and local governments, to bring the contrast between ghetto life and middle-class suburban opportunities into sharper focus.

Most blacks in the Atlanta area still live in segregated neighborhoods and send their children to separate and unequal schools. Many are more isolated from the mainstream of white middle-class society than was true a decade ago.

Most black influence is within the black community, which has become even poorer relative to the white community since the mid-1970s. The basic dynamics of both residential and business investments are working to make the separation more profound and its consequences worse. Wealth, jobs, newly constructed housing, and the best educational opportunities are moving farther and farther out into the overwhelmingly white part of suburbia. The powerful contemporary racial barriers, operating through the housing market and through unequal education attached to residential location, have not been significantly challenged.

The social and economic despair of the underclass residing in the core ghetto is devastating. To an extent that was not true even in the worst periods of Jim Crow laws, there are very large blacks areas where Depression-level joblessness is the norm in "good times," where few children are born into two-parent families, where the infant mortality rate is higher than in many Third World countries, and where people grow up with almost no real contact with middle-class role models, black or white.

Central-city black children have legal rights, but they have no real connection to the opportunity systems of the society. Atlanta's Hyatt Regency would welcome them if they had $125 a night for a room, but their families are terribly worried about being evicted again from dismal ghetto apartments because they can't pay $200 a month rent. Though their children need the most help if they are to have any chance, they have the least adequate schools, the most limited and impoverished local job markets, the most dangerous and disruptive neighborhoods, the worst health care, and the most tenuous knowledge of what it takes to make it in the mainstream.

Black children in the ghetto dream of becoming doctors and lawyers and astronauts, but they will grow up in communities where no one knows how to enter these professions. Their schools and other institutions are so profoundly isolated that they can grow up without understanding what society expects of them or what kind of academic achievement is necessary for success in college or in a major company. Many of those who do everything that is asked of them in their neighborhood schools are performing at a level below minimum suburban standards, but no one tells them. This will be crippling when they come in touch with institutions and employers outside the ghetto, where almost all the good jobs are.

Nor has the black middle class been fully accepted in the social and economic structure. An extremely high level of school and residential segregation has persisted in spite of massive black suburbanization. A large sector of the black middle class depends on public and nonprofit sector jobs serving low-income blacks—jobs threatened by government cutbacks. The black businesses created by the city's affirmative action programs are threatened by court decisions against minority set-asides. The decline in the number of blacks going to college deeply threatens the future of the middle class. Middle-class blacks still face serious racial barriers.

When American cities exploded in riots more than twenty years ago, it was obvious that something was seriously wrong. Social control evaporated suddenly and black rioters looted and burned down businesses in their own communities. While cities were burning, all the major black leaders and some sympathetic whites perceived a crisis and recommended major policy changes to open up real opportunities within metropolitan society. Martin Luther King, Jr. spoke of the hopelessness of young people growing up in the prison of the ghettos. President Lyndon Johnson urged the nation to open up possibilities to those whose lives had been crippled by isolation and inequality. In the mid-1960s, the 1964 Civil Rights Act and the Voting Rights Act attacked racism head-on.

The economic miseries of the urban ghetto, however, were hardly

touched. And the two great forces that might have tackled them foun-
dered: the civil rights movement was pulled apart by a fierce internal
argument over the merits of black power versus integration and the Great
Society liberals ran aground on the rocks of the Vietnam War.

Atlanta has been a place where new ideas about racial justice were
born and it is an important place to find out how they worked. It was in
Atlanta that the two great black leaders of the early twentieth century,
Booker T. Washington and W. E. B. DuBois, expressed their very different ideas about the road to black progress. Dr. King preached many of
the sermons that helped ignite first the civil rights movement and then
the peace movement in Atlanta. It was in Atlanta in the early 1970s that
his disciples decided after his death to drop the goal of school integration
and accept, in its place, black power over the city schools. This was a
crucial test of a new separate but equal strategy based on seizing power
within the ghetto. Atlanta leaders announced that this approach succeeded in the mid-1980s, but its success was very much in doubt as the
decade ended.

On a national level, the racial crisis became a nonissue for all but the
most conservative of politicians after the late 1960s. Liberals were only
beginning to seriously face urban racial issues when they lost political
power in Washington. Although they enacted their civil rights agenda to
abolish southern Jim Crow laws and succeeded in changing those aspects
of southern life, liberals lost the campaign for a policy of urban racial
integration. The policy did not fail; in cities like Atlanta, it was never
implemented.

Conservatives learned how to score breakthroughs by exploiting white
fears of black violence and white resistance to change and held the political initiative for a generation. For the first time, the Republican Party
became the dominant party of the white South in national elections. The
decisive shift of the South to Republican presidential candidates was a
symptom of the change, beginning with the 1968 election of Richard
Nixon on a "law and order," anti-civil-rights platform and reaching its high
point in the Reagan years. The Democratic party reacted to this racial
polarization by suppressing discussion of racial problems with the hope
of holding essential white support.

The sweep and consistency of the conservative policies of the early
1980s reflected an ideological purity that was rare in American politics.
Unlike the Great Society policies, which held clear sway only for a few
years before yielding to conservative resistance and the Vietnam War cri-

sis, the conservative impulse dominated federal policymaking for sixteen of the twenty years from 1968 to 1988. All of the judges named to the Supreme Court during that period were chosen by conservative Republican presidents who had attacked civil rights policies.

The conservative movement of the 1980s had a sweeping effect on state and local governments as well. When the federal government took the posture that educational standards had deteriorated and priority must be given to raising them, the states eagerly responded. They adopted stiffer public school graduation requirements and became more tolerant of resulting inequities. Few states had ever paid serious attention to civil rights policy, except when under direct federal pressure, and now many adopted policies that had the consequence of limiting opportunities for blacks.

It was during this period that some local school districts sought, with the Reagan Justice Department's encouragement, to throw off the "burdens" of the school desegregation orders they had been under for a decade or more. During this period the movement to decentralize subsidized housing in the white suburbs virtually disappeared. In fact, programs to build subsidized housing for families anywhere were shut down. Welfare payments dropped by more than one-third in constant value dollars and work requirements were imposed on low-income mothers. Many social programs were curtailed.

Although conservative analysts often blame urban social problems on a long period of what they describe as liberal dominance, it was actually an era of conservative dominance and we are now in a position to analyze its effects. Liberals committed to civil rights reform controlled the national agenda only from 1963 to 1965; since Hubert Humphrey's defeat in 1968, except for one brief interlude, conservatives have controlled the federal executive branch. And the only Democratic administration took a moderate position on racial and social policy issues, offering few new initiatives. U.S. policies on welfare, crime, urban school desegregation, housing, and other issues became increasingly conservative during this period. The studies in this book show that the conservative assumptions have not worked and that they have caused a severe shrinkage of opportunities for young blacks.

Showing the negative effects of conservative policies is not, of course, proof that the old liberal policies were adequate. There was never, for example, anything like equal education or housing for blacks and whites in the metropolitan Atlanta area. The increasingly clear evidence that policies such as Head Start preschool programs and integrated education have benefits does not mean that they could, by themselves, end racial gaps. The employment and income situation of blacks was always profoundly unequal.

But, since the 1960s, the elective branches of government have been generally hostile to any attempt to attack the urban color lines or to redistribute opportunities to blacks in segregated and unequal training institutions.

There were some gains made in institutions in the 1980s, which show up in portions of the book. Genuine progress was made through the early 1980s, for example, by the Atlanta Public Schools' effort to toughen policies on attendance and dropouts. There were signs of progress in the early grades in inner-city schools. The economic growth following the 1981–82 recession reduced black joblessness. There were far fewer entirely white neighborhoods or schools than there once had been. The most prestigious white colleges had become more open to black students even while the doors were closing elsewhere. The existence of some positive trends in a very negative period is an important indication that more positive outcomes are possible with supportive policies.

Too often, however, whites take these limited breakthroughs as proof that racial problems have been solved and ignore the fact that, for many blacks, conditions have actually deteriorated.

As this book demonstrates, major changes are necessary if there is to be real opportunity for blacks. It identifies the awful economic and social costs of the long-term conservative experiment and raises nearly forgotten questions about the ghetto and the color line. It also outlines the steps that will be necessary to revive the forward momentum lost in the 1980s and to make the rhetoric of equal opportunity under the law a reality in metropolitan Atlanta and in the rest of urban America.

Acknowledgments

This book grew out of a large project studying the changing patterns of opportunities for white and minority youths growing up in five of the nation's largest urban communities. Obtaining and analyzing large and complex sets of data from a wide variety of sources in each area is a vast enterprise, completely beyond the reach of an individual researcher. This book reflects the work of many people.

Much of the data in this book was drawn from a series of working papers prepared for the Metropolitan Opportunity Project. These papers were released in metropolitan Atlanta during the course of the study and the public debate greatly aided the final stages of this study. The authors and their topics are as follows: Helene Slessarev, Job Training; Faith Paul, College Access; June Patton, Black Men in College; Larry Peskin, High School Attrition and Achievement; and James Fossett, Rental Housing. In addition, James Krusenoski prepared another background paper for the project, "Race and Homeownership in Atlanta, 1975–1982," which includes the logit analysis discussed in the chapter on housing.

Copies of the original papers can be obtained from the Metropolitan Opportunity Project, Gary Orfield, Director, University of Chicago, Chicago 60637.

Earlier versions of some parts of this study or including some of the Atlanta data developed for the overall project appeared in different form in the following publications: Helene Slessarev, "JTPA as a Mobility Program in Metropolitan Atlanta," *Evaluation Forum*, no. 2 (1987); Gary Orfield and Faith Paul, "Declines in Minority Access: A Tale of Five Cities," *Educational Record* 68, no. 4 (Fall 1987/Winter 1988); Faith Paul, "Access to College in a Public Policy Environment Supporting Both Opportunity and Selectivity," *American Journal of Education* 98, no. 4 (August 1990); Gary Orfield and Lawrence Peskin, "Metropolitan High Schools: Income, Race, and Inequality," in Douglas E. Mitchell and Margaret E. Goertz, *Education Politics for the New Century* (London: Falmer Press, 1990).

This book is not a compilation of the working papers, though they were very important. The editing, the addition of substantial new material in most chapters, all work on three chapters, the final writing of all chapters, and the judgments reached in the book are the responsibility of the co-authors.

This project was greatly aided by the generous support and understanding of two foundations. Much of the Atlanta research and editing was supported by grants from the Southern Education Foundation in Atlanta. The larger project was created by a grant from the Spencer Foundation, which supported much of the analytic work. The Institute of Government at the University of Illinois also provided resources for the housing analysis in this book. The study was greatly enriched by insights from the work of the Metropolitan Opportunity Project in other cities. This work would have been impossible without the cooperation of many government and educational agencies in Georgia and Washington in providing data that was essential for the analysis. We also relied on the assistance of community organizations and scholars in Atlanta, as well as the families interviewed. The library of *The Atlanta Journal and Constitution* was extremely helpful in our work. We appreciate the support of our colleagues at the University of Chicago, *The Atlanta Constitution*, and the *Chicago Sun-Times*, in particular Diane Hunter, Tom Bennett, and Tom Teepen.

Across the greater Atlanta area we found people deeply concerned about the patterns of shrinking opportunity for blacks in the region. They included many people who believed that their own institutions must do more. They were generous with their time and their advice. In the midst of what remains a deeply conservative part of the country, there were many people who were very uneasy with the bland assumption of the 1980s that everything would work out. We believe that when the nation's attention again turns to the unfulfilled social agenda that there will be many in Atlanta ready to contribute to opening up the door of opportunity.

1

Opportunity in Metropolitan Atlanta: Going Backward in the 1980s

The triumphs of the civil rights movement swept away the web of state laws mandating racial segregation in many aspects of life in seventeen states, but its successes were largely limited to the elimination of Jim Crow laws. When it tried to eliminate ghettos, it failed.

Martin Luther King, Jr. turned back from his last major effort, the Chicago campaign to integrate white neighborhoods, without piercing a system of racial containment he came to see as much more deeply rooted than the southern system of segregation laws. The country turned away in the 1970s and 1980s from King's vision and from the warning of a presidential commission in 1968 that we were building "separate and unequal" urban societies that would threaten the stability of our entire society. Tacitly, both parties embraced the hope that either racism was no longer a serious problem or that black leadership and economic growth would solve the problem indirectly.

This book shows, however, that even under the very favorable economic and political conditions of Atlanta in the 1980s, the basic reality was still one of schools that did not function, of families unable to get to jobs from isolated inner-city communities, and of black men burning with the frustration of never earning enough to support a family. It was still a world of white realtors pretending that fair housing was operating in housing markets where segregation was visible everywhere and discrimination was easily detectable. It was a community with more powerful black officials but less help for college training or good job training for young blacks.

King spoke of the despair and depression of ghetto life, calling the ghetto a "reservation" and a "prison" and pointing out that "even the new

1

Negro middle class often finds itself in ghettoized housing and jobs at the mercy of the white world" (King, 1968, 141). King said, in the title of the book published the year before he died, that we must choose between a future of "chaos" or one of genuine "community." This study shows that we have moved away from the idea of a community of equal opportunity and that the political and economic solutions are not working.

Close analysis of the most important city of the South is of utmost significance because change in the South has been seen as particularly remarkable under the dual stimuli of the Voting Rights Act and the economic boom of the Sun Belt. And some of the most optimistic reports have come from Atlanta, home of a number of the nation's most prominent and effective black business and government leaders. A substantial black return migration to the South, beginning in the 1970s, seemed to verify that equal opportunity had been achieved.

But this optimism never has been fully justified, and the statistical evidence on young blacks growing up in metropolitan Atlanta since the mid-1970s—presented here, and in the ensuing chapters, for the first time—tells a startlingly different story.

Our research shows not only that full equality of opportunity has eluded Atlanta, but that some of the gains made during the civil rights era are eroding rapidly. It shows that educational systems are no longer closing the gaps between whites and blacks and that there are profound differences between the schools that correlate with race. After strong earlier improvement, the number of city dropouts rose in the mid-1980s, especially among young black men. College access has declined sharply. And the Reagan federal job training program, designed to give the unemployed a second chance, focused not on education's failures, the hardcore unemployed, but, rather, on job-ready applicants who would be easy to train and place. State and local administrators reinforced those federal policies. The programs gave the appearance of success by ignoring those most likely to fail without training (Orfield and Slessarev 1986).

None of these trends was inevitable, and most were reversals of previously favorable trends. Some were caused by stiffer requirements for graduation from high school; others by changing college fees and financial aid structures. Still others reflected policy changes and cutbacks in appropriations for job training. All took place within a system of residential segregation by race and income and rapid dispersion of opportunity into wealthy outer suburbs.

Many of these policy changes were attributable to neoconservative ideas popularized by the administration of President Ronald Reagan and embraced by state and local officials who had similar goals or who were responding to similar political currents. These policies directly challenged and ultimately reversed the commitment of some previous administrations to expanding equal opportunity and assuring equal protection under the law.

This book has three broad objectives: first, to document the impact of those policies; second, to contribute to the national debate on the role of government in addressing social problems, a debate dominated in recent years by conservatives; and, third, to test some of the basic theories about the causes and solutions of contemporary black urban problems in recent research.

The root assumption of educational and social policy in the 1980s was that government could do little to produce social progress and that liberal reforms had unanticipated consequences that made a bad situation worse. Economic growth and the market mechanism, on the other hand, were seen as the only workable solutions for social problems. The evidence from Atlanta directly challenges those views.

The sharp declines in opportunities under conservative policies show that policies make a difference. The market did not solve inequities even during a long period of rapid growth. In fact, there is substantial evidence of separate and racially defined markets and increasing inequality as is shown in chapters 3 through 7.

The long-term trends in the urban markets were not benign. A basic reason why the value of liberal reforms was underestimated until they were reversed was that their positive effects were partially offset by long-time negative market trends in jobs and housing for urban blacks, even as the suburbs boomed. Even if a training program, for example, greatly increased the employability of a group of inner-city blacks for the electronics industry, its effect could be negated by electronics firms moving to inaccessible white suburbs, moves that were often subsidized by conservative economic development policies (Kasarda 1987; Chicago Urban League 1990).

After energizing the reform movement of the 1960s, liberalism was itself challenged by a rising conservative movement and by disaffected liberals who styled themselves "neoconservatives." During the last twenty years, ideas from the old and the new conservatives have dominated national policy and have played an important role in driving the issues of civil rights and urban policy off the national agenda.

The idea that government has both the responsibility and the power to make opportunities more equal in a highly stratified society, a central driving goal of the Great Society, gave way to the belief that government had gone as far as it could. The hope for a solution, if there was one, was transferred to the market. If the economy could expand sufficiently, by unleashing private capitalism, the jobs and income created would provide new opportunities. The savings would go into job-creating investments, not paternalistic services, and produce an economic boom that would put low-income minority people to work. Welfare cuts and work requirements would increase the incentive to work, and freezing the minimum wage for nearly a decade would lower the cost to employers of hiring more workers. Since neither liberals nor conservatives were happy with the operation of the existing systems of welfare, public housing, or urban schools, it was not difficult for the conservatives to seize the initiative in important areas of policy. Now it is time to find out how their ideas worked in practice.

Why Atlanta?

Atlanta is an ideal place to assess the changing patterns because it has all the basic ingredients for rapid black progress—if it is true that the explicitly racial social problems have been largely solved. Atlanta was so very successful in economic opportunity and black empowerment, and Georgia had such a vestigial welfare system, that it is something of a limiting case. If economic expansion and a tight labor market could create equal opportunity without targeted government action, it should have happened in the Atlanta area. If these theories didn't work in Atlanta, it is very doubtful that they will have application elsewhere.

Metropolitan Atlanta had a long, deep, and very large economic boom beginning in the mid-1970s. During the first half of the 1980s, the metropolitan area job-growth rate was much faster than the national and state averages. It was a major employment growth center for the South. Some parts of the outer suburbs had a growth rate of more than 500 percent from 1980 to 1985 (see chapter 3).

The Atlanta area is also a center of black power, with two nationally prominent black mayors running the city for more than a decade and with a great many prominent and successful black businessmen and professionals. Many national leaders of the civil rights movement remain active in Atlanta and its black community can draw on the unique intellectual resources of four black colleges, the Martin Luther King, Jr. Center for Nonviolent Social Change, and other institutions.

With a carefully cultivated national image as the "city too busy to hate," Atlanta has been celebrated as a black Mecca, where the doors are open and a critical mass of black leadership already exists. Atlanta's first black mayor, Maynard Jackson, expressed this in his frequent public promises to give minorities "a piece of the pie." (Jackson was elected again in 1989 to succeed Andrew Young.) The number of substantial black firms grow rapidly under the minority set-aside contracting policies of the city government. If economic growth and black political leadership were sufficient to resolve racial differences in the 1980s, tremendous mobility for the region's poor blacks should have taken place in spite of the conservative social and civil rights policies of the Reagan administration.

Indeed, some blacks made it. On average, however, the situation of the black population relative to whites became significantly worse in very important respects. Even those blacks who were able to obtain resources to move to the suburbs usually found themselves in different suburbs with fewer opportunities.

The beginning of the boom period saw the last vestiges of policies styled after Great Society liberalism. These reached their high point in the first years of President Jimmy Carter's administration. Carter, however, initiated cutbacks in his final years and 1981 ushered in the Reagan administration, the most ideologically conservative administration since the 1920s. State and local officials adopted many conservative policies in the late 1970s and 1980s. California's tax-limiting Proposition 13 in 1978 was a signal of a dramatic turn to the right. Conservative assumptions about the uselessness of social programs, the error of race-conscious civil rights policies, the need for rigid controls on poor people, the need for tougher standards in schools and colleges, and the primacy of the private market spread through many areas of policy. Such dramatic about-faces in social policy have seldom been effected in so short a period of time.

The policies and the sweeping economic changes brought by the emergence of a service-centered, suburban-dominated economy had highly visible impacts on Atlanta. The changes were particularly dramatic in areas dominated by the federal government: housing, job training, civil rights policy, and federal scholarship assistance. There were also important parallel changes in school and college reforms adopted by local and state officials, reforms of a type strongly advocated by the Reagan administration's education officials.

The rapid turn from the early Carter policies to intense conservativism in close sequence, against a backdrop of solid growth of local markets, gives us an unusual opportunity to examine the accuracy of the conservative assumptions. As the economy grew and government receded, opportunities should have increased for blacks.

The most underutilized source of labor should have experienced rapid mobility as new jobs mushroomed. Instead, the new jobs drew in huge numbers of white outsiders and the racial income gap grew.

THE DATA

The studies that follow required the collection and analysis of vast bodies of statistics and other information from state, local, and federal agencies: school-by-school enrollment and graduation statistics for all high schools since 1971 from the Georgia State Archives; thousands of pages of computer printouts on public colleges and universities obtained under a Freedom of Information request from the Office of Civil Rights of the U.S. Department of Education; higher education computer data tapes from the Center for Education Statistics; computer tapes from the U.S. Census Bureau's Annual Housing Surveys; special tabulations of state data from the state job training agency, the state department of education, and the university system; and reports from other agencies. Individual researchers worked for months on drafts of each of the chapters, developing ways of interpreting the information and submitting it to local officials and experts for comments and corrections. The authors and several of the researchers also questioned Atlanta officials about the impact of the broad social trends they observed on the lives of blacks and whites living in metropolitan Atlanta. The study is intended to help fill a vacuum caused by the drastic reduction of racial data and research produced by the federal government in the 1980s.

DECLINING KNOWLEDGE OF MINORITY OPPORTUNITY

Research and policy debates take place within a context of popular ideas, available information, and the predominant ideologies. In the contemporary United States, concern for civil rights violations has abated in part because less information is being produced and circulated about them. We actually know less about the current problems of blacks than we did a decade ago. A massive National Academy of Sciences study of the status of black Americans reported in 1989 that the study "had to cope with gaps and other inadequacies in the data, even for basic descriptive tasks. Recent changes in the collection and reporting of statistical data by federal agencies, and proposed changes in the national census, may seriously limit the information needed for analyzing demographic, social, and economic changes over time" (Jaynes and Williams 1989, 567). Among the steps taken in the 1980s to limit such data were the elimination of racial data in subsidized housing in the early 1980s, reduction of data collection and a virtual end of analysis of the racial composition of American public schools, the dissolution of the National Institute of Education staff and advisory committee working on desegregation and racial issues, the ending of funding for the major federally supported research center working on such issues, the Center on the Social Organization of Schools at Johns Hopkins, and many other changes. Government and educational institutions in a position to produce or demand information often have a vested interest in creating an impression that things are working out.

Research agendas and research funding tend to follow changes in public opinion closely and to reflect administration views. The Reagan administration discouraged studies of racial issues; thus, the flood of information on urban minorities that was produced in the 1960s slowed to a trickle in the 1980s. Private philanthropy, with few exceptions, tended to move in the same direction as the government.

The late 1960s' prophecies of dangerous racial separation have given way to a vague hope that racial inequalities are being resolved, perhaps through the election of black officials. Many blacks have reached positions of local power, such as mayor, county commission chairman or superintendent of schools, positions undreamed of thirty years ago. But these achievements do not necessarily produce success for blacks as a whole. In fact, they may contribute to our lack of knowledge about low-income blacks. Black officials, like their white predecessors, tend to publicize successes, not problems. Moreover, while it was considered anti-black to ignore institutional failings when these institutions were headed by whites, some now see it as anti-black to call attention to failings in institutions headed by blacks. Today, black-controlled bureaucracies may hesitate to disclose vital information about damage caused by federal and state policy rather than risk being blamed for the results.

Then, too, as central-city schools, colleges, and other institutions cease serving primarily white populations, the dominant white media may lose interest in close critical examination of their performance. These institutions no longer matter to whites and the media may be afraid of charges of racism by black administrators if they are too critical. Reporters often lack the technical training to challenge the bureaucracy's interpretation of its own performance. In metropolitan Atlanta, for example, the press uncritically reported extremely misleading test scores from the overwhelmingly black Atlanta public schools for years until the state government forced the release of accurate data. The city and suburban dropout rates were radically underestimated and virtually no local information was produced on the declining rate of access to college for black Atlantans (see chapters 5 and 6).

The community was happy to assume that the problems had been solved. When the black middle class follows whites out of city institutions, outside attention to the performance of ghetto institutions becomes even more limited. This pattern of unrealistic information and rhetoric of racial solidarity may be a temporary stage in the consolidation of black political and administrative power—a stage that is now coming to an end.

Many politicians and researchers reacted to the conservative victories of the 1980s by avoiding discussion of racial issues. Thus, the great number of whites personally isolated from poor blacks were less and less likely to get that information elsewhere.

The growing lack of direct personal knowledge puts a special burden on government to provide accurate and credible information so that people can reach informed judgments. However, when the Reagan administration came to Washington, there was a sharp decline in the collection and dissemination of data about racial problems and a continuous, high-pitched ideological attack by government officials on social programs and civil rights policies. The Education Department, the Department of Housing and Urban Development, and the Civil Rights Commission sharply curtailed research and data collection on racial problems. The National Institute of Education disbanded its Desegregation Study Group of experts from across the country, ended its research program, and hired a busing critic to write position papers for newspapers attacking busing (Schneider 1982).

The country had come to rely on the federal government's statistical offices, federally funded research, and federal civil rights monitoring and enforcement offices for basic information about racial issues—but much of that information was no longer being collected. In its place came an active disinformation campaign by Reagan administration agency heads opposed to busing and affirmative action. During the 1980s this was particularly true of the Justice Department and the U.S. Commission on Civil Rights. Both Assistant Attorney General William Bradford Reynolds and Commission Chairman Clarence Pendleton became famous for their sweeping attacks on Great Society initiatives and civil rights groups. The Civil Rights Commission stopped producing information on the extent of racial problems and on the need for more civil rights enforcement by the federal government, focusing instead on efforts to undermine pay equity, affirmative action, and school desegregation (Citizens Commission on Civil Rights 1989).

The decline in information meant that it was possible for large changes to take place almost undetected since no private institution could match the data collection capabilities of the federal government. At the same time that information on civil rights activity dried up, civil rights advances were halted and social programs that supported low-income minority families were slashed (Palmer and Sawhill 1984). There were little data to illustrate the consequences of these policy changes. The Reagan administration merely asserted that these programs were too expensive and no longer necessary and wiped out the federal data collection that could be used to examine those claims. When federal programs were eliminated, no one kept data on what happened to their former beneficiaries.

State and local governments often had no racial data apart from what they had been required to collect by the federal government. They almost never examined the racial impact of major policy changes. Thus, the sweeping reforms of the "excellence" movement in public schools, the rising college admission standards, and the declining resources in many programs were not studied for their racial consequences.

But the impact of many policy changes can be measured through untabulated and unpublished data that still exist inside many bureaucracies at several levels of government. Racial data are statistically combined with data on other issues. A great deal of this data is assembled and analyzed in the ensuing chapters.

In a number of important ways, this work is only possible because we are now in the era when government records are computerized and low-cost computing makes possible analysis of issues on a scale that was previously not feasible.

This book is the result, and it is the largest effort to date to study opportunity in metropolitan Atlanta. In fact, no comparable studies for any metropolitan area were published in the 1980s.

STRENGTHS AND LIMITS OF THE DATA

The data used in this book are very different from the data used in most national studies of black mobility, and the kinds of statistics reported here are not the same as those studies use. Most national studies rely on surveys—random samples of the national population or of a subgroup, such as students of a particular age. Most of the data on high schools and colleges in the 1980s, for example are based on a big national survey of the high school classes graduating in 1980 and 1982 called "High School and Beyond" or on yearly surveys of the entire population, such as the Census Bureau's Current Population Survey.

Surveys have great strengths, particularly a survey like "High School and Beyond," which follows the same sample over a six-year period. Surveys provide data at the individual level, provide information about plans, and enable researchers to look at the relationships between a number of possible causes of a problem over time.

Surveys also have serious limitations. They are extremely expensive, particularly when they follow people over the years. Sampling may produce errors and there must be statistical controls for the possibility of error. A statement in a survey-based research report that 35 percent of residents of inner-city black neighborhoods had serious housing problems could be shorthand for a real finding that it is highly probable that between 29 percent and 41 percent of residents in the neighborhood had such problems. Unless the sample was very large, the survey could probably support no statistically valid statement about housing of a particular group, such as black suburban women.

Very little good quality survey data exist for individual metropolitan areas because the money has not been available to collect such data. The samples for the national studies do not permit the data to be broken down to the local levels. Surveys can only validly explore populations included in the initial sample design and often can say nothing about very important questions which were not apparent when the survey was designed. The surveys are on such a high level of generalization that it is very difficult to understand the specific role being played by different institutions.

The data used in much of this study are not surveys but the official records of various major institutions and governments. When we report the trends in black enrollment at the four-year colleges, or the number of black women trained for a particular kind of job, for example, the data come from the actual official records, from the agencies' own data tapes. This is not a sample, it is the total population. The tape may include a million cases while an unusually large survey for a state would include two thousand. There is no problem of sampling error since all cases, rather than a sample, are examined by the computer. Since the data comprise the total population, they can be broken down several times, for example, to look only at black men in two-year inner-city colleges without statistical problems. Very specific local analyses can be done.

The actual data tapes also have limitations, which is why we have not used them exclusively and also draw on survey data, particularly in the housing chapter. Official records consist primarily of data on what actually happened and cannot describe motivation. The data tend to cover fewer issues than surveys and rarely follow individuals over time. Sometimes the agencies do not provide information on what seem to be the most obvious questions, such as what percent of junior college students came wanting to transfer and what percent are enrolled in a vocational program. The data are not appropriate for the sophisticated statistical modeling now used in social science research to try to assess causation.

The approach of this book, and of the related Metropolitan Opportunity Project studies in four other metropolitan areas, is to take advantage of the vast amount of official records that exist and to use them to show the broad outlines of the changing pattern of opportunities, thereby pinpointing the institutions where the changes were most substantial and the groups of people whose prospects were shrinking most rapidly. This study cannot answer all the questions of causation, but it can describe, in far greater detail, the broad processes of social change and the changing roles of various policies and agencies. When large changes in black access occur right after a major policy was changed, these findings permit a reasonable inference that the new policy had an effect. When possible, the findings in Atlanta have been checked against findings in the other areas studied in the Metropolitan Opportunity Project and national survey data, lending strength to the conclusions when all these sources show similar patterns.

BASIC FINDINGS

The evidence supports several conclusions of the greatest importance for the next phase of American social policy:

First, very serious racial barriers remain a generation after the civil rights laws were passed, and conditions are worsening in some basic respects.

Second, the market cannot by itself solve the social, economic, and educational problems of urban America even if economic growth is exuberant and continuous. When markets are segregated, growth can have perverse effects, increasing inequality.

Third, opportunities were significantly greater in some vital ways for the poor—particularly for low-income blacks—under the less conservative administrations of the 1970s.

Fourth, black control of central-city governments and educational institutions cannot in and of itself solve these deeply rooted problems, though it is important in other ways. City governments play a very limited role in many of the key policy issues affecting opportunity for young people, and black mayors are under great economic pressure to follow conservative economic development policies to retain business in the city.

Fifth, in the urban societies of the future, equal opportunity for blacks must mean access to opportunity in white suburban areas. Blacks in Atlanta are rapidly suburbanizing but are missing many of the benefits that came to white suburbanites because they are concentrated in less successful, racially changing suburbs. It is time to look very carefully at the effects of the color lines developing in the suburbs.

Sixth, there are powerful relationships between residential segregation and the quality of education, the quality of housing, the availability of jobs, and income level.

Residential segregation remains a fundamental underlying feature of urban racial inequality in this period after the abolition of the old system of de jure racial discrimination. Although it is now illegal for the government to treat blacks and whites differently, extremely different levels of education are routinely provided to predominantly black and white communities and maintained by residential separation. It is particularly easy to discriminate when black and white areas are separated by municipal and school district boundaries. A wide variety of public and private institutions treat these black and white communities differently, producing consequences that may be as severe as those produced by de jure segregation. If the basic findings of this study are correct, successful social policy will have to have a racial as well as an economic dimension recognizing the impact of the highly segregated metropolitan society. Separate urban societies remain profoundly unequal and a policy seeking greater equality must directly attack the color line and its continuing consequences.

The level of residential segregation in metropolitan Atlanta is very high and has not improved significantly since the enactment of the federal fair housing law. In 1980, one study accorded metropolitan Atlanta the highest level of residential separation of whites from blacks of any metropolitan area in the South (see chapter 3). Recent tests in Atlanta show widespread continuing discrimination in the housing market.

The Broader Implications of the Study

The broad conclusions about Atlanta directly challenge some basic conclusions in the most widely influential recent studies of black opportunity. Probably the most widely read intellectual justification for the Reagan administration's approach to black opportunity came in Charles Murray's book, *Losing Ground*. Murray was the leading neoconservative dealing with the effect of social policy on urban blacks. He argued that the cause of the problems of the black community was the expansion of welfare and other liberal programs and that the best way out was to dismantle existing social policies and increase the incentive for socially and economically productive lives for black families. Others, including Nathan Glazer, led the attack on color-conscious civil rights remedies including affirmative action and school busing (Glazer 1975). The movement was built around several propositions: (1) that change is very complex; (2) that there are often negative and unanticipated consequences of well-intended reform efforts; (3) that things will get better if government stops trying to intervene and the market is left to operate on its own; and (4) that inequality arises not from prejudice or institutional inequities but primarily from lack of aspiration and cultural deficiencies which are often exacerbated by governmental paternalism. These principles were central themes of the administrations of Presidents Ronald Reagan and George Bush.

Perhaps the most significant answer to the neoconservatives was William J. Wilson's 1987 book, *The Truly Disadvantaged*. Wilson, a preeminent black sociologist, responded that the basic causes were the isolation of lower-class blacks and the transformation of the economy. He argued that the best approach toward a solution was a policy of increasing jobs and creating tight labor markets, opening opportunities for blacks. Wilson did not see severe problems for middle-class blacks. He favored broad-based social policies that were not race-specific.

Wilson spelled out the political implications of his analysis of the problem in a 1990 article. He called for "new policies to fight inequality that differ from court-ordered busing, affirmative action programs and anti-discrimination lawsuits of the recent past." He recommended that the Democratic party try to form a coalition behind "race neutral programs such as full employment strategies, jobs skills training, comprehensive health care, reforms in the public schools," and others (Wilson 1990, 74). Wilson argued that civil rights policies had mostly helped the black middle class but that broad economic and educational policies, which had no specific focus at all on race, would produce larger benefits for low-income blacks.

Another widely shared idea was that the problems in the cities were basically the result of the racism of white officials and that many could be solved by the black mayors, school superintendents, policemen, and teachers who were displacing white ones. The 1965 Voting Rights Act embodied this hope of empowerment through representation as did the black power movement and the campaigns of many of the black candidates for office. The hope was that black political and educational leaders would be able to make large moves toward racial equity simply by devising policies and practices reflecting their understanding of the background and needs of black people. This theme permeated the struggle for black representation, the black power and community control theories of the 1960s and early 1970s, and was still very much present in the Atlanta of the 1980s. It was particularly evident in discussions about black control of the Atlanta schools.

If either Murray's or Wilson's analysis were correct, or if the argument about black political leadership was accurate, there should have been major progress for blacks in Atlanta in the 1980s. Government did withdraw. Very low welfare payments fell further in real value, diminishing financial incentive for welfare dependency. Law enforcement became more harsh and young blacks faced a high probability of imprisonment for crimes. With less government assistance and no visible civil rights enforcement, low-income black families had every incentive to become self-reliant. If white businesses had responded to their growing need for labor by reaching out for the black workers already in the labor market, their situation should have improved greatly. Murray's theory cannot explain what happened.

The period also tested the most important prescription of Wilson's book. It was a period of tight labor markets; jobs grew much more rapidly than the metropolitan area's population. The job growth in the greater Atlanta region probably exceeded that which could ever be expected in a similar period on the national level. It should have been much more efficient economically to hire blacks already living in the area than for firms to bring in workers from somewhere else.

This study does support Wilson's findings about the extremely negative consequences of the profound racial and economic isolation developing in the inner city. The evidence is abundant that the residents of the isolated high-poverty areas are fundamentally cut off from opportunity for an equal education or employment.

This analysis differs, however, from Wilson's in two vital respects. First, it finds problems of racial isolation and discrimination much more important not only for poor blacks but also for those in the working class and much of the middle class. Second, it argues that because of the consequences of racial segregation, unequal opportunity and discrimination, the nonracial solution of tight labor markets is not likely to work as expected. Increasing demand for workers did not increase the relative income of black families. The supply of labor is not fixed, information about jobs does not travel well across entire metro areas, and the distribution of added income is not necessarily equitable.

Prosperity drew in many workers from outside, many of whom did much better than the blacks already in the city. In an open and mobile society, local tight labor markets are very likely to have such effects. On a national level, changes in labor force participation and large-scale immigration would undermine the benefits of a nontargeted tight labor market strategy on black employment and income, even if inflation could be contained. For example, more suburban women would enter the job market if the suburban economy expanded. And, this project's forthcoming reports on metropolitan Los Angeles will show that much of the extraordinary growth of that region has redounded to the benefit of workers coming from outside the United States.

Wilson's work strongly deemphasizes the racial problems faced by middle-class blacks and sees isolation primarily as a problem of the inner-city "underclass" population. This study finds the vast majority of blacks in metropolitan Atlanta in segregated neighborhoods and schools, reflecting, in part, a very large pattern of segregated suburbanization. It reports evidence of continuing racial discrimination in housing and in mortgage lending. In a society where the maintenance of middle-class status is strongly dependent upon the provision of college education for the next generation, it shows sharp declines in college access. We estimate that racial barriers directly affect and harm a much larger portion of the black population than is suggested in Wilson's work.

This analysis is closer in some important respects to that of Georgia

Tech black economist Thomas Daniel Boston in *Race, Class and Conservatism*, which concluded that racial discrimination was still powerfully related to the unequal job status of blacks (Boston 1988, 3).

Blacks are overwhelmingly confined to low-status low-paying jobs with no established career ladders and with a great deal of job instability. Even controlling for levels of education, experience, and tenure, there is still this concentration of blacks in secondary jobs. (*Atlanta Journal and Constitution*, 13 February 1989)

Boston saw affirmative action as critical to the success of blacks and felt "very, very pessimistic" about the combination of a conservative federal government with a Supreme Court which was reducing black rights, particularly affecting affirmative action (ibid.).

These differences in analysis imply a need for different remedies. General policies of the sort advocated by Wilson would no doubt be beneficial to both blacks and many whites, were they politically feasible. Even with such policies, and, certainly, in the absence of them, however, this study shows a need for attempts to break down the color line and for race-conscious efforts to remedy past and present discrimination for a very large part of the black population. Unlike the blacks in central Chicago studied in Wilson's work, those in Atlanta have lived in the midst of an area of vibrant growth and many opportunities. They still need an assist to vault the walls of racial separation and unequal treatment.

The Findings and the Nature of Contemporary Discrimination

In the period from 1975 to the early 1980s, the gaps between city and suburban average income and between white and black income actually grew in metropolitan Atlanta. After a long decline, high school dropout rates rose in the mid-1980s and the gap between the city and the suburban rates grew. College access, the key to adult success in most professions, declined rapidly for blacks and rose for whites after 1980. The predicament of young black males in schools and colleges became particularly acute.

Black children became even more segregated in public schools, and inner-city black communities continued to have unequal housing and job opportunities. Housing prices soared faster than income, and development of new subsidized housing virtually stopped. Neither the economic expansion, nor the existence of black leadership, nor the fact that some blacks had crossed traditional racial lines were sufficient to bring down deeply rooted racial barriers for most blacks.

In the 1980s, the color line was still a prominent factor in metropolitan Atlanta; merely knowing the racial composition of an area was enough to predict many other vital aspects of local conditions with dismaying accuracy. The areas of most rapid growth in jobs and the highest-scoring schools, for example, were overwhelmingly concentrated in segregated white areas in the outer suburbs, which are not accessible from black communities, while the worst economic and school conditions were in the areas heavily populated by blacks.

From 1980 to 1985, the five predominantly black regions had a less than five-percent rate of job growth while the seven regions within metropolitan Atlanta with a greater than ninety percent white population had an average growth rate more than fourteen times higher. Nearer the center of the booming metropolis there are still areas that continue to lose jobs. They are usually predominantly black communities (see chapter 3).

HOUSING: PERPETUATION OF THE GHETTO AND DETERIORATING CONDITIONS

Atlanta has a racially defined dual housing market that leaves many middle-class blacks in housing that is worse than that occupied by poor whites and which channels those who leave the city into suburbs isolated from the best schools and the greatest economic growth. Recent studies show that discrimination remained severe in the late 1980s and that lending institutions were providing little mortgage money to black neighborhoods. Blacks faced an increasingly severe housing cost crisis even as prosperity grew in the overall region.

Even during a period of great overall expansion, the economic gap between whites and blacks widened and the concentration of poor families in the central city ghetto increased substantially. Between 1970 and 1982, a period of enormous population increases for metro Atlanta, the percent of central city households that were poor doubled. By the early 1980s, families living below the poverty level in either the city or the suburbs paid two-thirds or more of their cash income for housing (see chapter 3).

Rapidly rising housing costs, driven up by rising incomes areawide and the demand from thousands of families moving into the region, hit inner-city blacks particularly hard. The gap between the white and black rates of homeownership grew.

The physical separation of most blacks and whites into separate schools and school districts meant that few blacks had the opportunity to attend the most competitive schools, a factor related to their declining college enrollments. For blacks, getting to the suburbs tended to mean moving into resegregating neighborhoods and schools which did not offer the opportunities and level of competition available to the area's young whites (see chapter 5).

Most blacks lacked both geographical access to the booming new centers of employment and the kind of informal personal contacts and local knowledge that often lead to jobs. Residential segregation also meant that most blacks who did own homes would not be able to participate in the choice suburban housing markets where equity grew most substantially. Family wealth, in the form of housing equity, grew more slowly in the suburbs in the path of black migration. Housing segregation defined separate educational, social, and economic worlds in which young people and their families had profoundly different sets of opportunities.

SEGREGATED AND UNEQUAL PUBLIC SCHOOLS

A generation ago, Atlanta black leaders made a bargain to accept political and administrative control of the city's public schools rather than to pursue integration either within the city or on a metropolitan level. By the late 1980s, Atlanta's public schools were among the most segregated in the South. And two in five Atlanta Public School students dropped out— a much higher level than the school district has acknowledged.

Education is critical to college access and success. The first generation of black metropolitan school administrators was particularly anxious to show achievement on this front. People wanted progress. And yearly test reports claimed steady movement toward the national norm, although the gap between the city and the white suburban schools never quite declined.

This study shows that achievement scores for metropolitan Atlanta high schools were very highly related to the percentage of minority and low-income students in the school. Years of publicity that claimed the Atlanta students were well above the national norm, which focused national attention on the superintendent's claims that he had solved the problems of poor and isolated schools, were unsubstantiated. People wanted to believe that increasingly disadvantaged school districts could provide equal opportunities for students without changing any aspect of the more privileged districts. They demanded better scores and they got reports of better scores—as it turned out, through the manipulation of test data.

Schools with large black student populations have never been equal to schools with large white populations. Schools where most of the students come from low-income black families have been doing very badly. The high schools of metro Atlanta reflect and perpetuate inequalities in race and income. Some of the most successful schools in the city have magnet programs that automatically produce higher scores by selectively admitting better qualified and more motivated students. Many black children living in the suburbs are in segregated and inferior schools. These problems are even apparent in suburban schools which have black student populations without large low-income enrollments. School leaders have often systematically underreported the problems in the city and there has been little attention to the problems of black suburbs until recently. A federal court acted in 1989 to require the preparation of a new desegregation plan for the largest suburban district, DeKalb County.

DECLINING ACCESS TO COLLEGE

One of the most hopeful trends in metropolitan Atlanta during the period from the mid-1960s to the mid-1970s was the very rapid increase in the proportion of young blacks going to college. Some of the changes in the South were unprecedented, as previously all-white institutions became significantly integrated under federal pressure. Both the possibility of going to college and the range of college choices available to young blacks were expended to previously unimaginable levels. The combination of a massive increase in need-based financial aid and strong civil rights laws produced very rapid and peaceful change. Access to college education is one of the most basic dreams parents have for their children. The dream reached very large numbers of black families as federal support increased.

However, the years since the mid-1970s tell a much less optimistic story. The number of black high school graduates continued to increase in metropolitan Atlanta, but the probability that they would go to college shrank rapidly, even more rapidly than in some less prosperous parts of the country. White access to college increased. Opportunity fell most rapidly in the inner-city ghettos while new campuses grew in the suburbs. Black colleges serving low-income students were particularly hard-hit by changes in federal financial aid policy. The changes forced low-income students to rely more on loans; since black students were less able to repay loans, the colleges were threatened with losing eligibility for federal aid programs because of loan default rates.

JOB TRAINING AND THE HARD-TO-EMPLOY

A study of opportunity has to include employment. Work is the dominant source of both income and status for Americans. To be unable to find a job is to be a failure in the most dramatic way. Having a job without income or mobility sufficient to support a family is a major reason for family instability. Those who lack skills for a good job and who lack the critical basic credential of a high school diploma need training to have a chance to break out of a cycle of failure, stagnation, and frustration.

Federal job training programs from the mid-1960s until the early 1980s had upgrading the skills of the most disadvantaged workers as an important part of their goals. The Carter administration increased funds and focused the program on the hard-core unemployed. The Carter reforms of 1978 rapidly expanded training for high school dropouts and other severely disadvantaged workers. The Reagan administration dramatically reversed this policy, sharply cutting funds while demanding higher placement rates at much lower cost per trainee (see chapter 7). This led to a severe reduction in training opportunities for many thousands of high school dropouts, particularly black men.

High school dropout rates were much higher in black schools than in white or integrated schools. High school dropouts had little hope for decent jobs in the post-industrial economy developing in metropolitan Atlanta. For the two-fifths of inner-city young people who failed to receive high school diplomas, the best hope for a good job was some kind of training that would give them the skills to get jobs and eventually perform more than entry-level work. Nine-tenths of those in training programs in Atlanta, however, were high school graduates; there was no safety net for dropouts. Twenty years of evaluation of federal job training programs showed that it was just this kind of basic skills training that had the largest positive effect. In the 1980s, however, the training resources that still existed were targeted toward more educated workers, not those in greatest need.

The federal job training programs were used in Atlanta in the 1980s largely to prepare black women for the very kind of entry-level, low-mobility jobs they had traditionally occupied anyway. The Atlanta program actually trained an even smaller proportion of dropouts than its suburban counterparts. The federal performance standards and the preferences of the local employers, the only source of jobs since the public employment program was terminated in 1981, drove the city's training system and the city administration reflected business preferences even more clearly than its white suburban neighbors (see chapter 7).

The federal requirements for low training costs and high placement rates created a strong incentive to screen out dropouts because they required expensive training and, even then, were more difficult to place than those with diplomas. Since the federal program provided for loss of funding—the ultimate bureaucratic weapon—if the cost and placement standards were not met, most training officials felt compelled to exclude from training those with the greatest need and to take those who could be most easily placed in their programs. Under the Reagan administration there was no longer a risk of losing funds for patterns of discrimination in job training. No federal civil rights regulations for the Reagan training program were ever issued. There was, however, a serious threat of losing federal dollars if too much money was spent on trying to train and place the hard-core unemployed.

Black Men: Schools, Jobs, Training, and a Shrinking Future

The decline in opportunity was greatest among young black men. This trend threatened those directly affected and diminished hopes for stable two-parent families in the black community. The Atlanta studies show that black men fared the worst in job training and college access and completion. Research in other metropolitan areas shows the same pattern.

Recent federal statistics show, for example, that only one-third of the black students beginning college immediately after high school were men. Anyone concerned about the lack of black leadership and the rise in poor female-headed black households has to be concerned about the rapidly deteriorating situations of young black men.

Separate Black and White Economies

The metropolitan Atlanta data show that an urban area can absorb a tremendous amount of economic growth without substantially improving conditions for blacks if blacks do not really participate in the white economy where the growth is concentrated. The metropolitan Atlanta economy is not a single economy in which demand for labor freely expands to draw in available black workers but a divided economy with a color line that is not easily crossed.

One difference from the old Jim Crow days is that not all blacks are on the wrong side of the line, in the subordinate economy. Another vital difference is that the line of racial and economic separation has moved well out into the suburbs, making it much more difficult to understand. The complexities are further increased by the spread of gentrification in some once-depressed regions of the central city. Statistics show, however, that the basic situation has not changed. As long as a great many blacks remain isolated in a subordinate economy facing ongoing disinvestment amid overall metropolitan growth, growth in the white economy may not improve the situation of the black community.

The vast extent of residential separation in the rapidly spreading metropolitan area and the virtually all-white population in the outer suburbs where job creation is most rapid are key features underlying the dual economy of the region.

The exuberant economic growth within the white part of a dual economy may actually harm those outside the economic mainstream. For example, the current growth in the Atlanta economy is providing decent entry-level office jobs for women living in inner-city black areas but not for men, intensifying social instability. These new jobs tend to be in service-oriented businesses that provide many clerical jobs for inner-city minority women but few jobs above the menial level for young men without higher education. Factory, construction, and other good, low-skill, traditionally male jobs tend to be concentrated in growth areas on the suburban fringe, not near the city's black neighborhoods.

As more successful blacks move out of the inner city and create new segregated suburban areas they do not gain access to the real economic growth centers of suburbia, but they do escape the overwhelming problems of the inner city. The main black path of suburbanization is moving south, but the jobs are booming in the outer reaches of the northern suburbs. Meanwhile, those left behind in the declining inner-city ghettos are isolated not only from whites but also from successful blacks. This profound isolation from the middle-class life, and from the role models and institutions that tend to develop around it, are central elements of the "underclass" situation that is now receiving such intense scrutiny across the United States (Wilson 1987).

At its worst, the syndrome of racially defined markets means that young blacks are excluded from opportunities, embittered by the unshared affluence in nearby white areas, and burdened by the rising costs and skewed opportunities of white prosperity. Whites become more fearful of deteriorating black areas, worrying that the criminals there will prey on them, but the victims of the underground criminal economy are overwhelmingly black. There are signs of this happening in parts of Atlanta. The poor in the inner city are becoming more and more isolated from and victimized by the prosperity of another, much richer, but very different economy nearby. The isolation has been growing for a long time, but the sudden removal of many of the social policies designed to moderate its effects make the consequences much more dramatically apparent.

Local Black Officials

Some effects of segregation and discrimination are difficult to discern because of the highly visible leadership roles held by blacks in important inner-city institutions.

The most successful blacks now have the option of either escaping the ghetto and its institutions or holding power within them. Sometimes they can do both, living outside and having power within. The idea of a black mayor, a black school superintendent, and a black police chief in Atlanta would not have been taken seriously a generation ago. The fact that there are blacks in authority in major institutions makes it seem to many whites and blacks that the institutions are working in a way more favorable to minority interests.

People forget that those institutions face more difficult challenges with far more limited resources, thanks to the departure of the white middle class and much of the black middle class. In a 1989 speech to Leadership Atlanta, the city school superintendent, J. Jerome Harris, said that the city schools were doomed if the middle class abandoned them. It is very important to understand the severe limitations and the larger challenges that face black leaders.

Certainly there has been a very great change in black power since rigid overt segregation was dominant in public institutions. Not long ago, former Georgia Governor Lester Maddox, who became famous by resisting integration of his restaurant, would lower the flag at the State Capitol whenever the Supreme Court handed down a civil rights decision he didn't like. In the late 1980s, Martin Luther King, Jr. was honored in his city, prominent civil rights leaders of the 1960s—Andrew Young and John Lewis—served as mayor and the city's representative in Congress, and blacks played important roles in many institutions. When the Democratic

National Convention met in Atlanta in 1988, Maddox couldn't even pay to get his views aired while Mayor Young hosted the national party. These were changes of real importance.

Black leaders mobilizing support in their difficult campaigns to take power, however, tend to vastly overstate the potential influence of local government and of the central city in the metropolitan area. After losing power in the central city through demographic change and black political mobilization, whites tend to assume that the new black leaders should bear responsibility for any unsolved problems and be left to solve them without significant outside resources. Too often the inability of declining cities to compete equally with booming suburbs is defined as a failure of black leadership rather than of broader institutions. Such black "failures" can reinforce white stereotypes.

Local government is not nearly so powerful as state government, federal government, or the private sector in affecting broad social, economic, and educational problems. Local government controls limited resources and struggles every year to maintain existing staff and services. Cutting city budgets means cutting into the black middle class since city government tends to hire much larger proportions of blacks than other large employers. Much of the discretionary money that used to fund new programs came from federal grants that fell sharply in the 1980s. Some critical programs, such as job training, were turned over to state government. Many of the programs cannot be solved, at any rate, within the boundaries of a single local government.

In fact, local governments act more as supplicants than as powerful regulators of private businesses, offering subsidies in efforts to prevent business departures. What city leaders can do to expand black opportunity is significant but limited: provide fair employment and affirmative action within their own staffs, see to it that some minority contractors get included in public contracts, and try to prevent problems such as police brutality.

The institutions and policies that most directly affect the mobility of young blacks are almost all outside the control of city leaders. City governments have no control of the suburbs, where most of the jobs are being created and almost all of the new housing is developed. The best opportunities for pre-college education are suburban. Educational funding, welfare policy, higher education, job training, and many other critical issues are decided largely at the state and federal levels, where suburban power is growing and city influence is shrinking as population disperses.

Suburbanization and the Expansion of Segregation

Black suburbanization has occurred on a vast scale in the Atlanta area since 1970 and most metro Atlanta black children are now growing up in the suburbs. On the surface this trend suggests that blacks are following the traditional path into the suburban mainstream of contemporary American society. It also reduces pressure on failing central-city institutions. Protests in the civil rights era came largely from upwardly mobile blacks who recognized the threats to their children's future. Most middle-class Atlanta blacks are now suburbanites, some of whom financed their moves to the suburbs by working within and defending the inner-city's institutions serving poor blacks.

But, and this is critical to understanding what has happened in Atlanta, suburbanization for most blacks does not mean crossing the color line; it means the color line is moving out to incorporate parts of suburbia. Though they are still outside white society, blacks are now themselves divided by the city-suburban boundary.

The most rapidly growing Atlanta suburbs are almost all white. Astonishingly, the enrollment of half of the black metropolitan area students in suburban schools has actually produced increased school segregation for the metropolitan area as a whole; evidence that resegregation of families is occurring on a large scale within the suburbs. Atlanta's largest suburban black community is in DeKalb County, which is losing white enrollment faster than all but one of the nation's largest school districts.

What is actually happening is the extension of the system of segregated housing beyond the city limits. The color line is not shrinking but spreading in extremely important ways.

Black officials have little incentive to talk about these problems because many of them fear that the negative cycles may become even worse if they are publicized. The viability of their institutions depends to a considerable degree on retaining residents, particularly higher-income black residents, while they are trying to keep those institutions afloat. Thus the short-run fortunes of some black leaders and institutions may even depend on making segregation seem less threatening than it is.

Black officials act much like their white predecessors in trying to emphasize the positive, as Representative John Lewis, the city's black congressman, noted in 1988:

The city of Atlanta is very image-conscious. There [is] a great [deal] of pride, but we want to protect our community. We don't want any blemishes to come out into the public, and the business community is probably more sensitive than any other segment. (*Chicago Tribune*, 20 November 1988).

In fact, power on both sides of the color line is based to some extent on acceptance of segregation. On the black side of the color line, it is advantageous to keep blacks within black electoral areas and keep black-controlled resources within black institutions; integrationist policies are often viewed as posing larger threats than they actually do.

On the white side of the line, although it is never said in public, some residents in outlying suburbs see critical advantages in their almost all-white and all middle-class status; they see isolation from the problems of the inner city as a fundamental reason why billions of dollars are being invested in creating new suburban "downtowns" and vast duplicate new industrial, commercial, educational, and residential infrastructures. Already, downtown is not the economic center of the emerging metropolitan complex; a series of huge suburban complexes and office parks along the freeways have become much more important.

Suburban politicians realize that their constituents think of social and economic exclusiveness as a right and as an important community asset. They fiercely resist sharing the exclusive schools, neighborhoods, and job opportunities they have created. They blame inner-city residents for their own problems. Thus they will fight school integration, mass transit links, zoning for affordable apartments for families, and even small amounts of scattered-site subsidized housing. They have let their constituents assume that they have the right to all the best of a great urban economy and society with none of the social responsibilities.

While many economic forces and governmental policies push toward increased racial and class stratification almost no one in power has any strong incentive to act. Civil rights groups are hard-pressed financially, fighting to defend their goals against a hostile federal administration. The issues of segregation and inequality are as remote to many urban residents today as they were for generations of white southerners before the Supreme Court held in 1954 that segregated schools were "inherently unequal."

But the issues must be faced again. The inequalities are not gone; they are growing and they pose social and policy problems of the first magnitude. Racial separation is a root cause. Vast economic growth has not provided the solution.

This book sets the stage for a major debate on what is happening to opportunity for blacks in metropolitan America. The current system of racial inequality based on location within metropolitan areas is powerful and self-perpetuating.

2

Shattered Dreams

Social theory depends for its validity on statistics, but in an analysis representing the cumulative experience of hundreds of thousands of people, it should be remembered that debilitating social problems are not randomly distributed. They tend to be concentrated in certain neighborhoods in multiples of two and three—for example, joblessness plus family violence; teen pregnancy plus malnutrition, plus illiteracy—with devastating effects on individual families. Families like the Bretts and the Wilkersons, who in this chapter relate their struggles to overcome one problem, only to be engulfed by others.

These families, who in some cases fled shoddy homes in one community during Atlanta's "boom" years only to wind up in isolated ghettos served by inferior schools elsewhere, give the lie to the argument that societal gains "trickle down" to the poor. Families who were able to trade tenements in the inner city for neat split-level houses or apartments in the new black suburbs found segregated schools, substandard construction, unsafe neighborhoods, and discriminatory banking practices waiting for them there, too.

Like a shadow world, full of negative counterpoints to the bright surface reality in Atlanta, the chapters that follow show fewer black youths going on to college despite significant increases in the number earning high school diplomas; high rates of joblessness despite great increases in the numbers of jobs being created; youths with less understanding of what was needed to succeed in schools and communities under black leadership than in many places where blacks were still battling for the right to self-determination.

In subsequent chapters, attention is focused on one problem at a time: problems of joblessness, poorly managed schools or job training programs, residential segregation, and declining access to college. This is the way in which government agencies and researchers divide the world to render analysis and policymaking manageable.

People, however, tend to have more than one problem at a time and to carry their problems from one stage of life to the next, even across generations. Problems encountered in childhood can so limit their vision as adults as to make even the opening of full and fair opportunities inaccessible to them. It is not uncommon in today's cities to find black adults so badly abused by bureaucrats in the past that they shun social service agencies set up to help them—adults unwilling or unable to believe what any bureaucrat has to say.

Of course, the problems that cripple these people are not always of society's making; they are not merely victims of an evil system but also of their own missteps and errors in judgment. Their lives are full of complexities and contradictions.

But as their stories show, there is no easy recovery from mistakes made by people without resources in communities circumscribed by poverty and discrimination.

How could they fail to break the bonds of poverty, when jobs and new housing starts were exploding all around them? How could they have remained stuck, between prosperity and hopelessness, in black-run communities and school systems?

No individual can speak for the hundreds of thousands represented in the charts and graphs in the chapters that follow, and the voices heard in this chapter offer only brief summaries of a few lives. But the sometimes numbing trends and numbers to be found elsewhere in this book are made more vivid by the real-life experiences of seven Atlantans who talked frankly with us about the shattered dreams and stopping-places in their own lives.

Selena Brett

Where a family lives is the single most important factor in the quality of its members' lives. It determines what kind of schools the children will attend, what threats "ordinary" life poses to their personal health and safety, whether a simple trip to the supermarket will be a routine or a stressful experience, and whether there is access to public transportation, government agencies, and jobs.

When a family is forced, whether by discrimination or poverty, to live in areas that are unsafe and isolated from good schools and job centers,

life is hard and dangerous despite the hopes one brings to it, said Selena
Brett, after half of a century in the wrong neighborhoods. Her name has
been changed to assure her privacy, as have the names of others in this
chapter, but her story appears exactly as it was related to us by Selena,
who said it seems she has always been in the wrong place at the wrong
time.

One of seven kids, she remembers watching helplessly as her father
died, without access to medical care, in rural Alabama and growing up in
ill-fitting hand-me-downs donated by the affluent whites who employed
her mother as a maid. Selena defied expectations by becoming the first
in her family to graduate from high school and aiming for a profession.
Diploma in hand, she applied and was admitted to nursing school, to the
family's enormous pride.

But nursing school, with its irregular hours and late shifts, entailed
long waits in the dark on lonely corners in unsafe neighborhoods for a
long bus ride home, reason enough to deter many of her contemporaries
from making the effort. And it wasn't long before her schooling was cut
short, and her dreams dashed, in a violent way. She was brutally raped
on her way home from a night class.

Maid's work, performed during the day in the well-patrolled white
neighborhoods to which she received referrals from her mother's employers, was a relief after that, and it was what she did until she came to
Atlanta in the 1960s as a young bride, and for years afterwards.

It wasn't so bad, she says. She and her husband, twelve years her
senior, had the makings of a good life together. He had a steady job as a
factory worker, and she easily found maid's work. They lived simply, in a
tiny apartment with crumbling walls, in the predominantly black and
poor Vine City section of Atlanta, with derelicts and drug addicts for
neighbors. But is was "only temporary," they told each other, confident
that by working hard they would soon be able to afford a fine home in a
middle-class neighborhood with good schools, good transportation, and
good neighbors.

Those were heady times in Atlanta; its "Sweet Auburn" Avenue, a national center of bustling black enterprise, had been a source of inspiration
to several generations of southern blacks. The civil rights movement got
underway and was run from a storefront headquarters on Auburn Avenue
by the Southern Christian Leadership Conference, an organization
founded by a local preacher named Martin Luther King, Jr. A black man,

Maynard Jackson, ran for mayor and won, on a platform promising "a piece of the pie" to minorities.

Buoyed by those events, and by the unaccustomed stability in her life, Selena raised her sights after moving to Atlanta and began to think about nursing school again. Then tragedy struck and she found out how illusory her sense of well-being was.

Brett suffered three crippling strokes in rapid succession, each more debilitating than the last, until he was unable to talk coherently or perform the simplest functions for himself, much less work. This forced Selena to take on more maid's work and to work longer hours, despite the risks of traveling at night through a neighborhood frequented by thugs and drug addicts. She had not yet obliterated the memory of her first assault when she was mugged by a youth who struck a crippling blow to her neck with a hammer, leaving her unable to turn it without pain—and terrified of venturing out at night again.

It was at this point that bureaucratic inefficiency and federal policy changes combined with the couple's already stressful environment to make their modest living circumstances desperate. Administrators in the Atlanta offices of two federal agencies encumbered them with red tape, at first denying her husband's application for $431 a month in Social Security Disability benefits under stringent new rules promulgated by the Reagan administration to guard against welfare "cheats." Then, after determining that Brett was indeed eligible for disability insurance, they used it to reduce his $650-a-month Veterans' Administration pension proportionately. The net effect was to freeze Brett's income below the poverty line after he was permanently disabled and incapable of providing for his family.

All that kept the couple from homelessness at that point were the sacrifices of other family members, who dipped into their own meager resources of cash and Food Stamps to keep them afloat while Selena asked her congressman, former civil rights activist John Lewis, for help.

Dreams die hard, Selena said. But they died harder, somehow, in Atlanta in the 1980s, a place and a time so pregnant with possibilities—new housing starts, new office buildings, new hotels, amusement centers, exposition halls, sports arenas, and rapid-transit routes—that she felt doubly mocked by her failures.

Black men ran the city government, the county commission, the city schools, the police department, and the chamber of commerce. Yet the

Bretts were forced to crowd into a small, $200-a-month house in the even more dangerous Simpson section of crime- and drug-riddled Vine City. It was there that we found them living with six others: her husband's unmarried daughter, Janet; Janet's three young children; Selena's brother Stanley and Stanley's girlfriend.

There were framed pictures of Martin Luther King, an American Flag, and an Army discharge certificate on the walls; an inexpensive sofa bed and table the family was buying on time in the front room; and, on the night we visited, the sounds of a TV game show emanating from the darkened back room where the 62-year-old Brett lay waiting helplessly for his partially disabled wife to bring him supper.

At fifty, Selena considered herself poorer in some ways than she remembered being as a child: all grown up, but stripped of her dreams and still powerless to do anything but watch helplessly as somebody she loved weakened and grew worse.

It was humiliating to have come so far, to the very cradle of the civil rights movement, without bettering herself, she said. And she worried endlessly about the children.

Janet Johnson

Selena's adult stepdaughter, whom we will call Janet Johnson, learned first-hand about the interrelatedness of residence and role models.

Like her stepmother, Janet had entertained dreams of becoming a nurse, a role that seemed capable of fulfilling her youthful yearnings for respectability, nurturing, and self-sufficiency at the same time. But by the time she had entered high school, she admitted from the vantage point of a chastened 26-year-old, she found less peer support for playing by the rules than for breaking them. She knew no one who had actually made the journey from her ghetto school, in which studiousness was ridiculed, to the gleaming hospital corridors in which workers wore crisp, white uniforms, helped to make the sick well again, and were looked up to; she knew no one who had chosen that path. But she knew plenty of young girls who had traded dependency on their parents for more grownup roles overnight by having a baby, somebody to depend on *them*. And, so what if many of them were scarcely out of childhood themselves? Even in the projects, motherhood was respected and deferred to. And Janet, in a hurry to grow up, saw no quicker route to adulthood than becoming a mother, and a welfare householder, in her own right.

So it was only a matter of time before she became pregnant, at fifteen.

And when the baby came, there were plenty of "role models" to point the way: Following their lead, she dropped out of high school and applied for Aid to Families with Dependent Children, a step that, for all its negative implications outside the ghetto, meant she had left childhood forever. She didn't think seriously at that point about completing the requirements for graduation from high school or qualifying for a good job, she admitted, but if she had, the scarcity of outreach programs for teenage mothers would have discouraged it. The system actually encouraged dependency, and her parents' declining health and dwindling resources meant she couldn't count on them to help her out.

By the time we met her, at twenty-six, she was a single mother of three, resigned to leading the sort of life others led all around her. By that time, it was her children—ages nine, seven, and four respectively—who dreamed of becoming a teacher, a football player, a policeman; dreams as unlikely to be realized in the absence of role models, peer support, or caring teachers and guidance counselors to point the way as Janet's own. What her children lacked, she had come to realize, was not hope but the means to build on it. And their mother's example was not encouraging.

Janet still took out that old dream of becoming a nurse, every now and then, and looked at it; but it seemed more elusive than ever in the late 1980s. She couldn't enter nursing school without a high school or equivalency diploma; she had made inquiries. And for that, she would need to go back to school. But who would take care of the children? She couldn't afford child care without a paying job. And she lived too far from the parts of the city where most of the new jobs were being created.

Moreover, the only ones for which she was qualified were $3.90-an-hour jobs in suburban fast-food restaurants, two buses and a trainride (90 minutes) away, a wearying commute. And as her mother's experience drove home, it was too dangerous for an unescorted woman to go anywhere in the vicinity of Vine and Simpson Streets at night, on foot. Crime was so rampant in the area that women and children observed self-imposed curfews and barricaded themselves inside their homes after dark.

A car might have provided a way out, and a means of avoiding the nighttime waits at deserted bus stops, but she didn't have one. Nobody she knew had one. The booming suburbs and the new office towers might as well have been in a foreign country. And the constraints on her life were direct threats to the future of her children.

D. L. Fain

Without role models, mentors, or any realistic means of surmounting the circumstances they are born into, some people will grasp at any possibility of escape. So it was with D. L. Fain, lured from his south Georgia home in the 1930s by a Navy recruiter's promise of far-off adventures and a military education.

If even a fraction of those tempted by the invitation to "be all that you can be" learn a trade and attend college afterwards on veterans' benefits were able to do so, it would be an inspired solution. Unfortunately, many of those seduced by the prospect of a deferred education, as Fain was, never obtain one.

In the 1930s, a military career seemed like the only route for a bright and ambitious black Georgia youth out of a world bounded by Jim Crow. It still seems like an appealing alternative to many black youths thwarted by stiff college admission requirements and the shrinking of federal college grants. But the recruiters' siren call was no less deceptive many years ago than it is now, with recruiters seeking volunteers in the poorest inner-city neighborhoods for dead-end military jobs.

There is simply no alternative to a good education as preparation for the good jobs and the good life Fain dreamed of when he signed up; then, as now, college was a prerequisite even for most entry-level white-collar jobs.

But Fain, who had taught himself to read, washed cars and sold cosmetics door-to-door in black neighborhoods before enlisting, trained in radios and antiaircraft artillery in the Navy, under the impression that he was preparing for higher education or at least gainful employment afterwards. He saw enemy action in the South Pacific, survived a bomb blast and, over the years, three failed marriages; but came home to uninspiring work in the kitchens of a series of Veterans' Administration Hospitals, ending with the VA Hospital in Atlanta.

It was, simply, the best that his limited education qualified him to do after a long stint in the Navy. Not even in the booming Sun Belt state he had fled before the civil rights movement got underway could Fain, who never got past the eighth grade, make up for his lack of a formal education.

Well into old age, he dreamed about "one of those executive jobs with a desk and a secretary, where you get paid to solve problems"—only to be passed over, time and time again, until he was disabled in 1978 by spinal surgery and related health problems.

Retired by the late 1980s, with a pension amounting to $800 a month, he lived austerely, in a $220-a-month flat with a faulty heater, off Memorial Drive in black suburban DeKalb County, feeling cheated by the changes that made college grants and loans available to black youths when he was somewhere else. He missed entirely the rush by colleges and employers to recruit minority candidates when he was off in the Navy; then came home to a booming economy in which a man, black or white, without a sheepskin had little value. His last assignments, at what should been the pinnacle of his career, the rewards for long service to his country, were menial ones in the kitchens of VA hospitals.

It wasn't that he couldn't have gone back to school at some point, completed the requirements for his high school diploma, and qualified for admission to college. It was, rather, that he allowed himself to believe that he had found a way out of the ghetto and a shortcut to success in later life; that the rewards would come eventually. He could not have known how important a college diploma would become in his lifetime, to the point that it was as critical as a high school diploma had once been for admission to the ranks of the gainfully employed.

"I feel like I been robbed," he said, trapped in old age by the choices he had made as an ambitious, brighter-than-average boy. Not only did he miss out on youth opportunities that became commonplace in the 1960s, he lacked the comforts people who've worked all their lives have a right to expect at the end of their lives. No companion, after a military career that proved to be incompatible with marriage; no hedge against inflation; no accommodation even from a crusty landlord, who refused to reimburse him for repairs to a faulty gas heater; and, as a result of dental problems he couldn't afford to correct, no steaks.

He worried that many of today's young firebrands, distrustful of the system and in a hurry to grow up, would repeat his mistake of enlisting in the service under the impression that it was an acceptable alternative—maybe even a shortcut—to college. There is no such thing, he said. "I know."

Anita Wilkerson

Anita Wilkerson was not without role models, not without pictures of the way life ought to turn out for a young white woman growing up in the

Midwest. Home ownership was central to her dreams of financial security, stability, a safe and secure environment for her children. And it seemed to be within reach even of families with modest incomes in the 1970s, when she left her safe, middle-class environment to become the bride of a black cement contractor, who would bring her to Atlanta.

But she had married into a world of lowered expectations; her husband had not made it past the first grade and was so embarrassed by the jeers of younger children in his one attempt to learn to read that he never tried it again and remained illiterate all of his life. Ill health, financial problems, and the perverse brand of discrimination that is sometimes visited on biracial couples would follow them all of their lives. Her own daughter's education would be cut short because of their failure to make a $199 tuition installment in her first year at a small Michigan college. And the dream of home ownership would slip further and further from her grasp in the struggle to make ends meet.

Early in their married life, her husband had commanded $12 an hour as a cement contractor; literate or not, he could "read" blueprints as well as the next man. She made $5.25 an hour as a Goodwill store manager. But income kept pace with rising housing costs only for white Atlantans in the last two decades when, as chapter 4 will show, black prospects for homeownership deteriorated. As a result, they lived precariously with their little girl in a series of rented houses. They failed to put down roots and were sometimes driven out by sheer bigotry, until health problems— he suffered a heart attack and she was stricken with cancer—forced them to scale down their labors and their ambitions.

As the decade of the 1980s drew to a close, Anita and her 65-year-old husband lived in the Center Hill section of northwest Atlanta, an integrated neighborhood, on public assistance with the two grandchildren— aged nine and eleven—their wandering daughter, a migrant worker, had left in their care, a fresh heartache. At a time when they should have been enjoying the fruits of their life's labors, life was particularly hard.

Together, they brought in $584 a month in cash benefits and $150 a month in food stamps, which covered the bare necessities but was not enough to qualify them for such ballyhooed homesteading programs as Habitat for Humanity, which was popularized by former President Jimmy Carter and his wife Rosalynn. Habitat purported to offer low-income renters a chance to get off the tenants' treadmill, but you had to have an income of at least $15,000 a year to qualify, Anita grumbled. "Poor people need not apply."

It sometimes seemed, she said, as if the system were set up to pull low-wage earners deeper into poverty and, having done so, to prevent them from ever achieving self-sufficiency again. The last adjustment in their AFDC allotment put an additional $6 a month in their benefit check but cost them $20 in Food Stamps.

Whatever benefits their countrymen saw fit to share with people who could no longer support themselves, Anita observed, home ownership wasn't one of them. And the fresh, new dreams of their grandchildren only served to remind them how far they all were from achieving the American ideal.

Tony, the older child, wanted to be a doctor and was already talking about medical school—something that, his grandmother said, "would take a miracle."

Brenda Mackle

What happened to Brenda Mackle is an example of how educational institutions sometimes fail people who are highly motivated to succeed by assuming that they come from middle-class backgrounds, know what questions to ask, and have all the grant and loan information they need. Sometimes they lead people who've grown up in poverty and made grievous mistakes to put all their hopes on an associate (two-year) college or vocational certificate that may not have much value in the marketplace. Sometimes they are so intensely engaged in the business of education that they fail to notice those who fall between the cracks.

Brenda had come to Atlanta in 1987 after serving thirty-nine months in the Women's Correctional Institution in Milledgeville, on bad check charges; the 35-year-old woman's only previous work experience had been as a maid.

But she had been a model inmate and student at Milledgeville, earning one and one-half years of college credits and a 3.5 grade-point average while in prison. She had acquired a variety of office skills and had learned to file, to operate a word processor, and to answer the phone professionally. She had a quick wit, an infectious laugh, great personal warmth, and was desperate to break the bonds of poverty, once and for all.

She should not have had any trouble completing the requirements for an associate degree, or landing a decent job, in Atlanta, "the city too busy to hate." For the first time in her life, she had something to put on a resume, academic credits, and something to look forward to. She had learned to present the conditions of her parole—she could not be late for work, have any unexplained absences, or have a "bad work attitude"—to prospective employers as plusses, selling points in her favor.

Yet a year and a half after her release, she was still unemployed; still two academic quarters short of the requirements for her associate degree; still living with three relatives in a cramped $205-a-month apartment at the subsidized McDaniel-Glenn Housing Project, a bleak southside community of 610 low-income families near three other housing projects.

Atlanta employers were cool to ex-cons, no matter how highly motivated they were. And when she called Atlanta Metropolitan College to inquire about financial aid and enrollments, a harried admissions staffer cut the conversation short: Pell grants were available for students with "financial need," she said, but would cover only 25 percent of the approximately $8,000 the average AMC student spent in a year. The admissions worker did not think it was necessary to explain that this didn't mean $8,000 in instructional costs, and Brenda, overwhelmed by what sounded like an astronomical figure, didn't ask for clarification, campus employment, or advice.

No wonder so few people from her end of town went to college, she decided grimly. A loan seemed unattainable; and even if she could have obtained one, she had no way of paying it back. Without any other means of raising so vast a sum, she put her dreams on hold, applied for public assistance, and continued to look for work.

It wasn't until a year later that she was amazed to learn, through a chance meeting with a researcher, that tuition and books came to less that $1,300 a year at AMC for Georgia residents—a hefty sum for anybody on public assistance, but nowhere near the $8,000 she had been quoted by the preoccupied admissions officer.

The high figure had been an estimate of housing, transportation, meals, and incidental costs for an adult student living alone in moderately priced rental housing. There was no estimate for a student living in federally subsidized housing or with relatives, and eligible for Food Stamps, and the effect of the limited information Brenda was given was to discourage—and others in her circumstances—from applying.

She was never even told that a loan might not be necessary; that, in fact, loans were discouraged except as a last resort. She was not told about a variety of grants and work-study programs with which she might have supplemented her Pell grant.

The system had not been set up for people like Brenda, who did not receive any encouragement from her caseworker, her parole officer, or her neighbors at McDaniel-Glenn either.

It is a bitter irony that white middle-class 16-year-olds from college-educated families, in which higher education is talked about, promoted and generally affordable, are far more likely to be approached by caring adults with strategies for getting admitted and obtaining financial aid than are minority youths or unemployed adults starved for knowledge about paths to gainful employment.

If college wasn't an entitlement for somebody in Brenda Mackle's circumstances, reliable information and advice about college fees and assistance should have been. Unfortunately, AMC Dean of Students Charles Easley suspects, what happened to Brenda was not an isolated occurrence. Insufficient information about college aid is one of the biggest complaints about and, he believes, barriers to enrollment at the city's only two-year public college.

In fact, the only prodding Brenda ever got to raise her sights, after dropping out of school in Alabama in the ninth grade to have a child, was from a boyfriend who introduced her to the worlds of sex and fast money, in that order, before she was introduced to the world of work.

All she knew about living well was what the youth, who became her first husband, taught her; he would steal and forge checks and send her to the bank to cash them. It seemed so easy that, after trying it a few times without getting caught, she grew bolder, writing herself checks for $3,000 or $6,000, usually to buy things for herself and her baby daughters after her marriage broke up.

Eventually she was caught and imprisoned. The stint in Milledgeville had not been her first. But none of her previous efforts to start over had panned out. The first time she tried to enter college, "between incarcerations," as she puts it, in 1981, the school, South Georgia College in Douglas, refused to accept her Graduate Equivalency Diploma from Alabama. Following the school's advice, she obtained one in Georgia, but it wasn't until she landed in prison again, on another bad check charge, that she began to think seriously about college and careers. And it wasn't until after her release in the fall of 1987, full of pride in her accomplishments and enthusiasm about starting over, that she realized how little support there was on the outside, in Atlanta.

Brenda Mackle still sees that elusive associate degree, the goal she began working toward as an inmate, as the key to her future—the passport to the really good jobs, advanced degrees, a career in social work. It is a misconception she shares with more than a few caseworkers and guidance counselors, who sometimes discourage people with financial problems and interrupted schooling from applying to four-year colleges.

What they don't yet realize, but our studies show, is that even with an associate degree, a person is behind the eightball. Junior colleges are seldom the bridges to higher education enrollees expect. Few finish and go on to earn four-year degrees, and transfers from Alanta Metropolitan College, the city's only two-year college, have special problems—made even harder in the 1980s by Georgia's adoption of a Regents exam requirement for admission to the junior year in college. The state acted to stiffen the requirements for admission to the upper levels despite civil rights complaints about discriminatory effects on black students from weak high schools and colleges (see chapters 5 and 6). Nor would the two-year degree that Brenda dreamed of open many doors in a marketplace that, increasingly, demanded a bachelor's degree for good entry-level jobs.

At thirty-seven, Brenda was a grandmother and felt "more like sixty-five," she said, with a variety of health problems that have lately made looking for work difficult. Anxious to keep her teenaged daughters, students at Southside Comprehensive High School, and her five-month-old grandson, from repeating her mistakes, she wonders if it's possible. Her 17-year-old, who dreams of entering the service, expected to graduate as this book went to press. But her 19-year-old, back in school after a series of operations to correct the scars of a childhood accident, and the recent birth of her own child, did not.

At her daughter's age, Brenda had no education, no skills, no real incentive to make a way for herself and stay out of prison. She does now. But she grows weary of the struggle. And there is a man—a postal worker twenty-seven years older than she is—who wants to marry her, prison record, grandchild, and all. Perhaps in marriage she would be able to find the security that has eluded her all these years, she said. But he was so much older. . . . She was still pondering the question as this book went to press.

Eula Cohen and Frances Pinkston

It is commonly believed that a lot of the problems in inner-city schools plagued by low achievement scores and high dropout rates can be traced to lazy or incompetent teachers and administrators with low expectations of their predominantly black and poor students. And studies do show a correlation, in some cases, between expectations and achievements.

But we found poverty and its effects to be so pervasive in some Atlanta schools that not even the heroic efforts of some educators to prevent suicides or teen pregnancies could make a dent.

Guidance counselors could and sometimes did intervene powerfully to prevent children from dropping out and to get students and families thinking about college and the careers for which college is a requirement.

But in the schools serving housing projects like Carver Homes and East Lake Meadows, where as many as 40 percent of the students dropped out, guidance counselors had more critical problems to contend with on a day-to-day basis. Like drug abuse, unplanned pregnancies, family violence, and alcoholic or abusive parents. These counselors included Eula Cohen and Frances Pinkston (their real names), who entered the teaching profession with dreams of their own.

Cohen's caseload was three hundred, about the same as it was anywhere else in the metro area in 1989. The trouble was, a caseload of three hundred at the inner-city Price Middle School was not the same thing as a caseload of three hundred elsewhere.

It's hard to focus on the student who might, with a little prodding, become college material, she said, when others are suicidal; hard to motivate a student to fill out college loan applications when the student's paramount concern is to end an unplanned pregnancy or keep a parole officer at bay.

And even if these students could be inspired to aim for college, how would they pay for it? College aid for the academically average, disadvantaged student plummeted under the Reagan administration, which shifted increasingly from outright grants and scholarships to federally guaranteed loans and then spurred tighter control over those loans by penalizing colleges with poor repayment rates, a serious problem at colleges serving students from poor minority families.

Eula Cohen was a splendid role model by Carver Homes standards: highly educated, respected, continuously employed since completing her education twenty-five years earlier under a grant from the National Defense Education Act of 1960. But her dream—to empower the children of the students she grew up with to complete school and pursue dreams of their own—was shattered, too.

As the decade of the 1980s came to an end, she wondered if there was any point in encouraging a ghetto kid to attend a college, even on a scholarship, where the work would be tough, the competition fierce, the social pressures intense, and the climate hostile. Maybe the Price student should lower his sights, and his stress ratio. Maybe a guidance counselor should stress beauty school, auto mechanics, or secretarial training, rather than college.

"What's important is to have a diploma from somewhere, a technical school, a cosmetology school," declared Frances Pinkston, a guidance counselor at the declining East Atlanta High School, which had a rapidly shrinking student population (down from 1,300 a decade ago to 350 in 1988) and some of the lowest reading and math scores in the state.

This was not necessarily so, with the government cracking down on diploma mills that did not sufficiently prepare their graduates for even blue-collar careers; and our research demonstrates that only a small percentage of those receiving associate degrees from junior colleges ever go on to earn bachelor's degrees from accredited four-year colleges.

But the struggles of Pinkston and Cohen to find incentives for keeping them in high school long enough to earn their diplomas, prerequisites for any additional schooling, were understandable.

There have been some success stories along the way. Pinkston's students obtained $240,000 in scholarships to local schools in 1987; 30 percent went on to college, though she admitted, "The economic level of some of those [private, predominantly white] colleges up North is so far beyond them that I worry for the child who winds up there. That can cause a whole lot of other problems."

She counseled about two hundred eighth-, ninth-, and tenth-graders at East Atlanta, a school soon to be closed as a high school. Drawing most of its students from the nearby East Lake Meadows Housing Project— one of the most barren and economically distressed in the city—it racked up some of the most consistently low scores on Georgia's Basic Skills Test.

Her proudest recent accomplishment was working with burned-out teachers on improving literacy and test-taking skills so as to halt and reverse the downward trend. Yet the staff was still castigated by state officials for failing to do better, "a blow we staggered under," the dispirited counselor said bitterly. Those who try to serve children with desperate problems are often blamed rather than rewarded for their work.

Signs of burnout were everywhere. But Pinkston had covered an entire wall in her neat office with snapshots of "her" smiling graduates, "her" athletes and award winners: inspiration for herself, and any who come here to consult with her. She chortled with pride about her "star" graduates: a Macon physician, a University of Georgia basketball star, a biochemist, a news photographer for *The Atlanta Journal & Constitution*. But close to 50 percent of her charges would drop out before the twelfth grade, and this was nothing to brag about. In the past year, she had spent most of her time making house calls to abusive or neglectful parents, counseling students with romantic problems, and raising money to buy clothes for one student whose mother's boyfriend had sent fire to their home.

It is hard for people like Cohen and Pinkston to avoid feeling over-whelmed—if not by despair, then by the sheer volume of paperwork. In addition to counseling students and keeping records, it also fell to counselors in Atlanta to nominate students for Upward Bound, Talent Search, Adopt a Student, and Distinguished High School Students of America awards (time-consuming paper shuffling that takes precious time away form student interview) and to run "Duties in the Community" courses requiring seventy-five hours of volunteer work from each student as a condition of graduation.

At the moment, Pinkston said, her thoughts were on a 14-year-old admitted to Georgia Regional Hospital after a second suicide attempt. Treated with lithium for a chemical imbalance, the seemingly tough girl had been the target of vicious gossip and cutting remarks by other students.

And there have been so many pregnant ninth-graders, she sighed. "I always wonder what will happen to *their* kids."

She didn't leave her concerns on the schoolhouse steps either. A member of Planned Parenthood, the DeKalb Task Force on Teen Pregnancy, and the Council on Children, she spent her off-duty hours counseling sexually active teens and trying to persuade others to put off their first sexual encounter or use contraceptives.

Ghetto kids "require more from us" than other students, she said; more than is sometimes possible over and above a torrent of administrative and record-keeping responsibilities.

There should be less, not more, of this for guidance counselors in "disadvantaged schools," she believes, and more staff support. More counseling of these kids before they get to the middle schools, a luxury not supported by state funds or permitted by the tight budgets in many Atlanta-area school systems.

"Sometimes," she said, "I think we just don't get to them early enough."

The story of opportunity for black people in Atlanta today is a story of many thousands of individuals like Brenda Mackle, Selena Brett, D. L.

Fain—each struggling with problems identified again and again by researchers in the chapters that follow and often in profound isolation from the mostly middle-class whites who benefited from the extended economic boom. To parents who have failed because of discrimination or long-ago gaps in their educations, to families without support systems, to people living in conditions so dangerous, so precarious, and so far from the job centers they could scarcely be imagined by middle-class families, the economic boom of the past decade has been almost irrelevent.

Their dreams were as strongly held as the plans hatched across racial and suburban lines in the affluent white suburbs where houses and jobs were being created faster than people could be found to fill them; people tend to want similar things out of life.

But the dreams of the black and poor youths growing up in places like Vine City, without role models, without books in their homes, without knowledge of the steps that had to be taken by the tenth grade if they wanted to be doctors or filmmakers, were unconnected to any practical means of achieving them. And without the support systems taken for granted by youths in most middle-class white households, there was precious little margin for error. But inner-city youths could not concentrate in critical math or language classes needed for admission to college if they hadn't had enough to eat or had been kept up all night by the battles of alcoholic or drug-impaired parents; if they couldn't walk the short distance from the bus stop to their own homes without anxiety about their personal safety; if they couldn't even be sure that when they got there, they would not find a notice tacked to the door and the family's belongings piled at the curb.

Dreams were plentiful, but in the central city and south suburban neighborhoods where quality schools and information about career paths were in short supply, where institutions struggled to do more with less resources, there were countless people with no practical means of achieving them.

It is well, as the discussion shifts to consideration of trends, averages, and statistical cohorts in the chapters to come, to keep them in mind.

3

Metropolitan Atlanta: Economic Boom and Growing Inequality

When the dreams of poor people die they often blame themselves. The single mother without a job will often talk about how things could have been different if only she had tried harder. In the ghetto, as in the suburbs, Americans tend to think about things in terms of individual decisions. People's choices are very important, of course, but they are often shaped and limited by large social and economic forces. Life offers very different chances in the inner city than in the suburbs.

Although suburbanites strongly affirm the ethic of individual responsibility for poor people, their actions show that they understand and even overstate the importance of environment when it comes to their own children. They will often make their fears explicit in fighting anything that would disrupt the protected middle-class socialization provided by suburban communities. They believe that they have purchased the right to homogeneous middle-class neighborhoods and schools, which they see as vital to their children's futures. A suburban political culture, however, ignores the same concerns with regard to minority children.

To begin to understand why so many dreams are dying in the ghetto and why we can predict so accurately, for example, that the child of an inner-city teen mother will drop out of school even before that child is born, we must look at broad economic and social forces affecting the people in the communities left behind in an economic boom.

This chapter shows that there is still a color line that blocks the flow of jobs and resources into the black community. The color line is rapidly extending its reach into suburbia. In fact, there is clear evidence that the relative situation of Atlanta-area blacks declined as the region's economy was surging. Solutions will probably require policies that open opportunities in white communities and white institutions to the families left behind in the area's older black communities.

During the last generation, the basic assumption of American policy, almost universally accepted in the conservative movement, has been that there are no more social problems that must be addressed by policies with explicit racial goals, no more major barriers that will only yield to a direct assault on contemporary forms of discrimination. Racial discrimination is seen as something that was solved in the 1960s.

During the 1988 presidential campaign, for example, polls showed that 71 percent of blacks but only 29 percent of whites believed that the federal government was doing too little to aid blacks. Seventy percent of whites said that blacks "have the same opportunities to live a middle-class life as whites" (*Newsweek* [Gallup Poll], 7 March 1988: 23; *Business Week* [Harris Survey], 14 March 1988: 65). Sixty-nine percent of whites surveyed in late 1989 believed that the quality of life had improved for blacks in the 1980s (*Washington Post Weekly Ed.*, 30 October 1989: 37). The black middle class is assumed to have no serious racial problems.

The problems of poor blacks, according to conservative assumptions, could be solved by the combination of a buoyant economy creating jobs and stronger, more demanding, educational programs. If enough jobs were created, it is argued, and blacks had the qualifications, blacks would have received good incomes and obtained access to jobs, housing, and the other essentials of life in the era of affirmative action, fair housing, and powerful black officials. It was impossible to test this theory effectively in the many cities that simply did not have enough jobs.

Metropolitan Atlanta, however, provides an extremely good test of this theory. Its economy boomed, creating jobs much faster than its natural population growth. In addition, it was a center of black political power and black educational institutions. It never experienced the violent racial conflict that wracked so many other cities in the 1960s. According to the conservative theory, racial gaps should have declined greatly in greater Atlanta. They did not, and in some critical areas, they grew.

This chapter describes the changing metropolitan area and discusses the deepening racial inequalities that have accompanied the region's unprecedented prosperity and the historic breakthroughs of black political leadership. It shows some of the large forces in the economy and in the housing market that limit the possibilities of ghetto families. It outlines a structure of inequality in which the color line in the metropolitan region plays a central part. It provides a framework within which the particular dimensions—housing, education, and employment—of a self-perpetuating system of racial inequality are explored in subsequent chapters.

The Economic and Political Importance of Atlanta

Each era in American history has its cities of destiny, areas formerly of secondary importance that become centers of economic booms and become key parts of the national and world economic infrastructure in a generation. This was the story of Chicago in the late nineteenth and early twentieth centuries, of Los Angeles after World War II, and of the great cities of the Sun Belt in the 1970s and 1980s. Only a few, such as Phoenix and San Diego, can rival Atlanta's recent surge, and none are becoming so visible and important internationally.

As the South finally became a fully developed and urbanized portion of the United States economy, it appeared that its great national city and critical regional economic center would be metropolitan Atlanta. There were also signs that Atlanta would play a decisive role in national politics and culture. Its role as the headquarters for the civil rights movement of the 1960s and for the first successful southern campaign for president since the civil war, Jimmy Carter's in 1976, reflected the city's political and cultural importance.

The city also had a very special role in the national black community and was seen by blacks as a center of success and influence. In 1980 the central city had one of the highest proportions of black residents, 67 percent, and the metropolitan area had a half million blacks. It was an area with much lower black unemployment rates in 1980 than the national average, although the black jobless rate was still 169 percent greater than the white rate (Joint Center 1988, 18–27). The city had a huge, visible black community doing better, in some ways, than blacks elsewhere, but still far behind whites.

Atlanta blacks did have a large amount of economic power; a University of Georgia study reported almost $8 billion in black buying power in the greater Atlanta area. There was $4.4 billion in Fulton County and $2.3 billion in DeKalb. Interestingly enough, however, the black share of total spending was only about one-sixth and in the Atlanta metro area blacks had a slightly smaller share of total spending power than in the rest of the state, which traditionally has been seen as more backward by blacks (*Atlanta Tribune*, April 1990, p. 19).

Metropolitan Atlanta is an excellent place to examine the changing structure of opportunity and the influence of policy changes. Mobility programs for blacks work best where there is a healthy economy creating jobs to provide opportunities for high school, college, and training-program graduates. With a metropolitan job growth rate of 43 percent between 1980 and 1987, the Atlanta area was one of the fastest growing job markets in the country. Its housing market was growing at an astonishing rate and new communities, without previous racial patterns, were springing into being. Employers who cannot readily find white workers are much more likely to be interested in considering the possibility of hiring blacks. It seems reasonable to assume that mobility policies would also work best where the disadvantaged groups have amassed political power. Atlanta's black leaders, for example, were early leaders in devising very strong affirmative action and minority set-aside policies.

Atlanta was the largest city in the region run by black elected officials. Atlanta had a black mayor since 1973, when Maynard Jackson was elected to the position by much the same coalition of blacks and affluent whites that had elected two earlier white mayors (Stone 1976, 31). In 1987 the *Christian Science Monitor* referred to Atlanta as the "mecca of the black middle class," describing the city as "the seat of black achievement in the United States for decades, from the post-Civil War elite black colleges, to the civil rights leadership of the 1960s, to Mayor Maynard Jackson's milestone successes in the 1970s at converting black political strength into economic advancement for black businesses" (*Monitor*, 29 May 1987: 1). The May 1987 issue of *Ebony* proclaimed Atlanta to be among the five best U.S. cities for blacks in business. The Atlanta economy is producing opportunities, and the region's black leaders actively seek a fair share.

The positive view of Atlanta as a center of black opportunity was still widely held as the 1990s began. An article on black mayors in *Black Enterprise*, for example, pointed to the preeminent role of Atlanta: "Since 1973, Atlanta has been the model of black mayoral power at work" (McCoy 1990, 150). A 1990 *Wall Street Journal* report on the black middle class described Atlanta as "a city with a thriving, self-assured black professional class." The authors concluded: "Since 1970, Atlanta, with its strong black political leadership and its high profile black colleges, has become a magnet for professional blacks in the North" (Hirsch and Alexander 1990, p. 1).

THE ECONOMIC SETTING

Capitalizing on a progressive racial image and a broadly diversified economy centered on the city's function as a major regional center of government, transportation, and commerce, the Atlanta area experienced unprecedented growth in population, employment, and income in the 1980s. Fueled in large measure by the in-migration of households, employers, and investment, this prosperity produced a very positive business climate. Louis Harris national surveys of corporate chief executive officers in 1986, 1987, and 1988, for example, ranked the Atlanta area first as a desirable business location (*Atlanta Constitution*, 14 July 1988: 1C).

Atlanta's success in becoming the South's dominant city was strongly related to the perception that it had solved the racial problems that hobbled the rest of the region. "With remarkable consistency," wrote *Atlanta Constitution* reporter Marilyn Geewax in 1987, "business leaders say Atlanta began to achieve its position as the region's leading city in the late 1950s and early 1960s for two reasons: the city's airport and its relatively harmonious race relations" (Geewax 1988: 34).

Our studies suggest, however, that what really distinguished Atlanta was not a better pattern of opportunity for black people but a better accommodation between black and white leaders in politics and business and much better public relations. The data indicates that there may be little relationship between the success of local black leaders and the opportunities of typical black families. In fact, local government may lack the power to make much difference on these issues.

Communities experiencing dramatic growth tend to celebrate the wonder of the expansion, the stories of fortunes made, the optimistic sense of progress and possibilities. They tend to have a politics dominated by development and a vision of government as a facilitator of investment. Business is at the center and is courted rather than seriously regulated by government. Business expansion is expected to solve many problems.

The Atlanta area is no exception. Much less public attention has been paid to the question of how benefits from the area's prosperity have been distributed. It is assumed that what is good for the overall economy is good for blacks.

Local observers described a kind of celebratory politics, where black middle-class leaders took the evidence of their own success as proof of progress and many low-income blacks accepted that as proof of the possibilities within the system. John Hutcheson, director of the urban research program at Georgia State University, said that the very visible success of the middle class greatly lower consciousness of black problems. "Nobody ever mentions that there are all these poor people here" (Hutcheson 1987).

"There is an Atlanta style about doing things," said Fulton County

Commission Chairman, Michael Lomax. ". . . I don't see our real problems now being put on the agenda when the black economic and political elites sit down with the white economic elites" (*New York Times,* 14 July 1988). The Atlanta style may be typical of the actual experience of blacks governing cities, as one black scholar wrote in 1990:

> . . . these governments . . . have generally pursued policies of fiscal conservatism and downtown development, coupled with policies and programs of minority appointments and employment, contracts to minority businesses, and efforts to restrain police misconduct in minority communities. (Smith 1990, 161)

In effect, black mayors found themselves trying hard in an often unsuccessful battle to attract white business interests being courted by many pro-business local governments.

The Movement of Population and Jobs, 1970–86

The Atlanta metropolitan area's major growth in population, employment, and income over the last ten years was unevenly distributed across neighborhoods and across racial and income groups. The bulk of the area's population and economic growth took place in the predominantly white northern suburbs in Cobb, Gwinnett, and northern Fulton and DeKalb Counties; the city of Atlanta and the southern suburbs did not do as well. Blacks are moving into the southern suburbs. There is substantial migration into all parts of the metropolitan area from out of state (see table 3.1).

Atlanta area whites had greatly expanded their suburban presence and had improved their economic position relative to blacks since 1970. Sub-

Table 3.1 Population Change from Net Migration and Origins of Population and Recent Movers, Atlanta and Suburbs, 1980

Unit	Net Migration 1970–80	Percentage of 1980 Population Born in State	Percentage of 1975–80 Movers from Different State	Percentage of 1975–80 Movers from Within State
Atlanta City	n/a	72.2	n/a	n/a
Fulton County*	− 54,873	66.5	14.2	9.2
DeKalb County*	24,684	54.8	18.6	15.0
Cobb County	74,749	55.4	20.8	14.9
Gwinnett County	78,993	59.4	17.9	25.1
Clayton County	33,928	63.6	13.1	21.3

*Includes data from Atlanta—most of the city is in Fulton County.

Source: Unpublished data furnished by Atlanta Regional Commission, *County and City Data Book, 1983,* table B.

Table 3.2 Population by Race: Atlanta and Suburban Counties, 1970–86

Unit	1970	1980	1986
Atlanta—City	495,039	425,022	430,100
white	240,093	144,507	135,460
black	254,945	280,514	294,640
Suburban Fulton	n/a	200,972	247,500
white		151,612	182,673
black		49,360	64,827
Suburban DeKalb	n/a	445,741	483,000
white		334,916	351,415
black		110,825	131,585
Gwinnett County	72,349	166,903	274,400
white	68,659	162,730	263,129
black	3,689	4,172	11,271
Cobb County	196,793	297,718	392,000
white	188,527	281,611	369,305
black	8,265	13,070	22,695
Clayton County	98,126	150,357	165,100
white	93,711	139,983	150,014
black	4,415	10,374	14,186

Source: 1970 and 1980 U.S. Census and Atlanta Regional Commission, 1987.

urban housing expanded even more rapidly than the population and very little housing was developed in the city. The white population in the city fell 44 percent from 1970 to the mid-1980s, but the great bulk of the decline took place before 1980. During the same period, the white population in booming Gwinnett County quadrupled while the black population remained very low. The broad outlines of this process of population change are shown in table 3.2.

The city's white population decline during the 1970s, through white outmigration to the suburbs, had leveled off by 1980. This relative stabilization stemmed from several sources, including a decline in the rate of white movement to suburbs. By 1982, the great majority of white suburban residents were longtime suburbanites and only one-tenth had come directly from the city. The large majority of whites in the metropolitan area had no recent knowledge of the inner city.

Among the city's remaining whites, a younger, relatively affluent group helped stabilize the white population. While gentrification in Atlanta was small on a citywide basis, it was larger than in many other cities (Berry 1985, 91–97). The housing opportunities available in such close-in neighborhoods as Inman Park, East Lake, Virginia-Highlands, and Midtown attracted or retained middle- and upper-income white households who might otherwise have located in the suburbs.

The growth in the size of this white professional group, together with the enormous growth in professional and service employment inside the city, increased the affluence of the city's white population. Median family income for Atlanta whites soared at a compounded annual average rate of 9 percent between 1975 and 1978 and 11 percent between 1978 and 1982, faster not only than the growth of black income but even of white suburban income.

The city's black population grew slowly after 1970 and became relatively poorer as the boom continued. Many middle-class blacks left. The annual growth rate of blacks within Atlanta was below one percent after 1970. Black births and movement into the city were counterbalanced by rapid black suburban growth in largely segregated and racially changing suburbs in southern DeKalb and Fulton Counties, where black population grew after 1980 more than three times as fast as in the city.

The Changing Income Distribution

This combination of middle-class suburbanization, first by whites and then by blacks, and in-migration by small numbers of upper-income whites, sharply increased the isolation of poor blacks inside Atlanta and increased the income disparity between blacks and whites remaining within the city. Like other relatively prosperous cities such as Washington D.C., Atlanta was increasingly characterized by a combination of poor blacks trapped in declining ghettos and affluent whites living in fashionable upscale neighborhoods.

The proportion of city households living in poverty almost doubled. Sixteen percent had incomes below the poverty level in 1970 but 28 percent were poor in 1982. Median black family income was two-thirds (68 percent) of white median family income in 1975, but it fell sharply to just over half (54 percent) of the white level by 1982. City poverty grew as jobs and income increased in the region (Fossett and Orfield 1987, 162–67). Even at the peak of the boom of the 1980s the intense poverty of Atlanta's inner city was virtually untouched. Georgia State University researcher, David Sjoquist noted in 1989: "The growing concentration of urban poverty is something one expects to find in economically depressed areas, not in the center of a booming area like Atlanta."

This situation creates a vicious cycle. Primary symptoms of poverty such as unemployment, poor health and welfare, crime and illiteracy, breed secondary symptoms of drug addiction and alcoholism, malnutrition, family instability, incarceration, illegitimate births and early death. (*Atlanta Journal and Constitution*, 13 February 1989)

For those who were poor and dependent on welfare, conditions were very harsh in Atlanta. In 1988, Georgia AFDC benefits ranked forty-first in the United States, with a family of three receiving just over one-third of the minimum income needed to escape poverty. Georgia provided no benefits to two-parent poor families. Georgia ranked thirty-seventh among the states in the adequacy of its low-income medical benefits (*Atlanta Constitution*, 19 May 1988). The total income of a family on AFDC was barely above what was needed to pay for a minimally adequate apartment in a poor and dangerous area of town, leaving nothing for other expenses.

Atlanta suburban population grew rapidly after 1970, with the most explosive growth in the northern suburban areas of Cobb, Gwinnett, and northern DeKalb and Fulton Counties. The southern suburbs, which had grown about as fast as the northern counties in the 1970s, expanded much more slowly in the 1980s.

Suburban growth over this period was driven by migration of jobs and of middle- and upper-income whites to the outlying areas where the housing stock grew rapidly. Initially, most Atlanta suburban residents came from Atlanta; more recently most came from outside the metropolitan area or moved from inner to outer ring suburbs. The economic boom brought a large migration of workers seeking good jobs directly to the Atlanta suburbs from suburbs across the United States.

The number of black suburbanites grew rapidly but only in suburban Fulton and DeKalb Counties. Blacks were less than six percent of the population in the prosperous and rapidly growing northern suburbs, reflecting both market discrimination and suburban resistance to low- and moderate-income housing and mass transit. Both Cobb and Gwinnett Counties refused to participate in MARTA (the Metropolitan Atlanta Rapid Transit Authority), the area transit system (Schmidt 1987).

SCALE OF GROWTH

The Atlanta Regional Commission estimated in 1988 that population and job growth accelerated again after 1985, reaching a yearly rate of 75,500 people and 68,500 jobs from 1985 to 1987. Throughout the 1980s the number of jobs was growing much faster than the working-age population. From 1980 to 1987, the population increased 23 percent and the jobs were up 43 percent (*Atlanta Constitution*, 13 June 1988). A national study estimated that by the year 2000 the area would have 600,000 more residents, gaining more than all but three other U.S. metro regions. The Atlanta Regional Commission forecasted even faster growth (*Atlanta*

Constitution, 29 June 1988). By all accounts there was vast growth and it was likely to continue.

Compared to other Sun Belt cities, Atlanta's population had a lower educational level and a higher poverty level. Earlier research showed that the city had one of the most unequal distributions of income in the United States (Bluestone, Murphy, and Stevenson 1973, 114). In 1980, the Census showed that 40 percent of Atlanta's population had not completed high school. The region's job boom did not produce strong outreach for black workers but drew many young, highly skilled, well-educated non-Southerners into the area, most of whom moved to the suburbs.

City Politics and Black Business

Atlanta had a significant black middle class with ties to a number of important black businesses and to the Atlanta University Center. Local government contracts were the bread and butter of black entrepreneurs. The contracts to build Hartsfield Airport awarded during Mayor Maynard Jackson's administration alone created twenty-one black millionaires (*Christian Science Monitor,* 29 May 1987: 32). Jackson recalled that "when I became mayor, zero-point-five percent of all the contracts of the city of Atlanta went to Afro-Americans in a city which at that time was fifty-fifty." When he announced the city's intent to foster minority participation through tough regulations, "we were threatened with litigation six, seven times a day." These much publicized contracts were a major reason for the favorable impression of Atlanta among many blacks, and the policy was vigorously pursued by Mayor Andrew Young in the 1980s.

Much of the very positive image of Atlanta's race relations grew out of its strong program for minority contracting on public projections. Mayor Jackson became famous across the United States for his aggressive minority contracting policy in building the city's new airport. The project, he recalls, "rewrote the books on affirmative action." The airport "accounted for 89 percent of all the affirmative action in all of America's airports" (*Atlanta Constitution,* 26 February 1990). The program was created in 1975 and expanded under the Young administration, with 37 percent of all city contracts going to minorities in 1988. "Atlanta is an enlightened city because of its pocketbook," said county board chairman Michael Lomax. "There's not a lot of social integration, but in the halls of commerce there's a lot of integration" (*Washington Post Weekly Edition,* 25–31 December 1989).

The spillover benefit for low-income, poorly educated blacks was modest. As the city's first black mayor, Maynard Jackson, neared the end of his second term, an *Atlanta Constitution* reporter observed that the situation of the poor was essentially unchanged. Michael Lomax, county leader and former aide to the mayor, said that poor blacks had expected a black mayor to "change significantly how they lived." The reality, he concluded, was that "you can't change the American economy and social system from a local unit" (*Atlanta Constitution* Staff 1981, "Black and Poor," 25).

Unfortunately, after the Supreme Court's 1989 decision against minority set-aside contracts in Richmond, Virginia, the Georgia Supreme Court rapidly ruled the minority contracting provisions in Georgia unconstitutional, curtailing at least temporarily a basic goal of Atlanta's black politicians (*New York Times*, 3 March 1989). The city immediately took steps to devise a new plan that would satisfy the court's requirements.

Compared to the long-delayed and very limited judicial response to desegregation cases filed in Atlanta by civil rights groups (see chapter 5), this was an astonishingly rapid response; the federal courts acting within weeks to forcefully apply the Supreme Court's decision in *City of Richmond v. J. A. Croson Co.*, 109 S.Ct. 706 (1989), seriously damaging a central accomplishment of black victories in city politics.

INCOME GAPS

The black political power of the 1970s had produced some large contracts but was not accompanied by growing equality between black and white families or neighborhoods during the 1970s. In fact, inequalities grew during that decade, after declining significantly during the 1960s, before blacks were elected. This does not mean that black political power was a negative influence; it means that the strategies of black administrations were too weak to offset very strong underlying negative trends in the economy and at other levels of government.

The 1970s brought a large expansion of the ghetto in the southern half of the city and growing differences among parts of the city, both between black and white areas and also among the black neighborhoods. Data show widening racial differences; in looking at income, housing value, overcrowding, years of schooling, and infant mortality rates, there were widening differences on three of the five measures. The data showed such rapid backward movement that the gains of the 1960s were more than wiped out. The research also showed special problems in tracts going through racial change (Smith 1985, 68–76).

Much of the inequality in the region's income distribution broke down along suburban versus inner-city lines. In 1985, 48 percent of Atlanta's households earned less than $15,000, but only one-seventh of suburban households did. In Atlanta, only 10 percent of all households had incomes in excess of $50,000 while 27 percent of suburban households did (Atlanta Regional Commission 1986). Although incomes rose in the region, 10 percent of the families were still below the poverty level. These poverty families were mainly concentrated in the city of Atlanta. Black families in the city were nearly eight times as likely as white suburbanites to be poor.

The percentage of families living in poverty in the city of Atlanta was four times as high as the percentage in the suburbs (see table 3.3). Eighty-eight percent of the poor were black. Close to one-third of the city's 65,808 black families were living below the poverty level. Although black families were only one-eighth of all families living in Atlanta's suburbs, one-third of the suburban poor families were black.

Among the nation's fifty largest cities, Atlanta ranked second in 1980 in terms of the percentage of its poor people concentrated in areas of high poverty. Only Newark was worse on this measure. In Atlanta, nearly one-half of the black poor, compared to only one-sixth of the white poor, lived in areas of concentrated poverty (Bane and Jargowsky 1988, 34, appendix 1).

Racial Stratification

One basic reason why the economic surge and black impoverishment co-existed in the metropolitan region was that blacks and whites were separated. The economic boom was concentrated in the outlying white areas while black homes and political power were concentrated in the center and in some of the southern suburbs.

This chapter shows the relationship of residence to economic opportunity and later chapters demonstrate how the major mobility institutions—education and job training—differed from white to black areas. If

Table 3.3 Poor Families in Metro Atlanta, 1980

Area	Total (%)	White (%)	Black (%)
Atlanta	24	7.0	31
Suburbs	6	4.3	17
Georgia	13	8.0	30

Source: 1980 Census data prepared by Lawrence Berkeley Laboratory.

segregation is severe and there are no mechanisms that transfer opportunities efficiently across the color line, then economic growth can occur on a very large scale without opening up major opportunities for minorities.

Metropolitan Segregation

Housing choice is strongly related to opportunities affecting the future of young people. The extreme stratification of housing markets by race and the increasing separation between the black lower- and middle-class areas is strongly related to the economic and social collapse of inner-city communities. The history of the city's ghettos produced very large areas where only blacks live. When fair housing became law, the boundaries of the ghetto expanded much faster, moving into parts of the suburbs, and most blacks with money left the older ghettos. A very small fraction of blacks moved into outlying white areas, but the basic results were rapid expansion of black residential areas and increasing impoverishment and isolation of older inner-city black communities. Children growing up in neighborhoods almost totally abandoned by middle-class blacks as well as whites are dependent on the metropolitan area's least effective schools, junior colleges, subsidized housing, and the most depressed labor markets.

The lowest-income communities tend to be unstable. Residents move often, frequently because of problems with the buildings or inability to pay rent, and children grow up in communities with few adult role models who have made it into the mainstream of society. Their communities are often dangerous and are places where the opportunities to make money in the criminal market are more visible than the paths to conventional success. These are the places most isolated from the effects of economic growth. Residential segregation, in other words, is the basic instrument by which the different societies and different opportunity systems available to most blacks and most whites in metropolitan Atlanta are kept fundamentally separate and unequal within a legal structure committed to equal opportunity. Residential separation creates separate societies.

Atlanta had long had a highly segregated housing market and the market remained far more segregated than could be explained by differences in black and white income levels. There were no stable integrated communities in the entire city, for example, as the contemporary metropolis was emerging in 1960. Every single area that blacks had entered in significant numbers had become a black community (Taeuber and Taeuber 1969, 109). Blacks were largely excluded from the post-World War II development of suburbia. Among the twenty-eight cities with more than 100,000 black residents at the time of the 1980 Census, Atlanta was among the most segregated. It had the largest fraction of blacks totally isolated from any whites. Measured according to randomness of its overall population distribution, it had the fifth highest level of residential segregation (Taeuber 1983, table 1). An analysis of all southern metropolitan areas by John Jakubs of the University of South Carolina found that metro Atlanta had a higher level of metropolitan segregation for blacks in 1980 than any area except metropolitan Miami (Jakubs 1986, 159). A study of the pattern of residential change in neighborhoods in a number of other metropolitan areas showed that only Atlanta and Chicago still had patterns of sudden, "panic" racial transition in which neighborhoods went from all-white to virtually all-black in a few years' time (Woolbright 1986). All of the measures showed a profound residential separation that had not been significantly altered by fair housing (see fig. 3.1).

There has not been a recent test of housing discrimination by realtors across the metropolitan Atlanta housing market. (A 1989 test of rental units within the city is described in the next chapter.) All major recent tests in other metro areas in the 1980s showed that discrimination remained very common, although it became more subtle and difficult to detect. It tended to involve not a simple denial of service or overt expression of racism, as was often true in the past, but different forms of treatment, such as steering black and white home-seekers to different communities and providing less assistance in obtaining mortgage financing. It is a sign of the low priority accorded fair housing in the Atlanta area that there was no private or public fair-housing organization with significant resources monitoring housing practices. Huge areas were urbanized, and vast changes structuring the future of the region's metropolitan society took place with no serious effort to break the power of the color line. A large study of lending activity in the metropolitan area by *The Atlanta Journal and Constitution* showed a clear pattern of discriminatory denial of mortgage financing to blacks. "Whites," the newspaper reported, "receive five times as many home loans from Atlanta's banks and savings and loans as blacks of the same income (see fig. 3.2)—and that gap has been widening each year. . . ." (1 May 1988). The housing market was still defined to a large degree by race.

School enrollment data provide an important way of looking at trends

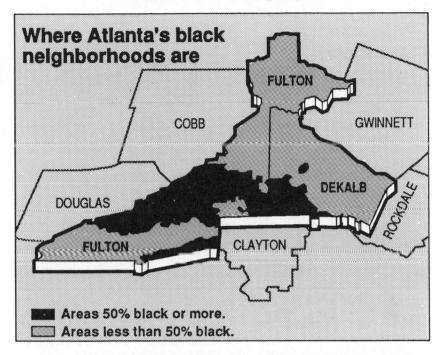

Figure 3.1. Where Atlanta's Black Neighborhoods Are. Reproduced from the *Atlanta Journal and Constitution*. Source: 1980 U.S. Bureau of the Census figures.

in segregation since the 1980 Census. In the absence of large desegregation orders, the school data primarily reflect neighborhood racial composition. Metro Atlanta schools in the mid-1980s were among the most segregated in the South. In spite of unusually large-scale black suburbanization, with more than one-half of black students in the suburbs by the late 1980s, metropolitan-level school segregation actually increased in the 1980s. School segregation reflected different patterns of white and black suburbanization which extended racial separation on a vast scale as first whites and then a substantial fraction of blacks moved out of the city in different directions.

By 1986, the Atlanta school district was 92 percent black and 41 percent smaller than it had been in 1967. Suburban DeKalb County schools, receiving the bulk of black suburbanization, were 57 percent black by the 1988–89 school year, and their black enrollment rose faster than all but one of the nation's largest school systems (a huge suburban Washington, D.C., district, Prince George's County, Maryland). Suburban school desegregation was spreading.

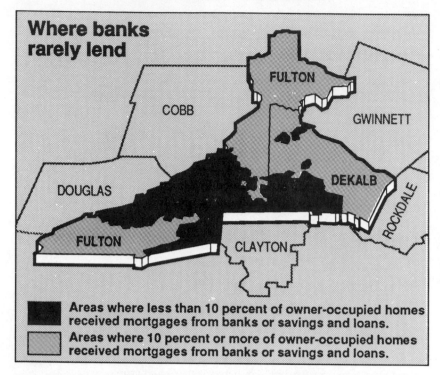

Figure 3.2. Where Banks Rarely Lend. Reproduced from the *Atlanta Journal and Consti-tution*. Source: Federal Financial Institutions Examination Council figures for 1981–86.

Segregation in housing helps to explain other findings. Blacks moving to the suburbs were much less likely to live in the areas experiencing high and rapidly increasing housing values. They were not competing for housing in the same market but in one with less desirable housing and amenities.

Within a system where economic growth provides jobs primarily for newcomers from out of town, while excluding many low-income inner-city residents, prosperity can actually make things worse for the poor.

Recent economic trends have made these problems worse. Like many other urban areas, Atlanta experienced major decentralization of eco-nomic activity, including low-skill, entry-level employment. Table 3.4 shows that a major suburbanization of employment has taken place in almost every economic sector since 1970.

The city's share of total private employment in the metropolitan area declined from 54 percent in 1970 to less than 33 percent in 1985. Private suburban employment more than doubled, and suburban growth rates in every major industrial sector were far in excess of those in the city.

Manufacturing jobs were the most desirable jobs for economic and social mobility by those without higher education. They were particularly critical for young men with relatively little education because they offered a wage adequate for supporting a family. Such jobs, however, have declined in the city of Atlanta by one fourth even as they were rising by two-thirds in the suburbs.

The Location of the Suburban Boom

Growth of all types of jobs varies greatly across sections of the metropolitan area. Although the downtown skyscrapers create an image of vibrant downtown expansion, growth is highly concentrated in the outlying counties. Many of the new jobs are far removed from black and low-

Table 3.4 Employment Change by Sector, Atlanta and Suburbs, 1970–85

Sector	Employment Numbers for Atlanta	Percentage Change from Preceding Period	Employment Numbers for Suburbs	Percentage Change from Preceding Period	Percentage in Atlanta
Manufacturing					
1970	56,494		67,109		45.7
1975	44,275	− 21.6	66,418	1.0	40.0
1980	48,917	10.5	80,981	21.9	37.7
1985	42,174	− 12.3	108,526	34.0	28.4
Retail					
1970	55,474		50,734		52.2
1975	47,417	− 14.5	72,509	42.9	35.5
1980	45,635	− 3.8	96,819	33.5	32.0
1985	47,080	3.2	146,320	51.1	24.3
Services					
1970	63,507		36,420		63.6
1975	66,337	4.5	64,076	75.9	50.9
1980	84,179	26.9	95,370	48.8	46.9
1985	102,726	22.0	140,674	47.5	42.2
Finance, Insurance, Real Estate					
1970	32,377		14,191		69.5
1975	31,037	− 4.1	27,847	96.2	52.7
1980	31,008	0.0	40,075	43.9	43.6
1985	33,637	8.5	52,563	31.2	39.0

Source: Calculated from tract data reported in Atlanta Regional Commission '85 *Employment.*

income areas. The geographic separation of jobs from black communities has created new barriers to opportunities for work which existing social programs, including job training, cannot remedy. The decision to break the metropolitan region into four separate areas for job training programs (discussed in chapter 7) further separated black Atlantans needing train-ing from the growing suburban labor market.

Fulton County, which includes most of the city of Atlanta, contained the largest percentage of jobs in the metropolitan area. In 1980, slightly more than one-half of all the jobs in the Atlanta region were located in Fulton County. However, by 1985 its share fell 7 percent. Cobb and Gwinnett Counties, located on the northern perimeter of the urban re-gion, experienced the largest increases in their share of jobs (see table 3.5). A continuation of these trends will make the outer suburbs the dom-inant force in the future labor market.

The trend can be seen even more clearly by comparing job trends for the part of Fulton County inside the city of Atlanta with suburban Fulton. Between 1970 and 1985 there were 61,100 new jobs created in suburban Fulton County but only two-thirds as many in the city. Thus, during the period when Fulton County's overall growth rate had slowed and its per-centage share of total metro jobs had declined, the remaining growth was mainly suburban (see tables 3.6 and 3.7).

The numbers of jobs in the city grew 12 percent from 1970 to 1985. Suburban jobs grew five times as fast. Even though downtown Atlanta was full of building projects, and was much better off than many other large downtowns, it captured only a small share of the new economic opportunities. Over half of all area jobs were located within the city in 1975, but by 1985 the city's share was reduced to slightly more than one-third of the total jobs.

Table 3.5 Counties' Shares of Jobs

County	1980		1985	
	No.	%	No.	%
Fulton	445,341	51	490,000	44
DeKalb	218,142	25	279,000	25
Cobb	96,685	11	151,900	14
Clayton	52,841	6	80,000	7
Gwinnett	48,514	6	89,400	8
Rockdale	10,834	1	15,300	1
Douglas	9,075	1	12,800	1

Source: Atlanta Regional Commission, May 1986.

Table 3.6 City of Atlanta's Share of Total Metro Jobs

Area	1970		1985		Growth	
	No.	%	No.	%	No.	%
City of Atlanta	338,054	55	379,597	34	41,543	12
Suburbs	281,639	45	738,803	66	457,164	162
Metro Area	619,693	100	1,118,400	100	498,707	81

Source: Atlanta Regional Commission, May 1986.

Table 3.7 Distribution of Job Growth in Metro Atlanta*

County	1975–80		1980–85	
	No.	%	No.	%
Fulton	56,947	10	44,659	9
DeKalb	50,303	23	60,858	22
Cobb	24,373	25	55,215	36
Clayton	17,725	34	27,159	34
Gwinnett	20,000	42	40,886	46

*Percentages based on 1985 figures.
Source: Atlanta Regional Commission, May 1986.

Much of the new office space located in downtown Atlanta was occupied by established, locally based companies such as Coca-Cola, Georgia Power, and Southern Bell. Branch offices of national corporations and business services such as data processing usually located their regional offices in suburban office parks.

Between 1960 and 1975, the share of total metropolitan employment in the central business district fell from 20 percent to 12 percent. The downtown Atlanta share of total retail sales in the region was reduced to just 7 percent by 1972 due to the explosive boom of suburban shopping centers in the mid-1960s (Abbott 1981, 180). The great retail and office booms were located around the largest suburban shopping centers, the real "new downtowns" of the greater Atlanta region. Many of these good new jobs that were locating downtown required high levels of education and went to suburbanites.

Job-growth rates were highest in segments of the northern suburbs. Overall, the five majority black areas had an average job growth rate of 5 percent while the areas where more than 90 percent of the residents were white had an average growth rate of 71 percent, a rate fourteen times higher than the black areas enjoyed (see table 3.8).

Table 3.8 Metro Atlanta's Employment Growth Rate (%) by Region and Race, 1970–85

Geographic Area	Job Growth	Black
City		
SE Atlanta	3.6	74.2
SW Atlanta	27.0	96.1
NE Atlanta	6.1	34.6
NW Atlanta	−2.5	76.2
Central Business District	6.0	69.4
Buckhead	77.0	6.0
Suburbs		
Sandy Springs	398.0	3.0
North Fulton	377.0	2.5
South Cobb	81.3	4.6
North Cobb	514.0	3.4
Southwest Gwinnett	866.0	3.0
Northeast DeKalb	304.0	4.7
Tri-Cities	−4.4	54.2
South Fulton	294.1	45.4

Source: Atlanta Regional Commission, 1985 Update.

The isolation of Atlanta's low-income black population on the city's south side, far removed from the main areas of job growth, is no accident. Local decisions in the 1950s and early 1960s blocked proposals to build public housing on the city's north side or downtown. Poor blacks were moved into outlying areas of the city in "areas that were already black or in areas adjacent to black residences; but, by long-standing 'agreement,' relocation facilities were not to be placed on the prestigious Northside— not even in or adjacent to scattered pockets of black residences in that section of the city" (Stone 1976, 79).

Low-income blacks were concentrated in segregated public housing and isolated from jobs and good schools. The lack of moderate- or low-income housing in many suburbs effectively barred many blacks from taking advantage of the suburban job growth.

Some suburban politicians sought to increase the separation between the suburbs and the city. The counties located on the city's northern perimeter refused to participate in MARTA (the Metropolitan Atlanta Rapid Transit Authority). They prevented public housing construction in the suburbs by refusing to establish their eligibility for federal funding and by enacting zoning that effectively excluded low- or moderate-income housing. These trends erected employment barriers for many black workers.

For almost two decades, national studies on the suburbanization of jobs projected that if trends continued unabated there would be a growing separation between the central-city labor market, in which the majority of blacks sought employment, and the suburban labor market, in which the vast majority of jobs went to whites (Kain 1968; Mooney 1969; Gold 1972; Masotti and Madden 1973; von Furstenberg et al. 1974; Wilson 1979). The predictions became a reality in the metropolitan Atlanta of the 1980s and the trends were all toward more severe isolation.

The ability to commute tends to expand job choices for middle-class families with reliable cars. Most outlying suburban jobs are only accessible by car. Many low-income families, however, have cars that frequently break down or no car at all. Thus, suburban whites can commute to jobs in the city while many low-income blacks in the city are excluded from suburban jobs.

According to the 1970 Census, 90.3 percent of the blacks working in the city of Atlanta also lived within the city, in contrast to only 33.6 percent of the whites who worked in the city. Even then, 74 percent of middle-income jobs in central Atlanta were held by suburbanites (Nelson 1974, 72).

Commuting to the central business district for good-paying jobs is feasible. Commuting to the suburbs for low-paying jobs is not. There were no efficient mass transit links between the ghettos and most of the growing job markets.

The situation was particularly grave for the factory jobs that provided the first step of mobility for poorly educated inner-city immigrant men in the past. In striking contrast to the dying industrial cities of the North, Atlanta was blessed with continuing industrial growth. By 1985, for every one manufacturing job within the city of Atlanta there were 2.5 jobs located in the suburbs, and the trend was toward greater dispersion of such jobs. This shift had a particularly adverse effect on black employment since blacks had long been highly concentrated in blue-collar jobs, with one-half of all southern black men employed as laborers in 1970. A 1974 study of this trend concluded, "Although the intent to discriminate may not be evident, the discriminatory impact, given the inner city-suburban racial polarization which is taking place, is nevertheless occurring, as jobs follow white workers to the suburbs" (Niemi 1974, 138). This loss of job opportunity for young black men is doubtless related to many aspects of the decline of black neighborhoods and basic institutions, including the family structure. The particular difficulties confronting black men in job training and employment in the Atlanta area, discussed in chapter 7, were strongly linked to the transfer of good jobs far out of the city.

The Atlanta area was relatively unaffected by the major recessions of

1981–83, the worst national economic downturn in the last half-century. Even in the center of the metropolis, conditions were better than the national pattern. Conditions were best, however, in the outlying northern suburbs. The 1982 unemployment rate in Fulton County was 2 percent below the national average, and annual unemployment in other area counties was still lower. The lowest rates were in the rapidly growing northern suburbs in Cobb, Gwinnett, and northern DeKalb counties.

The economic boom of the mid-1980s brought employment growth inside the city, especially in high-skill service, technical, and clerical jobs that minority and low-income governments frequently lacked the skills to fill. While Atlanta was spared the absolute loss of jobs that many northern cities faced and while the large absolute shrinkage of employment that afflicted some of them was not present in the inner city, there was an increasing mismatch between the locations of low-skill jobs and housing for low-skill minority workers.

Employment in lower-skill industries inside the city declined rapidly over the last fifteen years. Manufacturing and retail provided large numbers of jobs to relatively unskilled workers while most positions in services, finance, and government required more education or training. Within Atlanta, manufacturing employment declined by almost one-third between 1970 and 1985 and retail employment fell by one-seventh; service employment inside the city grew by more than two-thirds and government employment increased by over 40 percent. The bulk of suburban employment growth in manufacturing and retail trade occurred in the outer northern suburbs.

Employment and the Economic Boom of the 1980s

No matter how unequal the distribution of jobs and income may be, it is, of course, much better to live in a metropolitan area experiencing vast growth of jobs than in a less prosperous area. There were significant increases in labor force participation but no decline in the level of joblessness for black men in the metro area during the 1978 to 1988 period (see fig. 3.3). Black women had a slight increase in labor force participation but a significant rise of joblessness. The situation of white males was virtually unchanged. The largest winners during this period were white women, whose labor force participation rates and percent employed rates shot up by about one-fifth while their unemployment rate fell. White women lived closer to where the jobs were being created. Both blacks and whites had a higher percentage of their total working-age population working in 1988 than a decade earlier, but the white rate rose slightly faster. Overall, black joblessness rose 1 percent while the white rate fell .6 percent. Even though prosperity and in-migration meant that 192,000 more blacks were employed by 1988, the racial gaps had widened a littler further (U.S. Bureau of Labor Statistics 1989). Even at the peak of the economic expansion in Georgia, blacks were three times as likely as whites to be jobless. In 1987 10.3 percent of blacks were jobless compared to 3.6 percent of whites (*Atlanta Constitution*, 4 June 1988).

This study concentrates on the period from the mid-1970s to the mid-1980s and focuses attention on the nature of the economic boom in the 1980s. No economic miracle, however, continues indefinitely. By the end of the 1980s, after the period of this study, growth slowed. The job growth in 1988 and 1989 was about one-third that of the mid-1980s, and the northern suburbs faced a substantial slowdown. Manufacturing jobs actually dropped by 6 percent between 1987 and 1989. The area was hardhit by cuts in domestic auto production facilities and defense production. Lockheed Corporation cut employment at its Marietta aircraft facility from 20,000 in 1987 to 9,100 in mid-1990 (*Atlanta Journal and Constitution*, 1 January 1990, 14 February 1990; *Gwinnett Daily News*, 23 March 1990; *Marietta Daily Journal*, 11 April 1990).

The suburban housing market began to experience severe problems. Hundreds of millions of dollars of foreclosures on construction loans took

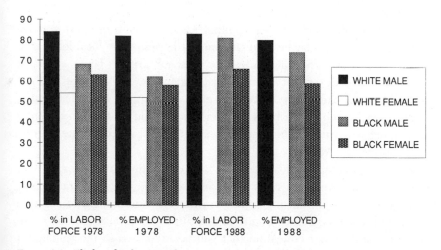

Figure 3.3. Black and White Employment in Atlanta, 1978–88

place in the Atlanta suburbs in 1989 and 1990 (*Atlanta Journal and Constitution*, 5 March 1990).

All communities go through economic cycles. All speculative booms lead to periodic overbuilding and reversals. Firms that flourished under the defense buildup of the early 1980s faced a very different environment as the decade ended. In political terms, however, the problem is that local officials are too busy and too optimistic about the market as a solution to all problems during boom periods to pay attention to social costs. When the issues are raised again during downturns, they then say they are sorry because it is too late and government must be cut back. This book examines the lost opportunities of the boom period.

Summary

There was a geography of opportunity in metropolitan Atlanta. New jobs, new housing, new schools, new shopping centers, and vast new wealth were mushrooming a few miles away from deteriorating slums and abandoned buildings. Dreams were dying in neighborhoods not far from where farmland was being paved for great malls, factories, and freeways. A color line separated these areas, and that color line was a line that defined radically different opportunities. The economic boom was a boom in white Atlanta. Where black Atlanta was reaching into the suburbs, the opportunities that were usually part of suburban migration were shriveling. Race remained a central factor in the opportunity system and the problem of racism was written out across the landscape of the metropolitan area.

The economic boom of metropolitan Atlanta during the past generation was formidable, far beyond the fondest hopes of the local leaders in most urban areas. The data show that even job growth far in excess of population growth did not narrow racial disparities. A rising tide will not ✔ float all boats if part of the harbor is walled off from the tide. Residential segregation, which is the basis for racial separation, is the fundamental underlying structure for the inequalities that persist and continue to grow in contemporary Atlanta.

Widening income gaps by race and by area within a rapidly expanding economy were important signs of the nature of the persisting racial barriers. The system of housing separation must be understood to come to terms with the inequalities in public education and in access to job training, jobs, and higher education that will be examined in the remainder of this book.

4

Housing and Opportunity

Housing provides the framework for many forms of inequality in metropolitan America. A home is the largest single cost families bear and their most important way of accumulating wealth. The home and what is linked directly to housing choice—the neighborhood—are key elements of status in American society and are basic in the allocation of opportunity in urban areas. The kind of housing and the kind of neighborhood in which a family lives are the most tangible and immediate signs of the success or failure of the family in the economic and social systems. Home ownership, for those who can afford it, is the basic source of a family's net worth and credit for large investments, such as college education for children. And housing location helps to determine social connections and the environment in which children grow up; it is strongly related to schools, jobs, safety, crime, and many other important aspects of life.

Segregated housing and neighborhoods are still fundamental realities in metropolitan Atlanta. In a period in which there would be an instant uproar over a "whites only" sign on a restroom or a racial comment by a governmental official, there is very little public discussion of the much more fundamental problem. A generation after fair housing became law, residential segregation stubbornly prevails, despite strong black preference for integrated neighborhoods.

Segregated housing and communities are still widely accepted as natural. So, too, are the things based on segregated housing. People who would be outraged by a proposal to provide unequal education by race within a school district accept without question unequal schooling among separate white and black districts built on residential segregation. In fact, many accept that pattern as normal and strongly object to plans that permit students to leave the black areas. Residential segregation has become the basic way in which we can openly and legally offer unequal opportunities to young people on different sides of the racial boundaries. The differences have very tangible effects.

The inner-city black mother who dropped out of a terrible and dangerous school and has to take three buses to get to a minimum-wage job in the suburbs feels the negative effects of living in the ghetto; the positive effects of segregation in a privileged community are apparent in the experience of the suburban child who attends a school and lives in a neighborhood where everyone begins preparing for a competitive college in elementary school. White suburban areas have the schools most able to prepare students successfully for college, while inner-city neighborhoods tend to be served by inferior schools with extremely high dropout rates. Housing has long been a fundamental barrier in the greater Atlanta area, and the problems associated with isolation have become worse in the 1980s.

Ghettos and the Perpetuation of Inequality

Housing remains segregated and highly unequal, discrimination continues in the market, and this research shows that blacks have a diminishing chance to own homes in comparison with whites in similar circumstances. Black renters do much worse than whites with less income; low-income families, who are very disproportionately black, face crises in the rental market. Black families continue to be denied a fair chance at a location that ties their children into the educational and economic opportunities routinely provided in white areas.

This is particularly worrisome since inequalities become self-perpetuating, in part through the stratification of neighborhoods, restricted access to housing in white areas, and unequal family wealth growing out of less frequent ownership and the more slowly rising values of homes in black areas. If housing and neighborhoods are basic levers for family success and mobility of children, exclusion from quality neighborhoods can mean a cumulative white advantage over time—even for black families with similar incomes and educational backgrounds.

In Atlanta, the income gap between city and suburban residents is growing. And, as later chapters will show, the schools and job training systems reinforce rather than compensate for neighborhood inequalities. The system of residential segregation confines most upwardly mobile blacks to neighborhoods that function as downward escalators for many families while exactly the opposite happens for young white families located in the all-white suburbs. Just the location of their homes can strongly affect the economic and social future of their families.

Housing inequalities seriously affect middle-class black households who flee city ghettos in search of suburban opportunities, but end up in racially changing suburbs with far fewer jobs, weaker schools, and more limited long-term prospects than is true for families in the white suburbs. Within the segregated housing market, their aspirations are directed toward suburbs that, at the beginning, have the physical appearance of typical suburbs but tend over time to develop problems much more like racially changing inner-city communities.

PUBLIC POLICY, RACIAL BARGAINS, AND THE CONSOLIDATION OF THE GHETTO SYSTEM

Residential segregation in Atlanta was not the product of black preference but rather the result of government-supported white resistance to integration. One-fifth of Atlanta's population had been black before the civil war and the black population increased by more than 500 percent by 1870. Before the war, blacks had lived where slaveholders allowed them to live. Afterward many settled in communities outside the old city, which were later annexed, or in areas shunned by whites. Segregation rapidly became a basic fact of life. Seventy-three percent of all city blocks in Atlanta were totally segregated by 1870, just five years after the war ended. By the 1890s the system of segregation covered large parts of the city; there were few integrated blocks, and those tended to be blocks in transition. In some cases, blocks appeared to be integrated because of the servants' quarters in the alleys (Rabinowitz 1980, 19, 100–115).

Within a few years after the war, the nuclei of Atlanta's twentieth century Negro districts had already been formed. These areas were located in the valleys and bottoms of the six wards, the same wards in which the whites lived along the ridges and atop the hills. The sole exceptions were the areas around the black colleges. (Rabinowitz 1980, 115)

Blacks were confined to separate neighborhoods, black educational and other institutions were located there, and whites resisted blacks' entry into white areas. The system was well established a century ago and segregation became the norm.

Atlanta had a race riot in 1906 followed by a tightening of the residential segregation of blacks. The city passed three laws requiring residential segregation in 1913, 1917, and 1922. Atlanta was one of the instigators of a national push for racial zoning, promoting it even after it was outlawed by the U.S. Supreme Court. Although these laws were struck down eventually, they helped define the city's residential patterns (Stone 1989, 19). A detailed study of the city's zoning ordinances shows that zoning continued to be used to reinforce residential separation. (Flint 1977). The basic policy of the city in the first part of the twentieth century was one of residential apartheid.

When the era of subsidized housing and urban renewal came to Atlanta, these tools were embraced by the business leaders as ways to insulate the downtown business district, and to carry out the program of separating it from the larger black communities. Atlanta had a long history of renewal and replacement of old housing. In the 1930s a coalition of downtown interests mobilized to wipe out slums near downtown (Stone 1989, 16).

Unlike some parts of the Deep South, blacks were not politically powerless in Atlanta, and some kind of bargain had to be struck if the business leaders were to receive black support for their plans. The bargain was built on black acceptance of the color line and the displacement of poor blacks from most downtown areas in exchange for construction of subsidized housing in black neighborhoods, acceptance of the expansion of black areas around their earlier boundaries in the southern and western parts of the city, and assistance for important institutions, such as the city's black colleges.

Blacks accepted apartheid and tried to create a more equal context by building on the power of some institutions within their own community. The bargain seemed to make sense because it provided some gains and the black community's power was insufficient to force a fundamentally different outcome. Nonetheless, it meant accepting and expanding a residential system that had never worked well—one that became the foundation for a metropolitan society with profound and deepening inequalities.

The residential foundation was critical because it had very powerful self-sustaining features that preserved and expanded the system even when overt discrimination was no longer permissible. The residential division of the social space of the urban community meant that the great majority of blacks were confined to communities with declining prospects and that almost all of the residents of the communities with the most buoyant prospects were white. As the system grew, most urban residents accepted it as normal and grew up with virtually no knowledge of life on the other side of the color line. Blacks knew very little about housing or other opportunities in white neighborhoods and black realtors and builders learned to live with segregation and did not participate in the much larger white markets. The residential pattern fostered racial politics, since segregation excluded black leaders from the larger community and white politicians in the suburbs were unconcerned with black interests because they had virtually no black constituents. The acceptance of the system of residential separation in return for some immediate gains turned out to be a Faustian bargain for black Atlanta much like the one described in the next chapter involving black control of the schools.

The city had an early and large commitment to subsidized housing and developed the nation's "fifth largest public housing program" (Stone 1989, 162).

The Atlanta Housing Authority and the Metropolitan Planning Commission both participated in identifying areas for black expansion; and, in building the projects of Carver Homes (opened in 1953 on the southside) and Perry Homes (opened in 1955 on the westside), the Housing Authority was integral to the opening of residential land for blacks. By one estimate, between 1945 and 1956, 3,450 new owner-occupied homes, 3,100 new private apartments, and 1,990 new public housing units were built for blacks. . . . Not only did the Mayor's Committee negotiate disputes, but other elements of the mayor's alliance played strategic roles as well. The support of the police department was crucial, and the mayor and the police chief were apparently inclined to hold back protection unless an expansion was part of an approved plan. (Stone 1989, 35)

The broad agreement between black and white leadership that dominated Atlanta politics during this era was based on white demands for segregation and downtown renewal and black demands for land and housing to accommodate population expansion in areas including newly constructed residential communities outside existing ghetto boundaries (Stone 1989, 36).

When urban renewal came to Atlanta on a massive scale under the federal housing act of 1949, the plan that was implemented followed the previous bargains and provided for clearing the land of black areas near downtown and expanding black housing in the southern and western parts of the city. Black colleges received "room for expansion and a diminution of substandard housing in the areas around them" (Stone 1989, 40). The plan called for moving 10,000 families by the early 1960s and a large expansion of public housing, which was largely confined, because of white resistance, to the inner part of the black community. Sometimes the only site that could be approved meant adding a new concentration of low-income housing right next to existing projects (Stone 1989, 41, 44). Public actions had a great deal to do with the establishment and expansion of the system of residential separation, even some black civil rights

leaders were active participants in the arrangements to expand segregated housing in the city (Stone 1976, 66–72). Nine renewal projects in
the 1960s cleared 900 acres of land, the equivalent of 450 blocks, and
they were followed by a series of additional projects. In the poorest low-
income parts of the city, 41 percent of the housing units were lost during
the decade. The new stadium and the interstate highway system were
primary consumers of the cleared land. Since the city did not provide
adequate replacement housing and discrimination in the housing market
remained largely untouched, the forced eviction of thousands of low-
income blacks had totally predictable effects—it expanded the ghetto and
led to the conversion of nearby neighborhoods into new slums. Most of
the people moved less than two miles, often doubling up in housing a
single household could not afford (*Atlanta Constitution* staff 1981, "Black
and Poor," p. 13).

By the mid-1980s there was a substantial body of subsidized housing
in Atlanta. One-eleventh of all the housing units in the city were publicly
owned, the highest concentration in the United States, but the public
housing system was in deep trouble with nearly 15,000 families trapped
in decaying buildings in dying parts of the metropolitan economy (Dedman 1988).

When Atlanta confronted intense serious crime in the late 1980s,
many of the worst problems occurred in the segregated housing projects.
The FBI reported in 1989 that Atlanta had the nation's highest crime rate.
In protest meetings residents of the city's forty-two projects demanded
that the National Guard be called out to protect them. Others asked for
creation of a special police force to protect the 50,000 project residents
(*New York Times*, 14 December 1989).

The Atlanta Housing Authority was the fifth largest in the United
States, with 33,400 residents, fewer than one out of twenty of whom were
employed. There were also 16,000 people living in other forms of subsidized housing in the city. Subsidized housing provided homes for about
one-eighth of the city's people (*Atlanta Journal and Constitution*, 8 February 1990).

The housing authority spent $85.3 million a year housing a population
in which only 5 percent had jobs and 98 percent of the families were
headed by single mothers. There were 4,500 tenants who had lived in
the projects for more than ten years. During 1988 and 1989, fifty people
had died in drug-related incidents in the projects (*Atlanta Constitution*,
2 February 1990).

Much of the subsidized housing was seriously deteriorated and lacked funds for needed repairs. This was true not only of public housing but also of some of the projects put up by community groups as a means of neighborhood development. The Wheat Street Baptist Church constructed a complex of three subsidized projects, beginning in 1963, in the heart of the black community. Many residents were among those displaced by urban renewal. The projects experienced major construction and management problems that the church and its hired managers and investment partners failed to solve. By 1981, 70 percent of the units in two of the projects were vacant, maintenance had virtually stopped, renovation money was lacking, and a lawsuit had been brought by tenants against the minister and the managers (*Atlanta Constitution* staff 1981, "Black and Poor," 14). It is not just housing authorities that have had problems managing high-density projects for low-income families in isolated inner-city areas. HUD reported many problems like those in the Wheat Street Garden Apartments in other parts of the United States. Investigators for the U.S. General Accounting Office reported to Congress in 1982 that problem projects tended to be "in isolated areas where the project constitutes a neighborhood to itself" or in "densely populated areas characterized generally by physical, economic, and social decay (U.S. General Accounting Office Letter Report 1982).

Housing Discrimination and the Contemporary Color Line

Whatever the history of segregation may have been, cities have been under the federal fair housing law since 1968. Much of metropolitan Atlanta's growth has taken place since housing discrimination became illegal. Research shows, however, that fair housing is far from a reality. In 1979, rental housing practices in metropolitan Atlanta were studied as part of the first national effort by the federal government to assess the extent of discrimination in the U.S. housing market. The study included 119 apartment complexes in the metro area. Only 27 percent of the complexes provided equal treatment for similar black and white families. In 45 percent of the tests, white families were given preferential treatment, a rate considerably above the national average (*Atlanta Constitution*, March 1989: A8; Wienk et al. 1979: ES-2). Since a typical family looks at several housing units in its search for housing, the chances that a given family would encounter discrimination somewhere in its search were extremely high.

There was no detailed study of housing discrimination across metropolitan Atlanta in the 1980s, but a federally funded study of apartment complexes within the city in late 1988 and early 1989 found substantial discrimination two decades after the enactment of a federal fair housing law. In the largest test ever within the city, 31 percent of all inquiries produced discrimination by the rental agents. The audit by Metro Fair Housing Services, Inc., also found out that 77 percent of the complexes in the city had policies against families with children (Metro Fair Housing Services 1989).

It is likely that tests of discrimination in the suburban housing markets would have found greater problems. In the city, more than two-thirds of the people are black and many housing complexes, which already house mostly blacks, could not be expected to discriminate. Atlanta is a city with a fair housing law administered by a black mayor and a black police chief. It is a city with many black property owners and managers. "We feel sure," said the MFHS, "that no other local jurisdiction would test as well" (ibid.). Based on his organization's experience in the area, the group's executive director, Joe Shifalo, estimated that as many as 70 percent of all complexes discriminated (Bronstein 1989, A8). For a black family seeking housing in three apartment buildings there would be more than nine chances in ten of discrimination.

The group also did an analysis of real estate advertising. It reported that the dominant metropolitan news paper, *The Atlanta Journal and Constitution,* carried no publisher's notice of fair housing rights. Its analysis of 3,277 ads in a Sunday edition in 1989 showed that 99.8 percent contained neither the fair housing assurance nor the equal housing logo (Metro Fair Housing Services 1989).

Fair housing was a weak movement in metropolitan Atlanta. There were no county fair housing laws in the entire state until mid-1988, when the Fulton County Board enacted a law following a newspaper investigation of discrimination in the mortgage lending business (*Atlanta Constitution,* 5 May 1988).

There was no systemic metropolitan housing testing. Since overt discrimination has been illegal, most cases of housing discrimination take the form of steering or unequal treatment, which often can only be detected by comparing the treatment accorded to similar black and white clients by the same broker or rental agent. Serious enforcement in such a situation requires professional-quality testing that can stand up in court or in an administrative proceeding. The Task Force for Housing Discrimination, working on some of the problems of discrimination and steering in the suburbs, got some money for testing but could not do a systematic job of auditing market practices (Hutcheson, 1987).

DISCRIMINATION AGAINST BLACK BROKERS

Part of the problem was the general exclusion of black brokers from the white suburban business. Atlanta had some two hundred black real estate brokers, organized in the 50-year-old Empire Real Estate Board. Its President, Edward C. London, said in 1990: ". . . blacks are still selling to blacks and whites to whites. We have no more access to the white market now than before. When blacks move to white neighborhoods, the agents are often white, so we lose opportunities for our agents and our customer base" (Jackson 1990, 17). Members of the black broker group were excluded from the Multiple Listing Service listings in white areas; membership was limited to realtors in the overwhelmingly white Atlanta Board of Realtors. The black group had an anti-trust case pending in this issue (ibid.).

The fact that black brokers could make their living only within the system of segregation by encouraging black clients to consider listings, for example, where their children would almost certainly face inferior, segregated schools is one example of the way different forms of discrimination interact with and support each other. Black real estate brokers became agents for the spread of ghettos because the racial separation of the market meant that only there could they get the listings they needed for clients who wanted to move outside of the existing black community.

HOUSING VIOLENCE

Blacks moving into some areas still faced racial attacks. Between April and October 1989, for example, there were six publicly reported incidents of racial vandalism in Clayton County. "KKK" was written on some homes, a cross was burned, and others had sayings including "Nigger Get" and "Die Tomorrow" written on their homes or cars (*Atlanta Constitution*, 18 October 1989).

A U.S. Civil Rights Commission staff member, Bobby Doctor, told an Atlanta meeting in early 1989 that the rise of violence and discrimination against blacks in the housing market was directly related to the slashes in federal civil rights agencies. His own agency, he said, had been "teetering on the brink of annihilation" (*Atlanta Constitution*, 30 April 1989).

RACE AND CAPITAL FOR HOMEOWNERSHIP

One of the basic problems affecting the destiny of neighborhoods and families in the late 1980s was the critical shortage of capital for families and communities in the black neighborhoods of metropolitan Atlanta. A massive analysis of the flow of mortgage money into black and white neighborhoods in metropolitan Atlanta won a 1988 Pulitzer Prize for the *Atlanta Constitution*. The series, "The Color of Money," was based on the records of the area's lending institutions, which were obtained under the federal Freedom of Information Act. The records for mortgages between 1981 and 1986 were matched with data on the racial composition of various parts of the housing market. A detailed study was made of the flow of mortgage money to sixty-four similar middle-income black and white areas. The study included 82,600 mortgage loans and 26,700 home improvement loans made by banks, savings and loan institutions, and large credit unions—a total of $6.2 billion in housing capital (*Atlanta Constitution*, 4 May 1988).

The study showed massive inequalities in the flow of housing capital. "In the white areas lenders made five times as many loans per 1,000 households as in the black areas," it said. The newspaper also conducted a detailed analysis of sixteen neighborhoods in 1986 and found that home purchasers in black areas were only one-fourth as likely as those in white areas to receive conventional financing (*Atlanta Constitution*, 1 May 1988). The research also found that loan application offices were "almost all located in predominantly white areas" and that a number of offices had been closed once the areas they served became predominantly black. In Mayor Andrew Young's own neighborhood, Cascade Heights, only one-fifth of the homes sold in 1986 received conventional financing (ibid.).

The effects of a lack of conventional financing were severe. Housing markets required a large and continuing influx of credit to provide well-maintained housing. "Without a good mix of credit to fuel it," reporter Bill Dedman concluded, ". . . the housing market in the neighborhood sputters and property values stall" (ibid., 2 May 1988). The consequence, said Sherman Golden of the Fulton County planning and economic development staff, was a transfer of money from savers in black areas to investors in white areas. "We're talking about disinvestment, capital flight from the Southside. . . . Southside residents put money in the bank and pay taxes, but their money is spent on the Northside (ibid., 1 May 1988). Middle-class black neighborhoods had to survive on a much weaker system of financial support and middle-class families wishing to own homes had far fewer options.

THE DECLINING SITUATION FOR BLACKS IN THE HOUSING MARKET

The extreme stratification of housing markets by race and by income is strongly related to the economic and social collapse of inner-city communities. Middle-class blacks who want better opportunities are spurred to leave and those who cannot afford to are more profoundly isolated. Children growing up in neighborhoods almost totally occupied by low-income blacks are much more likely to be exposed to crime and family pathology, which tend to be concentrated in those areas. (If there were large areas where whites suffered from highly concentrated, long-term poverty in metropolitan Atlanta, they would also, doubtless, experience these problems.) While children growing up in older ghetto areas have the same legal rights as their suburban counterparts, they will lack essential preparation for opportunities because of where they live.

Atlanta has long had a highly segregated housing market and it remains far more segregated than can be explained solely by differences in incomes. In 1980, it was one of the most intensely segregated housing markets in the United States, which helped account for our findings: blacks moving to the suburbs were much less likely to live in the areas with high and rapidly increasing housing values, and typical middle-income black families in rental housing were still living in housing that had as many or more defects as that occupied by poor white families. Blacks were not competing for housing in the same market but were concentrating in the black or racially changing areas with less desirable housing choices, areas where disinvestment in the maintenance of rental stock may already have been under way.

This chapter uses data from the Census Bureau's Annual Housing Survey and other sources to examine the situation of Atlanta area blacks in both owner-occupied and rental housing. The Housing Survey offers more information on housing conditions than the 1980 Census and collects data much more frequently, thus permitting a more accurate assessment of changing housing conditions. Extensive analysis of the survey data tapes from the mid-1970s to the early 1980s provided much of the data for later sections of this chapter.

At the bottom of the economic spectrum, the problem of housing was not an issue of choice but of crisis and the absence of any workable solutions. Many families could not afford any private-market housing without severe defects, and there was far too little subsidized housing available to meet their needs. Additionally, subsidized housing usually was limited to locations that were extremely unfavorable for families, in part because of decisions by the political leadership to isolate the poor in order to encourage the redevelopment of the downtown area (Stone 1976). The families needing the most help to make a connection with a good job or a good school were forced by their desperate need for housing to live where there were few opportunities for jobs or education. Furthermore, subsidized housing was severely isolated from middle-class contacts of any sort.

Poor families unable to obtain a subsidized unit simply did not have enough income to pay a landlord the reasonable costs of maintaining any form of standard housing. In Atlanta's tight housing market, where there was growing competition for what housing was available, the poor were squeezed both by rising costs and their own declining real incomes. The poor blacks were much more likely to remain impoverished in comparison with whites, who tended to be temporarily poor during a family crisis; thus, the blacks faced long-term housing problems. Most ended up in deteriorating flats in isolated areas where they often could not afford to pay the rent for long.

By the early 1980s, as this chapter will show, housing costs in the Atlanta area were extremely high for families in poverty. City or suburban, white or black—poor families could expect to pay two-thirds or more of their cash income for total housing costs.

Within a system where economic growth provides jobs primarily to well-educated, white newcomers but acts to exclude many low-income inner-city residents, overall prosperity can actually make matters worse for the poor in the housing market. In Atlanta, it created strong incentives for gentrifiers to convert lower-cost housing to middle-class use and for landlords to raise rents sharply as the demand greatly exceeded the supply.

By 1982, poor families faced a nearly hopeless situation in the private housing market, and costs have risen rapidly since then. Many of these families lived precariously, frequently forced to choose among absolute necessities: Would they pay the rent, buy their children shoes, or pay for needed bus tokens out of their small incomes? Such families had no choice about schools, often were exhausted and discouraged, and their children grew up in a depressing and insecure setting. Many had only one parent or lived through severe family disruption.

When entire schools and neighborhoods are dominated by children whose families face this level of impoverishment, local teachers and school officials face enormous problems and often feel helpless in the face of them. What can a school do, for example, if half of its students move away during the year to other schools and most of those who remain go home to very poor families in communities with few resources? In spite of the official rhetoric about equal opportunity, few children from such neighborhoods ever get to a good college and a great many never complete high school. Many live on blocks with no families who have what suburbanites consider normal: two parents with good educations and decent jobs who live in a home they own.

Housing and neighborhood choice was also seriously limited for higher-income blacks. The rental and homeownership markets, particularly in the more desirable suburbs, remained largely closed even to blacks with sufficient incomes. The housing element of middle-class mobility was not working for blacks.

Since the 1930s there has been a very strong federal policy encouraging homeownership. The basic idea has been that a nation of homeowners would enhance stability and commitment to communities and millions of families would be able to invest in their own futures rather than pay off their landlords' mortgages. This policy, which included large tax subsidies and special federally insured mortgages, produced an extraordinarily high level of homeownership which reached about two-thirds of the nation's families in 1980 before declining slowly during the 1980s.

Exclusion of blacks from homeownership in many areas meant that the benefits of the housing subsidies went very disproportionately to whites. Blacks were almost totally excluded from the first waves of post-World War II suburbanization when prices were low and veterans' benefits meant that families could own homes with no down payments. The effects of this exclusion became much more severe as the price of housing rose very rapidly. Many new suburban communities were built without any rental housing, and the opportunities for those left behind in the inner city deteriorated.

If racism was no longer a basic problem in the Atlanta area, the gap between black and white homeownership levels should have narrowed among families with similar incomes. Data in this chapter show that this

did not happen. In fact, the homeownership prospects of black families
fell in the 1980s.

The Context of the Housing Crisis

Understanding housing problems begin with an awareness that development of new suburban housing and jobs is the basic mechanism for
growth of the metropolitan Atlanta area. Fueled in large measure by the
in-migration of households, employers, and investment, this prosperity
resulted in the area's frequent ranking in business-climate and quality-of-
life surveys as among the most desirable in the country. Louis Harris
national surveys of corporate chief executive officers in 1986, 1987, and
1988, for example, found metro Atlanta ranking first as a desirable location for a business (*Atlanta Constitution*, 14 July 1988: 1C). In fact, however, metro Atlanta, by their terms, consisted primarily of certain parts
of suburban Atlanta. The suburban economic surge has brought the conversion of mile after mile of farmland into new suburban subdivisions
near mushrooming suburban factories and office buildings.

Communities experiencing dramatic growth tend to be strongly focused on the wonder of the expansion, the stories of fortunes made, the
optimistic sense of progress and possibilities. Their politics tends to be
dominated by proponents of development with a vision of government as
a facilitator. The Atlanta area was no exception. Much less public attention was paid to the question of how benefits from the area's prosperity
were distributed or whether anyone was hurt.

Economic growth has long been seen as the most efficient and lasting
means of improving the conditions of lower-income and minority groups.
It is difficult to conceive of a politically feasible policy that would produce
greater mobility and better education in a shrinking economy. In his influential 1987 book on the urban underclass, *The Truly Disadvantaged*,
William J. Wilson argued that the decisive policy initiative for solving the
problems of the urban underclass would be economic growth policies that
created "a tight labor market and economic growth" together with a childcare strategy (Wilson 1987, 163). The Atlanta region had had a job market
that grew much faster than its population. The data in this book strongly
suggest that the Wilson strategy would not have been sufficient for increasing minority opportunity. A more adequate policy would almost
surely require a serious attack on the racial dimensions of inequality in
the housing market.

A decline in the number of good entry-level jobs with adequate wages and a shift in the location of such jobs from cities to suburbs, some argue, sharply limited the benefits of overall economic growth to lower-income groups, particularly to geographically isolated minority groups.[1] In this theory, propounded by University of North Carolina sociologist John Kasarda, "spatial mismatch" within metropolitan areas skews the effects of growth.

Overall prosperity may serve to make the rich richer and the poor at least relatively poorer. The housing markets are key instruments by which these allocations occur. The rapid expansion of the metropolitan area may leave those confined to housing and educational institutions in the inner city even more isolated.

The analyses of homeownership in this chapter and of education and training in the following chapters suggest that the situation was worse than either Wilson or Kasarda believed. Even a very strong economy may not carry job opportunities across the color line. The spatial mismatch may not only limit the access to gains, as Kasarda argued, but if the area is sufficiently prosperous, it may actually make the condition of many black households worse; it may create so much competition for housing that the poor are pushed out.

Markets and Low-Income Housing: Theories and Evidence

High levels of expensive suburban residential construction of the type that have occurred in Atlanta during the 1980s were defended by economists as the most efficient way to improve the housing of lower-income and minority groups. Housing for those at the bottom was supposed to improve because the new housing would provide places for existing residents to move up in quality. The homes they vacated would "filter down" to the less affluent. Many critics of public subsidies for low-income housing construction argued that the "filtering" process was a more effective solution for the poorest families.

Federal housing policy in the 1980s was almost completely oriented toward a market strategy. No major area of the federal budget was cut more drastically during the "Reagan revolution" than construction of subsidized housing for families. Goals for newly constructed subsidized housing declined from about a quarter of a million units per year in the late 1970s to a few thousand in the 1980s. The Reagan administration

1. John Kasarda, "Urban Change and Minority Opportunities," in *The New Urban Reality,* edited by Paul Peterson (Washington, D.C.: Brookings, 1985), 33–67.

argued that it was much more efficient to rely on the market and to use rent subsidies through Section 8 certificates or housing vouchers (Struyk, Mayer, and Tuccillo 1983). President Reagan's Commission on Housing concluded that the government should rely on the market to produce housing for low-income families. Since funds for construction of new subsidized housing were virtually nonexistent by the mid-1980s, the only approach available for housing the poor was some variation of the filtering policy accompanied by a limited number of vouchers. The data from Atlanta show very severe problems with the market approach.

The filtering theory has some unstated assumptions. It could work if there were an expanding supply of housing and a constant demand, or if demand grew less rapidly than the supply. When the level of demand is growing rapidly, however, through both in-migration and growing real-income levels, the problem becomes much more complicated. For Atlanta area blacks, who faced both discrimination and income declines relative to whites, growing competition for housing meant that the real cost was likely to increase substantially even as the real income of many poor families fell. In such circumstances good, affordable housing did not filter down.

If the housing market in white areas is not open to black buyers and renters, the development of a new supply of housing in white areas may, in any case, have little relevance even for blacks with ample incomes. If there is a strong barrier between the white and black housing markets, and white demand is so strong that it supports conversion of lower-cost black housing in some areas of the central city through gentrification, the share of the city housing supply within the market actually available to low-income blacks may shrink significantly. As a city grows economically, there is a continual tendency to lose low-cost housing through public works projects, which tend to be built in low-income areas. Contrary to simple economic theory, in other words, there are a number of ways in which the tremendous boom of construction, migration, and jobs can leave those previously ill-housed with worse housing problems, less money, and more isolation than they had before.

At the same time, the tremendous expansion of suburban housing in outlying white areas weakens the city and the black suburbs as institutions and economic areas by drawing out more of the area's resources to where they will not support central-city businesses and cannot be taxed to support central-city schools and other vital public services. Suburban zoning and land-use policies mean that the outlying housing markets have a selective screen that welcomes high-income families and provides nothing for low-income households, households confined by lack of options to city and inner suburban neighborhoods.

This chapter first examines the effectiveness of the private housing market in the Atlanta metropolitan area in providing adequate and affordable housing to lower-income black households since 1975.

The potential effectiveness of filtering, even when the economic conditions make it possible, may be limited by various factors, including racial discrimination. Landlords or real estate agents may refuse to rent to blacks or to provide information and may even be willing to accept reduced rental income or vacancies in order to continue to discriminate.[2] In cities where black demand is strong relative to white demand, widespread discrimination producing strong racial boundaries could produce sharp increases in rents paid by blacks even if there were high vacancy rates and declining rents in the larger housing market.[3] "Reverse filtering," in which units that have been available to lower-income households come to be occupied by members of an upper-income group, may limit the impact of new residential construction on the supply of lower-income housing. The clearest example is gentrification, in which lower-cost units are purchased and upgraded by higher-income families, thus directly reducing the number of low-cost units.[4] Gentrification clearly occurred in some sections of Atlanta.

More complex versions of this process may occur in cities experiencing sharp increases in housing demand. Investors may react to the speculative cycle of rising housing prices by bidding up property in expectation of future gains.[5] Under such conditions, there may be a large net "filtering" of housing from lower-income to higher-income groups. Units that were affordable go up in relative price.

Both private development and public works projects in booming cities

2. For evidence, see John Yinger, "Prejudice and Discrimination in the Urban Housing Market," in *Current Issues in Urban Economics*, edited by P. Miezkowski and M. Straszheim, 430–68; and "Measuring Racial Discrimination with Fair Housing Audits: Caught in the Act," *American Economic Review* 76 (December 1986): 881–93.

3. For an example of this phenomenon, see James W. Fossett and Gary Orfield, "Market Failure and Federal Policy: Low-Income Housing in Chicago, 1970–83," in *Divided Neighbors*, edited by Gary Tobin (Beverly Hills: Sage Publications, 1987), 158–80.

4. See Brian J. L. Berry, "Islands of Renewal in Seas of Decay," in *The New Urban Reality*, edited by Paul Peterson (Washington, D.C.: Brookings, 1985) for a detailed discussion.

5. See Karl E. Case, "The Market for Single-Family Homes in the Boston Area," *New England Economic Review* (May/June 1986): 38–48, for a description of this process.

are likely to cut the stock of low-income housing by converting some residential areas to purposes that have become more valuable without replacing their low-cost housing supply; they may be converted into newly fashionable residential units or be replaced with office towers or shopping malls.

On the other hand, in isolated low-income communities without any prospects for gain, investors may choose another strategy whereby they "milk" their properties in ways that maximize cash flow, minimize maintenance, and eventually lead to abandonment of the buildings and a shrinkage of the supply. Such trends cut the supply of housing for low-income renters.

Under these market conditions, lower-income or minority households will likely experience increased costs and narrowing choices. If the stock of lower-cost housing in the black sector of the market stops expanding or starts shrinking, competition for the remaining units may drive up prices, even as landlords allow their property to decline.

The consequences of relying on the free market to create housing for lower-income and minority groups are troublesome. Discrimination, gentrification, and loss of low-income housing stock elsewhere mean that normal market operations may increase the price or lower the quality of units available to blacks. Even a strong metro housing market with large-scale new construction may see deteriorating conditions for the poor and very limited options for blacks at any income level.

In examining market conditions and their consequences for lower-income housing in Atlanta since 1975, this study relies on data from the Census Bureau, the Atlanta Regional Commission, and the Annual Housing Survey. Surveys were performed in Atlanta in 1975, 1978, 1982, and 1987. (The 1987 data were not available for this book.)

The ability of black families to compete for housing was declining, and family-income levels for whites grew much more rapidly in both city and suburban areas. In 1982, the average family income level for blacks was only 54 percent of the income level for whites in the city and 63 percent of the income level for whites in the suburbs.

Housing values in Atlanta's black neighborhoods had been declining relative to those in white neighborhoods even in the 1960s, but the trend accelerated in the 1970s. This does not mean that the property values in the black and changing areas fell but only that the housing in the white areas was increasing in worth more rapidly. During the 1970s, the value of housing in areas experiencing racial change declined relative to the value of housing in white areas. This meant that if a black family and a white family started out with similarly priced homes in black and white neighborhoods, on average, the white family would accumulate more wealth in housing value over time because of the differences between the markets.

David M. Smith (1985) analyzed area census data from 1960 to 1980 and looked at income, education, infant mortality rates, housing over-crowding, and value of owner-occupied housing. He found a modest de-cline in the gaps between black and white areas during the 1960s but widening differences in the 1970s.

Poor blacks were being left in greater isolation:

Greater inequality among black residential areas will have resulted, if the poorer blacks remain trapped in low-value inner-city housing. This appears to be the case, for the so-called urban renewal programs of the 1960s did not generate the scale of benefits to Atlanta's poor blacks which might have been expected . . . only about one-third of the 67,000 inner-city blacks displaced by "urban renewal" were rehoused by the city. . . . [The public housing that was built had problems] with respect to neighborhood environmental quality and social conditions. . . . [F]or the majority of the displaced population rehousing simply meant a move into the next zone of deteriorating property. Thus it would be hard to judge a relative (or even absolute) improvement in the housing conditions of many of Atlanta's poor blacks during the 1960s and 1970s, when compared to the increase in housing quality experienced by most of the city's population. (Smith 1985, 79)

A 1986 study of housing conditions in Atlanta by the city government showed severe problems in the city in terms of housing investment and the condition of rental housing. Nineteen of every twenty dollars of res-idential construction were spent in the suburbs. Only one-third of the city's housing was owner-occupied and more than one-fifth of all rental units were in substandard condition. There were enormous differences from one part of the city to another.

The prosperous white area at the northern tip of the city had 80 per-cent homeownership while at the other extreme was an area with 95 per-cent renters. Twenty-eight thousand of the city's 32,000 low-income households were paying too much, more than 35 percent of their income for gross rent. The typical family in poverty was paying almost twice this level. Housing in Atlanta was relatively affordable compared to other metropolitan areas in 1979 but costs rose rapidly in the prosperous 1980s. Very little new housing construction was taking place in the largely black southern part of the city.

The city had few resources to address the deepening housing crisis for

low-income families as the Reagan Administration shut down family housing construction programs (Atlanta Department of Community Development 1986).

The fact that subsidized housing is a federal rather than a local policy
question is one of the many reasons why black mayors and local officials
have little impact on the most vital concerns of ghetto residents. In the
first Reagan budget bill in 1981, for example, all the families in subsidized
housing in the United States had their rents raised to 30 percent from 25
percent of their income. Families dependent on low welfare benefits (set
by the state legislature) had to find housing in a rapidly inflating housing
market with incomes whose real value fell substantially as the cost of
living increased. Policy changes in Washington increased their costs and
radically limited their options.

The housing situation of low-income families in Atlanta was bleak. City
officials estimated in 1987 that 27,000 families were paying more than 35
percent of their incomes for rent. Ten thousand families lived in overcrowded buildings. City planners estimated that one-third of all of the
city's rental units did not meet minimum housing standards and one-fifth
needed major rehabilitation or demolition. In 1985 two children died in
an apartment fire caused by housing code violations. Two years later, Atlanta Public Housing Authority Executive Director Samuel Hider
summed up the situation: "For low-income people and poor people the
housing situation is worse. The units being built now are too expensive
for low-income people" (Dedman 1988, 68). The Housing Authority had
600 uninhabitable vacant apartments but no money to repair and reopen
them because of federal budget cuts (ibid.).

The housing authority was continuing to lose units to public works
projects and not building new ones; 160 units were leveled when a con-
nector was built between the city's two largest freeways, but the housing
authority did not receive enough money to replace them (ibid.). "In Atlanta," reported Dan Sweat of the Alliance for Human Services Planning,
"no new subsidized general purpose housing units have been built since
1973" though the local Task Force for the Homeless estimated that more
than 8,000 people were without homes in the area (Sweat 1989). "Now
we're relying," said city councilman Bill Campbell, "on a hodge-podge of
volunteer efforts and a few city-sponsored projects that are marked with
incompetence and mismanagement and outright fraud" (Dedman 1988,
68). One of the Atlanta responses came from a group of young professionals who called themselves the "Mad Housers": they built illegal huts

without utilities in isolated areas. Anita Beatty, of the Atlanta Task Force
for the Homeless, noted that some of the poor were relying on a "third
world kind of housing" (*Chicago Tribune*, 23 July 1989).

There was little political priority for this issue. City Councilman Rob
Pitts, who had headed the "slumlord commission" set up after the 1985
apartment fire tragedy, observed, "I don't think housing is a real priority
of the city. Not compared with the sexy projects—a new City Hall, a new
zoo, Underground Atlanta, a new stadium" (*Atlanta Constitution*, 16 August 1987). Council president Marvin Arrington observed that the city
was "failing" and that it lacked the "resources to fund housing" (ibid.).
The city government was not seriously planning for low-income housing
construction in the 1980s. Sabrina Freeney of the Planning Bureau noted
in 1987 that the plans for the center of the city for the next fifteen years
called for encouraging middle- and upper-income housing around downtown. She noted that there was "very little new low-income housing construction" in Atlanta and that substantial abandonment was still occurring
(Freeney 1987). In spite of huge waiting lists for public housing there
had been no significant developments in years. In 1987 the housing authority had to return a $3.5 million federal grant for new housing when
it failed to obtain a site (*Southline*, 21 October 1987, 13).

Mayor Andrew Young announced a goal of building or repairing some
80,000 units of affordable housing in the city during his final months in
office. He said, however, that the problem was not only of local failure
but one of "abandonment of a problem by the federal government." Without more federal subsidies and lower interest rates, he said, making real
progress on housing would "take a miracle" (*Atlanta Journal and Constitution*, 28 August 1989).

Housing was one of the most serious problems facing the huge population of low-income black families in the city's ghettos. The presence of
a black mayor in city hall, however, was virtually irrelevant. Housing
subsidies and subsidized housing construction are very high-cost policies
that have been almost entirely in the domain of the federal government.
With the radical shift in federal policy, subsidized housing programs were
devastated. Some cities tried to replace at least a small part of the lost
resources and some others attempted to protect low-income families
through rent control. Low-income housing was not a priority in Atlanta
city politics. At the end of the 1980s, there were an estimated 10,000
homeless people in the city, 7,000 households on the waiting list for public housing, and two-thirds of the city's renters were facing inadequate

housing conditions or being forced to pay more than they could afford. Housing was being built for affluent families, but the affordable housing for single homeless people—often single-room occupancy hotels—was rapidly shrinking. "I don't know that we can house the homeless in Atlanta, ever," the mayor concluded (ibid.).

The Atlanta Metropolitan Housing Market, 1970–89

The special analysis of the Annual Housing Surveys conducted for this study showed high rates of residential construction and sharp increases in housing prices and rents in metro Atlanta between 1970 and 1983.

As the result of nearly equal levels of construction and demolition, the number of housing units inside the city of Atlanta increased slowly and the residential vacancy rate declined slightly in the early 1980s. By contrast, there was a major increase in housing construction in the suburbs (see table 4.1). The number of suburban housing units almost tripled from 1970 to the mid-1980s, with the largest numbers of new units being built in Cobb and Gwinnett Counties. After 1980, the rate of new construction ran well ahead of population growth as real estate speculation grew. This exuberant growth reflected the rush of investment into the outlying white housing market, where a great deal of long-term growth was expected. In early 1989, metropolitan Atlanta was the fourth most active housing market in the United States, though it ranked only thirteenth in population, with a projected 37,000 units of new housing estimated for the year—many more than were expected in much larger metropolitan areas such as Chicago, Detroit, and Philadelphia (*Atlanta Journal and Constitution*, 21 January 1989). The new housing being built in the metro area in a single year equalled more than one-fifth of all the housing units in the city of Atlanta.

Poor people, however, were excluded from the boom areas. In boom-

Table 4.1 Housing Units in Metropolitan Atlanta, 1980–86

Jurisdiction	1980	1986	Change (%)
Atlanta	178,669	182,399	2.1
Suburban Fulton	81,039	107,541	32.6
Suburban DeKalb	167,831	194,527	15.9
Cobb	133,311	162,545	43.0
Gwinnett	58,109	109,321	88.0
Clayton	53,014	61,084	15.0

Source: Atlanta Regional Commission, *1986 Population and Housing Estimates for the Atlanta Region* (1987).

ing Gwinnett County, there was fierce resistance to subsidized housing. An arsonist burned a house used by subsidized tenants. The county government rejected zoning for a homeless shelter after residents protested about possible damage to their property values, and the homeless people had to move out. Millard Fuller, founder of the Habitat for Humanity group working on voluntary low-income housing production, said that "the problems in Gwinnett are unlike those experienced anywhere else in this state or country." This group, strongly supported by former President Jimmy Carter, was a religious-based, nonprofit organization working across the United States (*Atlanta Journal and Constitution*, 24 January 1990).

These increases in construction were accompanied by sharp increases in both sale prices and rents. The costs of both sale and rental housing increased much faster than either the overall local cost of living or the cost of housing in most other cities. The average sale price for a single-family home more than tripled over this period, increasing from approximately $38,500 in 1972 to just under $120,000 in 1986. By 1988, the figure was $138,000, an increase of 105 percent since 1979 (*Atlanta Journal and Constitution*, 21 January 1989: D1). Average rents grew more slowly, but also more than doubled from 1972 to 1986 (see table 4.2). Changes were even more dramatic in the most prosperous areas.

Rents and home prices followed similar patterns, with the most growth in the late 1970s and after 1984. The sharp increases were likely the result of white in-migration into both central city and suburbs. The region's rapid employment growth drew newcomers from outside the region and increased the population, spurring housing demand. Recent resettlers have generally been wealthier than natives and have been willing to pay higher prices for housing.

Table 4.2 Annual Increases in Rents and Sale Prices of Homes in Metropolitan Atlanta, 1970–86

Period	Yearly Rent Increase (%)	Yearly Sale Price Growth (%)
1970–75	3.3	6.2*
1975–78	2.7	4.2
1978–82	9.2	13.4
1982–84	6.6	1.2
1984–86	8.4**	10.4

*1972–75 only

**1984–85 only

Sources: U.S. Bureau of the Census (1981), *Statistical Abstract of the United States*, table 786, p. 469; unpublished data, Federal Home Loan Bank Board.

Table 4.3 White Income and Housing Costs for Local Residents and Newcomers 1975–82

Place Moved From	City			Suburbs		
	median income	mean rent	median home cost	median income	mean rent	median home cost
			1975			
City	9.9	2.3	40–50	13.6	2.7	40–50
Suburbs	10.0	2.0	20–25	13.1	2.5	40–50
Outsider	9.0	2.4	50–60	14.5	2.7	50–60
			1982			
City	21.8	4.6	90–100	19.5	4.9	55–60
Suburbs	16.0	4.2	40–50	17.5	3.2	60–75
Outsider	17.0	4.5	150–200	25.1	5.2	100–125

Notes: Income computed from grouped data in Annual Housing Survey; all data in $1,000s.

The influence of newcomers on housing prices is reflected in table 4.3, which compares average family income, gross rent, and housing values for nonpoor whites in both central city and the suburbs from 1975 to 1982 for outsiders and natives. These figures indicate that migrants from outside the Atlanta area have exerted a strong upward influence on housing prices. Those migrating to the suburbs were wealthier than established residents and generally paid higher prices for housing. The explosion of jobs drew in high-income whites who bid up housing costs.

LOW-INCOME AND MINORITY HOUSING, 1975–83

The Annual Housing Surveys from 1975 to 1982 show changes in the quality and cost of lower-income and minority housing.[6] The conclusions are largely pessimistic. Although housing quality and cost for lower-income and black households improved slightly during the mid-1970s, when the larger housing market was sluggish, housing conditions for both groups deteriorated sharply during the late 1970s and early 1980s. The large increase in housing prices and rents over this period, particularly in the suburbs, was well above income growth for blacks and the poor,

6. The presentation of Annual Housing Survey data here and elsewhere in the paper contains no standard errors or other tests of statistical significance. This information has been omitted partially to simplify the presentation, but largely because almost any relationship in this data set is statistically significant. Standard errors and other tests of statistical significance are largely a function of sample size—the larger the sample, the smaller the error of any estimate or the size of any difference required to be significant; and the sample sizes chosen in the Annual Housing Surveys for Atlanta are very large, approaching 15,000 in 1975 and 1978 and 5,000 in 1982. Those wishing more details should consult the statistical appendices to the published volumes of the Annual Housing Surveys for Atlanta, which are published by the Department of Housing and Urban Development.

with the result that they often had to pay more of their incomes for deficient housing in poor locations.

Rental Housing. The great majority of low-income families, except for the elderly, lived in rental housing. Black households were poorer, on average, and therefore less able to own homes. Blacks below the poverty line tended to be even poorer and to remain poor for much longer periods of time than whites.

Even among families with the means to own housing, blacks were much more likely to still be renters, probably because of discrimination as described earlier in this chapter. In any case, developments in rental housing availability and cost had very disproportionate importance for black households.

Rental Housing Quality. Increasing housing costs meant that lower-income and black households whose income grew more slowly than rent levels became increasingly concentrated in lower-quality housing, for which they had to pay a rising share of their income. The data show levels of structural inadequacy and overcrowding for unsubsidized housing units in both Atlanta and the suburbs. A housing unit is classified as structurally inadequate if it lacks either plumbing facilities or a kitchen, or if there are multiple minor deficiencies.[7] Units are classified as overcrowded if they are occupied by more than one person per room, excluding kitchen and bathroom, or by more than two persons for each bedroom.

The quality of rental housing occupied by lower-income and black tenants deteriorated between 1978 and 1982. The decline was clear for blacks in Atlanta. Among lower-income suburban black households, the proportion in deficient units increased steadily over this period, from 20 percent in 1975 to over 31 percent in 1982—indicating that suburbanization for blacks was often a very different experience than for whites.

There was a severe disparity in the quality of rental units. Not only did blacks occupy units of much lower quality than whites with the same income, but nonpoor blacks generally occupied units as bad or worse than those occupied by poor whites (see table 4.4). This dramatically refutes any claim that housing markets are now shaped by economics rather than race. These data strongly indicate discrimination.

7. Congressional Budget Office, *Federal Housing Policy: Current Programs and Recurring Issues* (Washington, D.C.: U.S. Government Printing Office, 1988).

Table 4.4 Housing Quality of Black and White Families with Rents over 30% of Income, by Family Income, 1975–82

	% Inadequate*			
	Poor Families		Non-poor Families	
	1975	1982	1975	1982
City				
whites	6.2	9.9	1.1	2.5
blacks	16.8	16.9	.9	1.7
Suburbs				
whites	5.0	3.0	.7	.3
blacks	12.8	26.7	3.3	.8

*Inadequate is defined as one major deficiency or two or more secondary defects.

Source: Computations from Annual Housing Survey Data Tapes.

Rental Burden. Lower-income and minority groups paid a larger share of their incomes for housing than higher-income and white people. This study examines trends in the average share of income paid for either contract rent or gross rent, defined as follows:

contract rent is the rent actually paid to a landlord and may or may not include utilities and fuel

gross rent is the total housing cost, including contract rent and other expenses for utilities and fuel

Rental burdens declined for low-income groups during the mid-1970s, but increased sharply over the late 1970s and early 1980s. On average, poor Atlanta-area households were paying more than two-thirds of their income for gross rent in 1982. This was more than twice the maximum rent burden permitted for low-income families in federally assisted programs (30 percent of income). In almost all cases the burden was above 1975 levels. Most of this increase in rental burdens reflected price increases, rather than income declines.

Poor whites in Atlanta, a small fraction of white households, experienced the largest increase in rent burdens over this period. Lower-income suburban blacks also experienced a sharp increase in rent burdens, particularly between 1978 and 1982. Their housing quality deteriorated while their rent burden rose.

This combination of worse housing at higher prices for poor people meant there was a significant decline in their overall housing conditions between the mid-1970s and the early 1980s. The rate of deterioration in housing status was largest among poor blacks. The share of the city's black low-income population with severe housing problems increased from 11 to 17 percent from 1978 to 1982.

The metropolitan Atlanta housing market, in spite of high levels of construction, did not provide adequate or affordable housing for blacks or the poor. In the suburbs, apart from relatively segregated areas in the southern section, blacks were effectively being priced out of the suburban rental housing market and burgeoning employment opportunities.

The Causes of Decline

The increasingly severe housing problem in Atlanta can be attributed primarily to three things: growth in income for black households and for lower-income groups has lagged behind rising incomes for whites and behind housing prices; discrimination has continued, and Atlanta has experienced considerable "reverse filtering" in some areas.

The most basic cause of the housing problems for blacks in Atlanta was that growth in their financial resources lagged behind overall income and housing-price trends. As real incomes fell, families might respond to higher costs by "doubling up"—putting more people in fewer rooms—a process that tended to speed deterioration of housing.

In addition to this increased income disparity, there was evidence of "reverse filtering" in some parts of the Atlanta housing market; over this period, newcomers, drawn by the good new jobs, helped bid up the price of existing housing. Because large numbers of suburban homes were occupied by families moving in from outside metropolitan Atlanta, the number of new local vacancies ultimately available for lower-income groups was limited.

Many of the added lower-cost units inside the city of Atlanta developed because of the migration of substantial numbers of middle-income blacks into southern suburbs, but this movement was not large enough in absolute terms to produce an adequate supply of lower-cost vacancies, and that migration may be much smaller in the future since the black middle class is now very largely suburban.

A decline in white out-migration from the city, while desirable for a number of reasons, appears to have further restricted growth in the supply of lower-income units. Calculations from the Annual Housing Survey indicate that the average rents paid by whites in the city increased more rapidly between 1978 and 1982 than those paid by blacks at all levels of the rent distribution. By contrast, landlords who rented mainly to minority groups were prevented from imposing similar rent increases by the weak economic situation of black families and instead allowed units to deteriorate in quality. These contrasting trends in income levels for whites and blacks in the city created a powerful financial incentive, where conditions permitted, for owners to transfer units from the black to the white or integrated housing markets. Unfortunately, this often led to a transfer of housing units in relatively good condition and in favorable locations out of the market for blacks.

Homeownership

Homeownership levels among most major racial and economic groups either remained stable or increased from 1975 to 1982. Ownership increased appreciably among both nonpoor inner-city blacks and whites over this period, with the largest increase coming between 1978 and 1982, while ownership rates remained level among suburban households of both races. Homeownership rates were approximately equal for black and white households in the city with incomes above the poverty level; white suburbanites were significantly more likely to own homes than were blacks.

The increase in homeownership in the city between 1978 and 1982 may reflect decisions to purchase smaller and cheaper central-city units by households who might otherwise have moved to the suburbs. After all, housing prices were increasing at an annual rate of 14 percent over this period, and area mortgage interest rates were also increasing rapidly, from 9.3 percent in 1978 to 14.5 percent in 1982. This combination of large price increases and high mortgage rates put many suburban units out of the financial reach of a number of city households and led them to purchase city units instead. Research on gentrification elsewhere shows that the basic motivation of the new middle-class, professional residents was affordability, not a preference for a sophisticated urban lifestyle (Palen and London, 1984).

The data on black homeownership are more difficult to interpret. On the one hand, levels of black homeownership were higher, and interracial differences lower, in Atlanta than in many northern cities. Blacks in the city owned homes at rates comparable to whites, even though the median black income level was lower.

On the other hand, these results may also conceal considerable racial disparities. First, the increase in black ownership may simply reflect relative declines in housing prices and a rapid short-term increase in offerings in the black housing market in areas undergoing racial transition.

Second, a number of studies in other cities have found that blacks are much less likely to own homes than whites of comparable age, position in the life cycle, and income. Blacks also tend to purchase lower-quality homes than comparable whites, in worse neighborhoods, with less access to employment and fewer amenities.[8]

Much of this research on housing was based on a statistical procedure known as a logit model. A logit model attempts to move beyond simply expressing the mathematical relationships between sets of numbers to exploring the nature of the relationship; it does this by postulating expected relationships, in terms of equations, and then checking the fit between those equations and the actual data. After finding a model that best fits the data, the relationships can then be more systematically explored.

logit.

Many statistical procedures try to show the relative strengths of the relationships of each variable measured to a particular outcome. Thus a correlation or regression equation might suggest that income has a stronger relationship than race to homeownership. One of the difficulties with such conclusions is that race and income tend to be themselves extremely highly related, and statistical controls tend to artificially separate their effects. Black families tend to differ from whites in many respects simultaneously; for example, they are poorer, younger, less likely to have owned homes in the past, more likely to have a single parent, and their members are less likely to have a college degree and a good job.

Logit models allow exploration of the relationship of different sets of specified variables to an outcome. They enable us to compare across several dimensions simultaneously. For example, we can estimate the comparative probability of homeownership by young black and white suburban families with two children, college educations, and $60,000 incomes at a certain age.

The question of racial equity in homeownership was analyzed using data obtained from the tapes of the federal government's Annual Housing Survey. The analysis, by James Krusenoski at the University of Illinois' Institute of Government, shows that the racial differences in homeownership cannot be explained by differences in income and stage of life. What follows is a summary of Krusenoski's report.

The differences in ownership have actually widened in some circumstances. During the period studied, the average income of black city

8. These studies are summarized in Yinger, "Prejudice and Discrimination in Urban Housing," 457–58.

households dropped by about one-sixth and that of suburban black families by about one-twentieth. The real income of white families living in the city rose while suburban white income remained virtually unchanged. By 1986, average sale prices were three times their 1972 levels and interest rates were significantly higher.

The cost-income squeeze helps explain the growth of inadequate housing among blacks. In the black sector of the low-income market, where owners had less latitude to raise rents, landlords may have increased income from properties by cutting back maintenance costs while maintaining or raising rents. Families may have responded to higher costs by accepting inadequate housing or by "doubling up." These responses may have accounted for at least some of the increases in inadequate housing among lower-income groups over the late 1970s and early 1980s.

EARLIER RESEARCH ON RACE AND HOMEOWNERSHIP

Three of the most notable studies of race and homeownership were completed in the 1970s; they are Kain and Quigley (1972), Birnbaum and Weston (1974), and Roistacher and Goodman (1976). This study asks similar questions but uses a more suitable statistical model. The logit model examines more than one year and uses more current data.

Kain and Quigley studied homeownership opportunities for a sample of 1,200 households in St. Louis. Their results show that after controlling for differences in stage of life, education, income, and employment status, black households were 9 percent less likely than whites to be homeowners. Analysis of recent movers, controlling for previous homeownership (home purchase is more likely for those groups who have already owned homes), shows that black families were still 9 percent less likely to own a home than whites who moved recently within the St. Louis market.

The Birnbaum and Weston study emphasized the importance of family wealth when developing a model of homeownership. They also argued that because white and black investment behavior was quite different, separate equations should be estimated for each group. Their results also showed a lower probability of homeownership for blacks with similar income levels and life-cycle characteristics than whites.

The Roistacher and Goodman article asked whether the findings of Kain and Quigley on St. Louis could be generalized to the nation as a whole. Studying 5,000 families from the twenty-four largest metropolitan areas and using 1971 data, they found that blacks had a lower probability of owning a home than their white counterparts. They found a larger racial difference than the St. Louis study: 17 percent. However, their more positive results about recent movers led them to suggest that discrimination was declining in the early 1970s.

The statistical model used in the Atlanta study attempted to build on earlier research while addressing some of its weaknesses. This study analyzed blacks and whites separately and compared those who relocated in the previous year to long-time residents to see if patterns were changing.

The model relates the probability of homeownership to a family's size, composition, income, present and prior residence, and the age, gender, and marital status of the head of household. The basic procedure was to specify various sets of household characteristics, such as income, age, number of children, and marital status, and use the logit model to calculate the probability of owning a home for black and white families with those characteristics. By choosing different characteristics, we can compare the probability of homeownership for families with different incomes and in different parts of the life cycle. Among those identified by the model as more likely to buy homes were suburban families, families moving in from outside the Atlanta metropolitan area, and families that had previously owned a home. Life cycle also made a difference. Older black families, for example, were more likely to own homes than younger black families.

The study selected types of families and then compared the homeownership chances of whites and blacks in each category over time. The types of households studied reflected a variety of city and suburban situations. The most important pattern was the decline of black homeownership probability after 1978. For nearly every family type considered, black probabilities of owning a home were at or above those for whites in 1975 and 1978. In other words, the homeownership problem then was not primarily that blacks with the same income and education as whites were not as likely to be homeowners but that blacks were so much behind whites in income and education that they could not afford homes. Even those with equal resources, of course, were not obtaining housing in the same areas. This relatively high possibility of black homeownership in the 1970s may have reflected the rapid spread of black communities following the enactment of fair housing laws in 1968, which made it much more difficult to maintain a rigid racial boundary.

As the housing market tightened and prices soared in the 1980s, however, homeownership probabilities for black households declined dramatically compared with white ones.

Older black families, where the head of household was over forty years

of age, did not fall so far behind. Black families who came from outside
the Atlanta metropolitan area did better. Among both city and suburban
residents, blacks whose previous residence was outside metropolitan Atlanta experienced no substantial disparity in the probability of homeownership.

The first family types studied were white and black suburban families
who had previously rented in the suburbs, with a married, 34-year-old
male head of household with a high school degree, an income of $15,000,
a wife, and one child of preschool age. Among such households, the
chance for a black family of owning a home trailed that of a similar white
family by about 8 percent in 1975 and 1978. By 1982, however, the disparity had reached 20 percent. The pattern was consistent for recent
movers.

Among more affluent and better-educated suburban families moving
into the area, the analysis shows that black households had a good record
of homeownership. Young, successful black suburban families from outside the Atlanta area were even more likely than similarly situated whites
to be homeowners in all three years, and this was true for both recent
movers and nonmovers. Even among those who had previously rented
housing, black homeownership probabilities were still comparable with
those of whites in all three years for both nonmovers and recent movers.
There was, obviously, a group of mobile, middle-class, suburban blacks
who were connected effectively to the housing markets. As the income
gaps within the black community grew, these families had a fundamentally different experience than ghetto blacks.

Local black families who had previously rented housing in the Atlanta
area showed a dramatic decline in ownership as compared with levels for
similar whites in the 1980s.

The last suburban family type considered was one which can clearly
afford housing. This type of family had previously rented in the suburbs,
had a college-educated, married, male head of household who was 30
years old, had an income of $29,000, and had one child of preschool age.
For this family type, probabilities of homeownership for blacks in the
1970s were only a few percentage points below levels for whites, for both
nonmovers and recent movers. In 1982, though, the black probability of
homeownership plummeted to 35 percent below the white level. This
decrease was also reflected among recent movers.

The last type examined was the family with a single female head of
household. Such households grew in number from the 1970s to the 1980s

for both blacks and whites in the city. This type of city family had previously rented in the city, had a female head of household who was 28 years old and had a high school diploma, two school-age children, and a 1982 income of $15,000. Black chances for homeownership kept pace with those of whites before 1982 and then fell off considerably.

The overall data suggest that black homeownership, across most types of families studied, sharply decreased between 1978 and 1982, both for long-term residents and for newcomers. Black income levels were falling relative to white levels during this period. Even for families with the same income, however, the possibility of homeownership fell for blacks. Perhaps this decline was linked to the patterns of discrimination in the real estate and mortgage lending markets discussed early in this chapter.

Housing Inequality

Black and white communities remained intensely segregated in the 1980s in spite of vast growth and hundreds of thousands of moves since fair housing became law. The rapidly growing, most prosperous areas of suburbia were developing as virtually all-white communities and a vast black community was developing at the other end of suburbia.

In the area's rental markets, one of the clearest signs of racial inequality was the fact that blacks with incomes above the poverty line were living in housing units with more defects than whites with incomes below the poverty line. Poor families in the rental market, a very disproportionate number of whom were black, faced a desperate financial burden unless they were able to obtain subsidized housing. Because the subsidized housing in the city had been concentrated in isolated, high-density ghetto areas, those poor black families who had to live there were denied access to decent schools, to healthy job markets, and to the black middle class.

Blacks also faced declining probability of homeownership. The effect of Atlanta's economic prosperity during this period was to decrease the probability for almost all types of black families. The private market did not provide equal housing for black households with similar needs and means. The situation appears to be worsening.

The housing issue remains one of overpowering importance for black and low-income families in metropolitan Atlanta. Housing opportunities are increasingly limited and housing is less affordable. Housing choice, or the lack of any real choice, determines schooling, safety, access to jobs, and many aspects of a family's experience. Inability to pay for decent housing in a safe area makes a normal family life extremely difficult and puts children at very great risk. Unequal housing for those blacks who are fully able to pay is one of the most serious aspects of contemporary discrimination, helping maintain self-perpetuating black and white societies within metropolitan Atlanta. Housing segregation, the suburbanization and stratification of white neighborhoods, and the abandonment of inner-city communities by middle-class black families combine to create a powerful foundation on which systems of unequal education and employment are built.

5

High Schools

High school is the last stage of universal public education in the United States and the key to almost all decent jobs in the American economy. High School is the pathway toward or away from college and the place where young people are expected to go beyond the basic skills to the higher-order skills that are the basis of reasoning, expression, scientific understanding, and civic leadership. High school is the time when young people have to work out their transition from childhood and begin to formulate plans for their adult lives, while dealing with all the stresses of adolescence.

Grade school is often a time of innocence and hope. In high school, the larger structures of the world outside the school penetrate more deeply as children on different sides of the race and class lines prepare for different realities. For a great number of minority and low-income Americans, high school is an experience that begins in failure in a dismal setting and ends without any evidence of achievement—in teenage pregnancy, a prescription for a self-perpetuating cycle of poverty, or in the illegal economy that flourishes in the inner city and leads to addiction, prison, and a life of failure.

These problems are exacerbated in schools that do not have middle-class connections and expectations, schools without the competitive example of students successfully positioning themselves for good jobs or colleges. The Supreme Court held in 1954 that legally segregated schools were "inherently unequal." And, as this chapter will show, Atlanta's city schools were among the most segregated in the nation. In fact, they were significantly *more* segregated in the mid-1980s than they were in the 1970s, when black community leaders and white political leaders put their heads together in an attempt to avoid busing in what came to be known as "the Atlanta Compromise."

The purpose of the Atlanta Compromise was to achieve educational equity without panicking whites. This could be done without busing, its architects decided, by putting the white-run city school system under black control. This was a heady prospect for blacks, as Atlanta had not yet elected its first black mayor. Some black schools were seriously run down and understaffed in comparison with the majority-white schools, and badly in need of books and blackboards. Under the controversial agreement (which the NAACP's national leadership opposed, and which ultimately cost local NAACP president Lonnie King his job), the school board promised in 1973 to hire a black superintendent and other black administrators in exchange for a plan that left many schools segregated. "In hindsight, I think it was a terrible mistake," said Julian Bond in 1987; Bond took over the local NAACP leadership after Lonnie King's ouster (Hansen 1987, 1).

The strategy was, in effect, the very model of the approach championed by conservatives who warned that "forced busing" would lead to deteriorating schools and white flight. It also appealed to those advocates of black power who believed that only black leaders would solve the educational problems of black children. Its key elements were control of the school system by blacks strongly committed to improving black education and intensely focused basic skills instruction. Blacks got control of the dollars spent by the school system and—with the support of conservative business interests keen on avoiding busing at any cost—Atlanta found itself in the unusual position of being a central city that actually spent more per student than the suburban average. Power, money, and expectations were directed toward accomplishment of the conservative reforms, under which standards were raised and tests became all-important. Performance was expected to rise and middle-class whites to stay put.

A generation later, evidence from across the metropolitan area showed that the best educational opportunities went to white suburban families with the most resources and that low-income inner-city students were concentrated in isolated and inferior schools. By the high school level, black students found themselves falling severely behind and with few of the options routinely provided in many suburbs. Educational inequality remained deeply linked to race and class differences among schools. A long decline in dropout rates ended and abruptly reversed itself. Whites and middle-class blacks abandoned the city system in droves. Huge num-

bers of children flunked grades and became more likely to drop out before completing high school. The data showed no relationship between
expenditures and student achievement and, as subsequently became apparent, much of the "progress" reported by the longtime black superintendent of schools turned out to have been illusory.

As the 1980s ended, not only was it becoming increasingly apparent
that the schools were segregated and unequal in Atlanta but also that the
problems were rapidly deepening in the suburbs. The number of segregated schools grew rapidly in DeKalb County. In late 1989 the county
schools faced a federal court order to devise a new desegregation plan.

The Black Struggle for Equal Education

The history of black schooling in Atlanta has been one long, unsuccessful
struggle to obtain equal education. With few exceptions, that struggle
operated within the context of segregation. During the city's desegregation struggle from the late 1950s until 1973, the federal courts in Georgia
were hostile to civil rights claims, were solicitous of white concerns, and
left the system of segregation virtually untouched.

Public education in Atlanta was unequal at its inception after the Civil
War. For many black students, no schools or part-time schools were provided, and there were great differences in class sizes, facilities, and types
of instruction. In the early twentieth century, per-student spending was
three times higher in white schools (Plank and Turner 1987, 588–90).
Generation after generation, blacks struggled to get schools built for their
children and black teachers hired. Blacks filed a federal court suit in 1943
to try to equalize salaries for black teachers, but the court never reached
a decision (ibid. 592–96). In the 1940s, blacks finally began to get a fair
share of spending from school bonds, a long-time demand of the black
leaders (ibid., 597). After eight decades of experience with inequality in
"separate but equal" schools, it was not surprising that blacks sought desegregation.

After the Supreme Court's desegregation decision in *Brown v. Board
of Education*, Atlanta NAACP leaders repeatedly asked the school board
to act but the board did nothing. A 1958 NAACP lawsuit led to a very
limited plan, delayed until September 1961, because of the court's worry
about a state law that would have required the cutoff of state funds for
education when the first black student entered a white school (*Calhoun
v. Members of the Board of Education of Atlanta, Georgia*, 188 F. Supp.
401 [1959]; *Calhoun v. Latimer* 188 F. Supp. 412).

From the beginning, the judges hearing the Atlanta cases gave a great

deal of attention to the problems of white resistance. If whites were de-
termined to defy the law and disrupt the city or its economy, then the
law was enforced in the most limited possible way.

The court concluded that most of the segregation in the city was not
caused by illegal actions but "on account of geography and residential
patterns" (188 F. Supp., at 406). Extreme residential segregation was assumed to be a fact of nature. This would be a problem until the end of
the case. The judge noted that the residential segregation was one reason
why Atlantans were less fiercely opposed than rural Georgians to desegregation plans. Such a plan would cause "little mixing" because it "would
result in the schools located in the white areas being practically all white
and those located in Negro areas to consist almost altogether, if not totally, of Negroes" (188 F. Supp. 412, at 414).

The progress of desegregation was almost invisible. In 1963, at the
peak of the national civil rights movement, only 54 of more than 45,000
black students attended school across racial lines in Atlanta. Each year
one grade was opened to applications by black students, who could transfer only by passing a test (Isherwood 1987, 10).

Great changes took place in the integration of southern cities in the
late 1960s and early 1970s, but Atlanta was virtually unaffected. Between
1968 and 1971, federal desegregation standards were transformed as the
Supreme Court announced that the goal was complete and immediate
integration; the court authorized the use of busing, approving a plan calling for racial balance across the city and suburbs of Charlotte, North Carolina, a few hours' drive from Atlanta. Hundreds of southern communities had to rapidly devise new desegregation plans.

When the civil rights groups went back to federal court in Atlanta,
however, they were blocked again by the judge's concern about white
reaction. Although the Supreme Court had concluded that courts must
take very energetic action against segregation, making "every effort to
achieve the greatest possible degree of actual desegregation" (*Swann v.
Charlotte-Mecklenburg Bd. of Ed.*, 402 U.S. 1), the local federal court
simply refused to bus white students and found the district innocent (332
F. Supp. 804). The court blamed housing segregation, calling it "the un-
conquerable foe of the racial ideal of integrated public schools in the cities" (ibid., 806), simply ignoring the Supreme Court's Charlotte busing
decision. The court ruled that "Atlanta now stands on the brink of becoming an all-black city" and that a busing order would make it happen "in a
few months time" (ibid., 808).

The court noted that in the thirteen years of the case, Atlanta schools had changed from 30 percent black to 70 percent black. The policy of constructing new schools on racial boundaries had been futile. The black ghettos were expanding so rapidly that many of the "line schools" were all-black within two years (ibid., 806). The court concluded in 1971 that the "critical point" had been reached for the city school system and that "the situation calls for a sweeping examination of its relationship to housing, planning, finances, rapid transit and all the other external factors which vitally affect its role in the community." The court recommended that city leaders consider the possibility of consolidating the schools with the surrounding Fulton County system (ibid., 809). Nothing was done to explore that option.

It became apparent in many big cities that full desegregation would require involvement of the suburbs, something that had been ordered by lower federal courts in Richmond and Detroit. The plaintiffs in the Atlanta case proposed in court in early 1973 that students be bused between the city and the suburbs, saying that such a remedy would permit substantial desegregation with shorter bus rides (*Atlanta Constitution*, 17 January 1973).

That proposal was attacked fiercely by the press and local political leaders. Under enormous pressure, including the active involvement of Governor Jimmy Carter, the local NAACP negotiated a compromise with the school board in February of 1973. This plan entailed busing less than 3 percent of the students, producing some integration in the small number of white schools and leaving all of the black schools segregated. The agreement opened the path for the city to have its first black superintendent. The price of gaining administrative control of the overwhelmingly black system was signing away rights of black children.

While the "Atlanta Compromise" was being implemented, and after the NAACP dropped out of the case, another effort to desegregate across city-suburban boundaries was pursued by the American Civil Liberties Union. The ACLU carried out the case in opposition to the black-led Atlanta school board, chaired by Benjamin Mays, long-time president of Morehouse College and a mentor of Martin Luther King, Jr. The local ACLU eventually took the case to the Supreme Court. A three-judge federal court issued its decision—ending the metropolitan Atlanta case in September 1979, twenty-five years after the *Brown* decision; the Supreme Court affirmed the Atlanta ruling in 1980, without even hearing the parties. The decision, by five of the nine Justices, offered no explanation, just the words, "Affirmed on appeal from D.C. N.D. Ga." (*Armour v. Nix*, 446 U.S. 930).

Just two weeks earlier the court had let stand a massive desegregation plan consolidating and fully integrating all the city and suburban school districts in metropolitan Wilmington, Delaware, where the black-led school board had fought for integration. The Delaware plan meant that virtually all segregation was ended in the Wilmington region (*Delaware State Brd. of Ed. v. Evans*, 446 U.S. 923). By 1986, black students in metro Wilmington attended schools with an average white enrollment of 64 percent, compared to 22 percent for students in metropolitan Atlanta and 4 percent for blacks in the Atlanta Public Schools (Orfield and Monfort 1988, 20; Orfield, Monfort, and Aaron 1989, 22). Successful metropolitan cases, including those in Louisville and Indianapolis as well as Wilmington, and the settlements in St. Louis, Little Rock, and Milwaukee, all had been brought with the support of central-city school boards.

The evidence presented in the Atlanta case was massive. Civil rights lawyers filed vast numbers of documents with the court claiming that "prior governmental actions" of many sorts had produced segregated housing and, therefore, segregated schools "throughout the six-county metropolitan area." The court conceded the violations but refused to order desegregation. The court noted that Atlanta had adopted zoning by race after the Supreme Court had ruled such zoning unconstitutional. The city had even adopted an ordinance in 1931 setting jail terms for blacks who moved into previously white housing within fifteen blocks of a school without an official city permit. The court found that the city had also created physical barriers between white and black neighborhoods as late as the early 1960s. Through the 1950s the court held that the city had been actively involved in controlling the expansion of black residential areas on a segregated basis. The court found that the city of Atlanta had 83 percent of all subsidized housing in the metropolitan area and that it had been openly segregated through the mid-1960s. The suburbs had resisted subsidized housing construction and several had used urban renewal and other land-use powers to bulldoze existing low-income black communities, often forcing their residents to move into the inner city. The net effect was to help concentrate blacks within expanding ghettos in the city. The court agreed, in other words, that there had been sweeping use of a wide range of governmental powers to create and maintain racially segregated communities.

The court held, however, that history was irrelevant to the present conditions; that "the causes of residential patterns can never be fully explained" and that much of the segregation resulted from "economic restraints and personal preferences."

It is obvious to the most casual observer that integrated housing patterns do not prevail in the Atlanta metropolitan area. It is also patently obvious that there is an interface between housing patterns and school populations. What is not clear, however, is that there is a remedy in the federal courts for all the problems of racial prejudice, even when those problems contribute to disproportionate racial concentrations in some schools. . . . The persistent social patterns which develop and crystallize due to the interaction of members of society over long periods of time are not matters within the jurisdiction of a court unless the involvement of government in these patterns causes a constitutional violation to persist. (*Armour v. Nix*, Slip Opinion N.D. Ga. [1979])

Throughout the legal proceedings, the focus of the local federal courts was never on black educational problems but on the threat to the city which would be created by driving out white families. It was assumed, incorrectly, that whites would stay if neighborhood schools were preserved. Ghettos and ghetto schools were accepted as facts of nature. Past practices were assumed to have no important contemporary effects. Local school authorities were never required to actually integrate the schools. The outlying suburbs were permitted to remain all white.

After years of futility and dramatic racial transition in a school district where major desegregation was no longer feasible, the local black leaders decided to bargain for black control. Eventually, they tired of foot-dragging and white business leaders began worrying that bad press would scare away new industry. So a cadre of white business and civic leaders, including then-Governor Jimmy Carter and Federal Judge Griffin Bell (who later became President Carter's attorney general) supported a compromise agreement with black leaders.

Defenders of the agreement point out that it redefined the equity issue. The belief that black students needed access to white schools with superior resources, competition, and better prepared teachers now gave way to the hope that black administrators would understand the needs of black children and would find ways to make segregated, low-income, inner-city schools equal to the middle-class white schools. Back in the 1880s the black community had struggled for black teachers; now they won black control.

Atlanta Superintendent Alonzo Crim, selected to implement the agreement, insisted that equality could be achieved within the system of segregation. Lyndon Wade, Urban League Executive Director and chairman of a biracial group appointed by the U.S. District Court to advise both sides in the lawsuit concurred: "I have always believed that if you could ever achieve equity in the administration of the school system, then it would improve the chances of black kids getting a better education" (Hansen 1987).

Part of the reason for black leaders' abandonment of the goal of busing across suburban lines was political. Lonnie King, president of the local NAACP at the time, put it this way: "If the metropolitan plan had come about it would have meant there would have to be some power sharing . . . blacks would still have gotten the short end of the stick" (*Atlanta Constitution*, 1 October 1987). A 1981 survey of Atlanta residents showed that blacks were more positive about their schools than whites. Fifty-one percent of low-income blacks and 38 percent of those with higher incomes, compared to only about one-fifth of whites, ranked the city schools "excellent" or "very good."

In spite of this more positive view of the schools, however, low-income black families strongly supported desegregation, even if it involved long-distance busing. They disagreed with the policies of the area's black leaders, favoring "busing across the metro area" by a two-to-one majority (64.4 percent to 35.6 percent). Higher-income blacks, many of whom would move to the suburbs in the 1980s, were evenly divided on the issue (*Atlanta Constitution* staff 1981, "Black and Poor," 22).

Some black leaders thought that funding rather than access to middle-class schools was the basic need. "It was really the integration of the money to provide a quality education for all children that was black folks' goal," according to Andrew Young, the civil rights leader who later became Atlanta's congressman and then its mayor. "Racial balance was [just] a means for achieving the goal."

"[Lonnie] King was the 'real hero,'" Lyndon Wade said, for having the courage to compromise and avoid the violence of integration that plagued other southern cities. "What went wrong," said Wade, "was that the support of the plan was not forthcoming from the white community. The white kids continued to leave the system" (Hansen 1987). No one thought about the possibility that the black middle class would also flee the segregated city system.

Black and white negotiators had accepted the premise that if "white flight" was caused by busing, a system of neighborhood schools would hold white students. In fact, however, Atlanta's decline in white enrollment was among the most rapid of all large school districts. Between 1967 and 1986 the total Atlanta enrollment dropped 41 percent. The school district was 38 percent white in 1968 but was only 15 percent white by 1974 and was down to 7 percent white in 1986 (Orfield and Monfort 1988, 11, 16). Clearly, the compromise didn't hold whites and reinforced continued high levels of segregation. The big cities that best held white enrollment were part of mandatory metropolitan-wide desegregation programs (Orfield and Monfort 1988, 11, 13, 16). What happened was not white flight from busing, since there was no significant desegregation plan, but a rapid fall in white and black middle-class students as the wealthier families of both races abandoned the city system, which became progressively poorer and blacker.

During the 1986–87 school year, 98 percent of Atlanta's black students were in majority black schools and 91 percent were in schools that were 90 to 100 percent nonwhite. The typical black student in the city was in a school where only 4 percent of the students were white. No city in the South was more intensely segregated and only New Orleans came close (ibid., 20, 24). On a metropolitan level, the Atlanta region was one of the few major southern metropolises that became more segregated for black students during the 1970s and whose segregation continued to intensify in the 1980s even as the number of black suburbanites rapidly climbed (Orfield, Monfort, and George 1987, 17–18).

Black leaders' tolerance of the persistence of segregation combined several elements: the futility of pursuing integration after the vast expansion of the ghettos and the departure of most whites, the assertion that black leadership would solve the problems, and a desire to avoid overt conflict with white business interests. Mayor Young, who had been one of Martin Luther King's closest associates in the 1960s, said that it was "tragic" that integration had not been achieved but that the compromise had been basically wise:

Instead of pushing for massive busing across county lines, we worked out a compromise agreement with the court that allowed a predominantly black administration to basically take control of the system.

It was good and it was bad. What happened when that occurred was that too many whites pulled out of the school system and too many middle-class blacks did. (*Atlanta Journal and Constitution*, 4 October 1987: 4)

The compromise, he argued, had helped in the political and economic success of the city: "One of the reasons the city has succeeded is that it has been able to make racial compromises" (ibid.). Atlanta has blossomed economically in the last generation but so too have a number of the southern metropolitan areas which implemented massive city-suburban desegregation plans—areas including metropolitan Orlando, Charlotte, Tampa-St. Petersburg, and Nashville.

Still, the irony is clear. Atlanta—birthplace of the civil rights movement, crucible of black leadership and economically booming metropolis of the future—failed to integrate its schools. Its black leaders agreed to accept segregation in return for power within a deteriorating and increasingly isolated system. Moreover, the hope that segregated schools could be made equal has gone a-glimmering.

There were already signs in a 1979 report by a research center at Clark College in Atlanta (now Clark-Atlanta University) that the bargain had failed. The study reported drastic enrollment declines, rapid racial transition, racial and class isolation, diminishing business interest in the schools, and little community involvement. And it found the lowest test scores in low-income black schools (Hadden et al. 1979).

The school district had attacked that study, promising to rapidly move the students toward national norms. But the data reported in this chapter show that the pattern of segregated and unequal schools was still striking, on a metropolitan scale, in the mid-1980s. The compromise had traded away the opportunities of low-income blacks in the metro area to pursue access to high schools operating at or near national grade-level norms.

Race and Educational Opportunity in the 1980s

Our study, the first systematic analysis ever done of racial, income, and performance data for all the high schools in metropolitan Atlanta, shows that in every category one could predict the success of a school in the region in the mid-1980s given only the percentage of black students and the percentage of poor students, so divided were these schools by race, class, and academic achievement levels. This analysis is based on data obtained from the U.S. Department of Education, the Georgia Department of Education and the school districts themselves. School funding did not explain the differences. This research shows that Atlanta was actually an area where there was relatively strong funding for central-city schools and where even more money was spent on low-income schools, but deep inequalities remained. The city, with its high concentration of poverty and related health problems, did have special needs, such as a higher proportion of physically and mentally handicapped students requiring expensive special services.

Distribution of Students by Race and Income

The Atlanta city schools are at the core of the five-county Atlanta metro-politan area and had a student population that was more than nine-tenths black and far and away the poorest in the region; the city schools were surrounded by eight suburban school districts. Several of these suburban districts rivaled the Atlanta city school system in size, and one, DeKalb County, actually had several thousand more high school students. In fact, certain suburban districts exhibited spectacular growth in comparison with the shrinking Atlanta system.

Between 1972 and 1985 the city's high school enrollment dropped by 25 percent while nearly every other district in the region grew. By 1985, 80 percent of all public high school students in the region attended sub-urban schools. In 1986 just over half of the region's black students went to school in the suburbs as did 98 percent of the white students.

The two districts which accounted for most of the suburban growth in that time period were in the regions of economic boom, Gwinnett and Cobb Counties. Between 1975 and 1985 Gwinnett's high school enroll-ment nearly doubled while Cobb's increased by about 15 percent.

Although an increasingly large proportion of metropolitan Atlanta's black public high school students attended suburban schools, Atlanta city schools had very few whites, and most suburban schools had very few blacks. Unlike many northern cities, by the mid-1980s Atlanta's schools had been overwhelmingly black for well over a decade. As far back as 1972 Atlanta's high schools were 77 percent black; by 1986, 92.9 percent of the city's high school students were black, and only three of its twenty high schools had a student population more than 10 percent white.

In contrast, blacks made up less than 20 percent of the suburban high school population and were concentrated in the less prosperous southern suburbs. The DeKalb County school district was 47 percent black by 1986 (Orfield and Monfort 1988, 10). But in some suburban districts, most noticeably the burgeoning Gwinnett and Cobb County systems, blacks represented a tiny minority. In 1986 they made up only 2.2 per-cent of the Gwinnett County high school population and represented 4.6 percent of Cobb County high school students. In Gwinnett County one major high school did not have even a single black student (see table 5.1).

All but one of the ten metropolitan Atlanta high schools with the larg-est proportion of black students were located in the city of Atlanta. That

Table 5.1 Distribution of Black Students in Metropolitan Atlanta in 1986

System	% black	% of area black students
Atlanta	92.9	49.4
Decatur	71.9	1.0
DeKalb	43.1	32.2
Fulton	37.4*	10.7
Marietta	29.2*	0.9
Buford	29.1**	0.3
Clayton	12.4	2.3
Cobb	4.6	2.3
Gwinnett	2.2	0.8
Metro Total	36.6	

*1986 data unavailable, 1984 substituted.
**1986 and 1984 data unavailable, 1982 substituted.

one school, Gordon High, was located just to the east of the city in nearby DeKalb County. These ten schools had black populations ranging from 99.3 to 99.9 percent.

The shrinkage of the city system meant that suburban schools enrolled a larger share of the area's black students; in 1986, just over half attended suburban schools, although only 22.5 percent of the suburban high school students were black. The overall percentage of black high school students in the region was 37 percent in 1986.

The bulk of suburban blacks attended a handful of high schools in nearby Fulton and DeKalb Counties. By 1986 these two counties combined had almost as large a black high school population as the Atlanta Public Schools. A number of the schools in these county systems were just as segregated as those in the city, but in several notable cases black students in these districts attended integrated high schools.

The economic disparities between inner-city and suburban schools in metropolitan Atlanta are even greater than the disparities in racial backgrounds. The correlation between being black and attending city schools, .6, was quite high (in social research, a correlation of 1 indicates a perfect statistical correspondence between two factors, a correlation of 0 indicates no relationship, and a correlation of .5 is considered a strong relationship). But the correlation between low income and enrollment in city schools was an astounding .86. Nearly three-quarters of the students in Atlanta city schools came from families with incomes so low they met the federal guidelines for receiving completely free lunches in their school cafeterias. By contrast, not a single suburban school district had more than 20 percent of its students qualifying for free lunches except for the small majority-black Decatur city system (see table 5.2).

Changing the focus from districts to individual schools, the contrasts become even more extreme. The ten poorest schools in metropolitan Atlanta—schools where from 83 to 94 percent of the students qualified for free lunches—were all located in the Atlanta city school district, while all of the region's ten wealthiest schools were located in suburban districts. So great was the difference between city and suburban schools that not a single suburban school had as many of its students receive free lunches as the average Atlanta school. There were no schools without significant poverty within the city; even at the city high school with the fewest low-income students (a selective magnet school), 27 percent of the students received free lunches.

At the opposite extreme, Cobb and Gwinnett Counties had, on average, fewer than 5 percent of their students receiving free lunches, and Clayton County had only a few percentage points more. At all of the region's ten wealthiest schools less than one percent of the student body received free lunches. All but one of these schools were more than 90 percent white.

Throughout metropolitan Atlanta the percentage of low-income students in a school correlated very strongly to the percentage of black students (.78), but several schools did stand out as notable exceptions. In partially integrated Fulton and DeKalb Counties, the correlation was significantly lower (.56 in both districts), although black schools still had more free lunch recipients than white schools. In DeKalb County three high schools, Cedar Grove, Southwest DeKalb, and Walker, were more than 90 percent black but had less than one-fifth of their students receiving free lunches in 1987. Lakeshore and Westwood High schools (since

Table 5.2 Percentage of Students Receiving Free Lunches in 1986

District	Percent
Atlanta	74.7
Buford	12.8
Clayton	6.6
Cobb	1.9
Decatur	37.0
DeKalb	18.1
Fulton	15.9
Gwinnett	3.8
Marietta	17.7

combined into one school) in Fulton County showed similar percentages. In addition, several integrated high schools in these districts were relatively well-off economically, and integrated Riverwood High in Fulton County was among the region's ten wealthiest. Another exception was the Atlanta city high school with the fewest free lunch recipients, Mays High, whose science and mathematics magnet program draws students from throughout the city; its student body was 99 percent black in 1986, with 27 percent of its students getting free lunches. The average city school had about three times as high a concentration of students in poverty.

Not all suburban schools were white and wealthy and not all city school were poor and black; however, every poor school in the region was black, and virtually all of the wealthiest schools were white. The few exceptions were mainly in those suburbs to which the black middle class has fled. As Atlanta's blacks suburbanize they are separating along class lines. Thus, instead of a split between relatively wealthy white students and poor black students, metropolitan Atlanta exhibits the characteristics of a region segmented into three parts: the poorest is overwhelmingly black and attends city schools; the largest is made up of wealthier white suburbanites in outlying white districts; the last, composed mostly of middle-class black suburbanites, many living in areas of racial change, stands between them.

Test Scores

It is always difficult and often controversial to measure student performance. No single statistic can ever give a clear picture of a school's success in educating students, and there is no single criterion for a successful school. Different schools receive students with very different levels of preparation. And standardized tests have been plagued by criticism that they are racially and culturally biased and that they are poor predictors of academic success, particularly for some types of students (Crouse and Trusheim 1988). A recent federal court decision in New York State found, for example, that the SAT (Scholastic Aptitude Test) tended to underpredict performance of female students in math (*Sharif v. New York State Education Department*, 709 F Supp. 345 [S.O.N.Y. 1989]; *New York Times*, 4 February 1989). Tests results also are confusing because they reflect what students bring with them from home and not merely what they learn in school.

Nonetheless, just about any criteria for success must include a stu-

dent's ability to learn basic subjects and advance steadily toward graduation and to score reasonably well on standardized tests. And standardized
tests are the only measures of educational achievement that are available
for comparison across the metro area. They should be interpreted cau-
tiously.

THE DATA

The data on test performance across the metropolitan area were difficult
to obtain and analyze. Since different districts used different tests, procedures, and norm years in their internal testing programs, the only comparable data came from tests required of all districts by the Georgia Department of Education. In 1972, 1975, and 1976, the scores reported here
are the sum of three TAP tests given to high school juniors in the Georgia
statewide testing program. (The Riverside Publishing Company's standardized Test of Achievement and Proficiency, or TAP, measured math
and reading skills and was administered throughout the state.) The 1982
scores cited here combine the eleventh-grade reading and math scores in
the Georgia Criterion Referenced Tests. For 1986 and 1987 the data rep-
resent the composite standardized scores for the TAP tests. Systemwide
data were obtained by averaging the scores of all high schools in the district. These measures are imperfect, but the consistent patterns
throughout different testing programs lend confidence to the general
findings.

TESTS AND THE EXCELLENCE MOVEMENT

The school reform movement, including the Atlanta programs of Superintendent Alonzo Crim and the state government's Quality Basic Education Act, gave extraordinary importance to testing. Progress in test scores
was used as both the central measure of the success of schools and school
districts and as an absolute requirement for graduation or even for pro-
motion from grade to grade.

Reforms adopted in the 1980s took the fascination with test scores to
extremes. By the late 1970s most of the major central city districts in the
United States had been hit by movements strongly emphasizing test
scores. Big city superintendents became famous and public support of
their programs increased when they could report excellent test score
gains. Georgia's obsession with tests became apparent when it became
the first state in the nation to require an entrance test for kindergarten
students before they could advance to the first grade. In 1988 the state

made one-eighth of its 6-year-olds repeat kindergarten because their test scores were too low. The state board dropped the pencil-and-paper component of this test in 1989 but continued to require proficiency in a variety of skills as well as personality and physical development assessments for admission to the first grade (*Education Week*, 15 March 1989).

ATLANTA'S APPARENT ACHIEVEMENT

One of the most remarkable and widely praised set of achievement test claims of the early 1980s came from the Atlanta Public Schools. The pronouncements by Atlanta school officials that a substantial majority of the city's virtually all-black enrollment was achieving over national norms were cited as proof that strong, committed, black educators could overcome the problems of race and poverty within a context of racial and economic segregation. If this were true, the claim that educational methods had been discovered to make segregated low-income schools equal would be strongly supported. Such claims were made, but they turned out to be premature.

Atlanta School Superintendent Alonzo Crim pledged in 1980 to bring Atlanta school children to national norms in achievement scores by 1985. In June of 1983, he announced that the goal had already been accomplished. Fifty percent of the city's students, he said, were scoring at the national norm or higher in reading and 55 percent were doing so in math. "This is just the beginning," he said. "In an urban system where 80 percent of our students are poor and 90 percent are black, historically we've always been at the bottom. We're announcing today that we don't need any special considerations. We can achieve what any students anywhere can achieve" (*Atlanta Constitution*, 7 June 1983). He claimed that well-run schools could overcome all the disadvantages of isolation and poverty. He received awards and recognition from across the United States.

Crim summarized his theory in a 1983 "Community of Believers" statement, which received wide attention. When he had come to Atlanta a decade earlier, he said, he had wanted to move poor black children "to achievement levels equal [to] or better than the national average." He opposed metropolitan school desegregation and adopted a strategy in which each school would "develop a community of believers which would include peers, parents, educators at all levels, business persons, members of the clergy, and citizens at large." Students had to be seen as "winners" and given evidence that achievement led to success. He called for "thousands of conscious, decentralized experiments that caring adults will attempt to drive students on." The end of the desegregation order, he said, brought a "sense of relief" and the focus turned to test scores, which were the leading concern of parents in community meetings. Plans were developed and carefully monitored to focus attention on skills and achievement.

Crim wrote in early 1983 that the effort had produced "continuous improvement" since 1976 and that the goal of meeting national norms in five years of intensive effort beginning in 1980 was being realized faster than expected. He said that the "involvement of parents and the general community in the job of positively developing the minds of our children" would have the district at "national norm at all grade levels by 1985." Crim pointed to praise from Ernest Boyer of the Carnegie Foundation, who was leading a national study of high schools: "We saw a school system that was healthy and where academic priorities were clearly understood and where progress was being made" (Crim 1983).

Dean Barbara L. Jackson, in her 1981 article "Urban School Desegregation from a Black Perspective," praised the Atlanta Compromise as a good model for the future, suggesting that "these black educators appear to have a different orientation from their predecessors. They want to make their school systems work for *all* children. . . ." She noted the reports of rising test scores (Jackson 1981, 212).

The record appeared so strong that many joined the chorus of praise. Harvard Professor Sara Lawrence Lightfoot praised the record in her important book, *The Good High School*, which included a study of one Atlanta school. She said that Crim had rejected integrationist dreams and was showing the way to solve the problems of poor inner-city schools. "Why spend money and energy on an unrealistic goal? He sees his challenge as difficult, but clear: to provide quality education for the city's poor and minority children" (Lightfoot 1983, 31). The book praised the values and reform methods put to use in Carver High School, which she saw as a successful reflection of the new philosophy. Lightfoot's book provided no statistical evidence of the achievement gains in the school. (In 1986–87, three years after her book was published, Carver High had average achievement scores in the eighth percentile—worse than 92 percent of U.S. students taking the test—according to the school system's report [Atlanta Public Schools 1987, A23].)

A 1987 *American Journal of Education* article on black education in Atlanta also praised Crim:

Under the leadership of a highly respected superintendent the system has committed itself to the goal of raising poor children, and in particular, black children, to achievement levels equal to or better than national averages. . . . System-wide programs of testing and remediation in reading and mathematics have been established, and achievement levels in these areas are increasing. . . . The Atlanta Compromise . . . does appear to have improved the quality of the educational services provided to the city's black children. (Plank and Turner 1987, 602)

The parade of announcements of success continued. In 1984 Dr. Crim announced that 53 percent of the city's students were performing above national norms in reading and 60 percent were doing so in math. "We have come a long way in a relatively short period of time," said Crim (*Atlanta Constitution*, 2 June 1984). The *Atlanta Constitution* called the results "gratifying proof" of the district's accomplishments (ibid., 15 August 1984). The 1985 data were even better; they showed 56 percent at or above national norms in reading and 63 percent in math (ibid., 7 June 1986).

A *New York Times* article about Crim, for example, was called "Urban Education that Really Works." Author Dudley Clendinen wrote: "As a result of his efforts, pupil performance levels in the basic skills are now above the national average; school attendance has risen 6 to 8 percentage points; automatic promotions are being eliminated; test scores are higher, and both the black and white communities are involved in support of the schools" (Clendinen 1986, 68). The *Times* credited Crim not only with reaching national norms in achievement but also with a high graduation rate.

The elimination of "social promotions" was warmly praised but later research within the school district produced warnings of problems. Augustine McDaniel of the district's research staff concluded that previous research did not show clear benefits from flunking students and that there were some reasons to worry about damage. Her study showed that about one-fifth of all Atlanta first-graders from 1980 to 1986 had flunked and that during the first five years of the policy 7 percent of students had flunked more than one grade. The study concluded that "the overall social adjustment of the nonpromoted students is significantly lower" and that they were rated sharply lower by their teachers (McDaniel 1987, 8).

EVIDENCE OF FAILURE

The claims that Atlanta's schools had overcome the problems of race and poverty began to break down, however, when the state government began to issue test data directly comparing school districts. The Georgia General Assembly mandated the use of the more demanding Iowa Basic

Skills Test and public release of scores. When the state policy was adopted, Crim predicted that the result would be a 10 to 15 percent drop in the city's scores, relative to the national norm (*Atlanta Constitution*, 7 June 1986). Obviously he knew the consequences of choosing different yardsticks for measuring achievement.

The first statewide data, released in 1986, showed that Atlanta children were doing well in the early elementary years, which may have reflected both Crim's intense basic skills emphasis and the policy of flunking children in the early grades if they did not achieve. By ninth grade, however, the test data found them twenty points behind the national norm. Even among the group of Georgia school districts with socioeconomic characteristics similar to Atlanta, this widely praised school district came in last in the state at the ninth-grade level (*Atlanta Constitution*, 7 June 1986). Atlanta high school students had the worst record in the state in passing the Georgia Basic Skills Test, a requirement for graduation from high school (ibid., 14 November 1986). A school district that had made proud claims of solving the whole achievement problem came in behind the state's poor, rural, majority-black districts. It was obvious that the gains made in the early grades did not carry over to high school.

The 1988 test results, reporting on the third year of the Georgia testing reforms, showed Atlanta slightly above statewide norms at the second grade, below at the fourth and seventh grades, and very sharply behind at the ninth grade. At the ninth-grade level, more than 140 Georgia districts scored higher than the Atlanta Public Schools. Atlanta ranked at the 36th percentile on the norms used by the state while Cobb and Gwinnett County schools each ranked at the 64th percentile. The DeKalb and Fulton County systems were also significantly above the norm. The state report showed that most large Georgia systems with more than one-fifth of their students eligible for free lunches were below the norm but that the Atlanta system had the lowest scores. On the required state math tests, 39 percent of Atlanta's tenth-graders failed as did 21 percent of those taking the writing test. In Gwinnett County the failure rates were 9 percent for math and 7 percent for writing (Georgia Department of Education 1988, tables 4, 6a, 6b, 11).

The publication of comparable data using the same yardstick for all school districts in Georgia consistently showed great differences between the city and suburban schools and school districts. This data shows a very strong persisting relationship between family income, race, and achievement levels across metropolitan Atlanta even after a generation of reform in city schools.

THE NATURE OF THE DECEPTION

The scores that the school system had been reporting prior to 1986 were deceptive. The district had been using a less competitive base test, the California Achievement Test (CAT) and norms established back in 1978 when average test scores across the nation were considerably lower than in the 1980s, particularly in the early grades. The new state testing program used a more difficult test, with a 1984 norm. Two other policies tended to increase the scores reported by Atlanta school officials: The school district had begun flunking very large numbers of students; a student repeating second grade and taking the second-grade test would, for example, look more successful in terms of his test scores than if he had to take the third-grade test. The district also allowed children functioning well behind their grade levels to take the test on the grade level at which they were functioning; a fourth-grader functioning on the second-grade level could be given the second-grade test and evaluated as a second-grader. Commenting on a draft of this study, Superintendent Crim explained the process:

The CAT was administered to Atlanta pupils based on their functional levels, not their grade levels. However, there were established parameters. First no child was administered a test level more than two levels below grade placement. Second, if a pupil in grade 6 took a fourth-grade test, he was compared to sixth-graders taking the fourth-grade test, not other fourth graders. Last, functional level norms tables, rather than on-grade level norms, were used for all functional level testing. (Crim, letter to author, 24 June 1988, 4)

Dr. Crim claimed that this procedure actually deflated scores and that the number of students tested on-grade increased until in 1985 it included almost all first-graders and three-fourths of the eighth graders (ibid.). It was nonetheless true that under this system a child old enough for eighth grade could have been retained two or more grades, been placed in sixth grade, given a fourth-grade test, and then compared only to other sixth-graders who had to take the fourth-grade test.

Such deceptive practices were not unique to Atlanta. They had been used by other urban school districts, and states, and, doubtless by suburban districts, to inflate apparent test-score accomplishments. This was one predictable result of an excessive focus on test scores.

A 1987 study showed that all states were reporting average test scores above the national norm, an obvious impossibility. A basic problem, according to the study, was the delay in updating test norms by the major test publishing companies (*New York Times,* 28 November 1987). This has enabled state educational leaders to take tough reform-minded policy positions and all come out winners. Atlanta Public Schools were in good company in reporting misleading test scores.

There is a major social problem, however, when such invalid scores are used to support a policy of accepting segregation. Parents and community leaders are lulled into thinking that school systems are doing much better in preparing children to compete at the later stages of education and employment than is actually true. A 1981 survey showed that 51 percent of low-income blacks and 38 percent of higher-income blacks in the city believed the schools were "excellent" or "very good." Only 10 percent of low-income blacks and 17 percent of those with higher incomes said the schools were "not so good" or "poor" (Mooney 1981).

If Atlanta students were actually achieving at national norms, however, the dismal problem of declining completion rates for black students in local colleges might not be so severe. One-eighth of Atlanta high school graduates entered the state university system and 43 percent of those who had taken college preparatory courses had to take remedial courses after they got to college (*Atlanta Constitution,* 11 April 1990).

Superintendent Crim's successor, J. Jerome Harris, continued the intense focus on test scores, seizing control of the schools with the worst records. He said, however, that Atlanta test scores were very weak and set his initial goal as simply moving out from the "bottom five" of school districts in Georgia. The transformation from the school district's sweeping claims of the recent past was striking (*Education Week,* 3 May 1989, 1, 23). However, within a year, Harris was reporting the schools over the national norms again. (This assertion came after the conclusion of our study.)

METROPOLITAN ATLANTA ACHIEVEMENT COMPARISONS

In the 1970s and 1980s, Atlanta-area students participated in a variety of standardized tests, and the differences between city and suburban scores remained striking while the variation among the suburban districts was modest. In 1987 the average student in the Atlanta city high schools received a standardized composite TAP score of 157.3, while the average suburbanite scored nearly twenty points higher. By contrast, there was less than an eight-point differential between the highest-scoring and lowest-scoring suburban districts. The correlation between dwelling in the suburbs and scoring well on these tests was .61 in 1986.

Similar findings were reported on the Basic Skills Tests administered annually to measure students' reading and mathematics skills. City and suburban districts both improved their scores slightly from 1982 to 1986, during a spate of education reform. The city/suburban gap was thirty-one points in 1983 and almost unchanged at twenty-nine points four years later (see fig. 5.1).

Most of the disparity between city and suburban performance on standardized tests was related to race and poverty. Low-income black schools almost invariably scored below their wealthier white counterparts and, in metro Atlanta, these poor black schools were concentrated in the inner city. The correlation between the percentage of black students in a school and low test scores was a remarkable .81 in 1987, while the correlation between low income and low test scores followed close behind at .80. These figures indicate that, given any group of metropolitan Atlanta high schools, one could predict with a great deal of certainty how they would perform on standardized tests solely on the basis of family income or racial data (since the two are so very highly related), without any information about their educational programs. The fact that race and income were so highly related means, of course, that it is all too easy to attribute to race what may well have been due to differences in family income, education, and other critical factors. If there were low-income white high schools in metropolitan Atlanta, they would doubtless also show considerable educational problems. Because of the extreme and growing racial

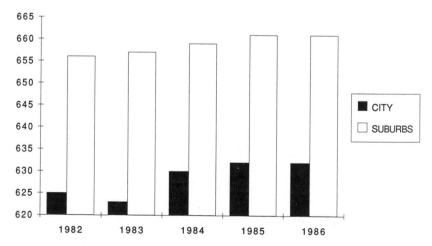

Figure 5.1. Basic Skills Test Scores

gap in income and the fact that poor whites rarely live in concentrated poverty areas, there were no such schools. The Metropolitan Opportunity Project found no predominantly low-income white high schools in any of the metropolitan areas in its national study.

The relationship between family income and educational success is one of the best-known relationships in educational research. In fact, a 1987 analysis of the schools in the entire state, carried out for the State Department of Education at the University of Georgia, found a strong relationship between the percentage of poor children in a school and achievement. (It did not include the racial composition of a school in the study.) The state's Quality Basic Education Act required comparison of achievement in districts "with similar demographic characteristics." The idea was to find out what factors outside the school strongly affected student performance and to take those into account in evaluating performance.

The study of schools in the state's 187 districts found no clear relationship to wealth of the district or expenditures per pupil. By far the strongest relationship was between the percentage of low-income students in a school and its achievement scores. There were similar findings in neighboring South Carolina (Wisenbaker 1987, 1–2, 8).

The study found that the differences between poorer and richer schools *within* large districts was even greater than it was across the state. Perhaps the multiple problems associated with living in an area of concentrated poverty in a big city with many such schools and large isolated neighborhoods made the effects of the isolation even worse (Wisenbaker 1987, table 2, appendix B). The Atlanta results show this pattern, with the Atlanta Public Schools following significantly behind the white suburban systems (see fig. 5.2).

The role of race and income in determining standardized test scores in metro Atlanta becomes strikingly clear when one notices the differences in scores between the region's richest and poorest schools and between those with the highest percentages of blacks and of whites. The ten area high schools whose students receive the most free lunches, Atlanta's most impoverished schools, had an average TAP score of 151 in 1987, ranging from a low of 143 at Price High to a high of 163 at Grady High. All ten of these schools were located in the city, and all except Grady, with the highest test scores of the group, were more than 90 percent black. Grady had a magnet program in communications since 1981. In contrast, metropolitan Atlanta's ten wealthiest high schools averaged

189 on the TAP in 1987, nearly thirty-eight points higher. The ten wealthiest schools were all suburban and all had substantial white majorities.
Only one of them, Riverwood High in Fulton County, had a significant
black population—9 percent in 1986, 16 percent in 1987; on average,
these schools were 6 percent black. *In none did the low-income student
population exceed 1 percent of the total.*

Comparing the ten schools with the largest and smallest percentages
of blacks, the difference in scores between these two groups of schools
was nearly twenty-nine points in 1987 (see fig. 5.3). Not surprisingly, five
of the schools with the highest proportions of whites were also on the list
of the ten richest schools, and three of the schools with the lowest proportions were among the ten poorest schools. Among the schools with
the highest proportion of blacks, TAP scores ranged from 147 at West
Fulton and Carver to 172 at Mays High (all in Atlanta), while among the
ten most white schools they varied from 171 (Dacula High in Gwinnett
County) to 196 for Gwinnett County's Parkview High (see fig. 5.4). Mays
High School in Atlanta, the one black school to score comparably to the
overwhelmingly white schools, included a select student body with fewer
free lunches than any other city school. Magnet programs screen students
and their higher test score results are built in by the selection process.

In metro Atlanta, suburban schools with a substantial black working-
or middle-class enrollment performed only a little better than their less-
advantaged counterparts in the city. In 1986 there were nine overwhelmingly (75–100 percent) black high schools in the racially changing parts of
the suburbs. These schools were not nearly as poor as the inner-city

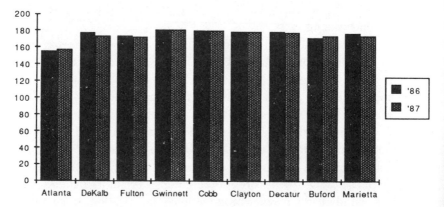

Figure 5.2. TAP Scores for Metro Atlanta

schools. With an average of 24 percent of their students receiving free lunches, they were slightly better off than any city school or the average metropolitan Atlanta high school. Yet these schools still scored far below the metropolitan average on achievement tests. The highest scoring of the nine schools, Southwest DeKalb High School, scored four points below the average metropolitan Atlanta school; as a group the black suburban schools averaged a score of 162, only seven points better than the much poorer city schools.

These segregated black suburban schools may well have been suffering the effects of past and continuing discrimination—among these, poorly educated parents, and teachers who didn't think black students can learn. The only optimistic findings were in schools that had been integrated. Racially integrated suburban schools (25–75 percent black) scored much better than their black suburban counterparts, despite the fact that they had almost as many low-income students (21 versus 24 percent). These integrated schools scored slightly above the metropolitan mean and almost twelve points better on achievement tests than the predominantly black suburban schools (see table 5.3). Thus, independent of student economic status, racial composition appears to help determine how well schools perform on these tests. In the Atlanta region, predominantly black schools, no matter what their economic composition, are normally clearly outperformed by integrated and white schools. It is important, however, not to overstate the racial factor; on average, black suburban schools had about twice as many low-income students as their white counterparts. Blacks have a much more difficult time maintaining a solidly middle-class housing market over an area large enough to populate a high school.

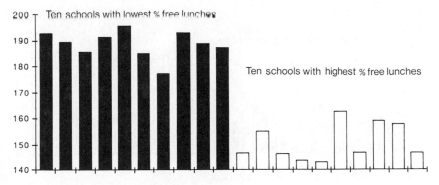

Figure 5.3. 1987 TAP Scores for Metro Atlanta High Schools

Since the mid-1970s, metropolitan Atlanta's top ten test-taking schools were overwhelmingly white, while the bottom ten were almost all-black. The percentages remained relatively stable, though both the best-scoring and worst-scoring schools were slowly gaining in black enrollment. The top ten schools moved from less than 2 percent black in 1976 to 6 percent in 1987 (see table 5.4). In 1976 not a single one was more than 5 percent black, but by 1986 three were about one-tenth black. Two of these schools, Riverwood and DeKalb County's Chamblee High School, had both been in the top ten in 1976, but at that time Riverwood had virtually no black students and Chamblee less than 5 percent. Despite significant integration, these suburban high schools remained on the list of the region's highest achieving schools. A tiny fraction of black suburban families gained access to the region's best schools, separating themselves from the vast majority of poor and middle-class blacks who remained in segregated, poorly performing schools.

In sum, test results were strongly related to both the racial composition and the income level of the student body. These factors were, in turn, very strongly related to each other since there was a large and growing racial gap in income. Race and poverty were also linked to other factors such as parental education, family status, health, and a variety of neighborhood conditions. Poor black students in the overwhelmingly poor black inner-city schools scored far below all other students in the region, yet some affluent suburban schools with large black minorities were among the highest-scoring. Conversely, a few suburban schools with virtually all black student bodies performed nearly as badly as their poorer inner-city counterparts. In metro Atlanta, white schools and integrated middle-class schools outperformed all other schools on standard-

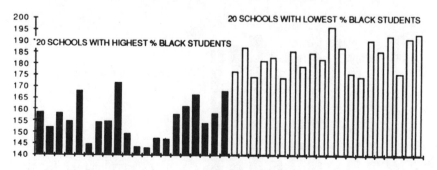

Figure 5.4. 1987 TAP Scores for Metro Atlanta High Schools

Table 5.3 Average Test Scores and Poverty Levels for White, Black, and Integrated High Schools in Metro Atlanta

	Black Population (%)	Free Lunch Recipients (%)	Average Test Scores
Black city schools	98.3	77.5	154.6
Black suburban schools	94.7	23.9	162.0
Integrated suburban schools	45.9	20.6	172.9
White suburban schools	7.0	6.0	180.2
METRO AVERAGE	36.6	27.2	171.9

Table 5.4 Percentage of Black Students in Selected Area High Schools

Ten Schools	1976	1982	1986	1987
with best test scores	1.7	4.9	8.0	6.1
with worst test scores	96.8	94.8	98.2	98.7

ized tests while overwhelmingly black schools, whatever their economic makeup, did worse.

COLLEGE PREP INEQUALITIES

Georgia provided special college preparatory diplomas for students who took additional coursework in high school to be prepared to meet collegiate standards. A state legislative study found, however, that only about one-eighth of the city's graduates enrolled in state colleges in 1988 and that those who did were far more likely to have to take remedial work even if they had obtained the special diploma. Of Atlanta graduates with college prep diplomas, 43 percent had to take remedial work in the state's colleges. In contrast, Cobb and Gwinnett Counties had about three times as high a proportion of their graduates enroll in state colleges, and their college prep students were less than half as likely to need remediation (*Atlanta Journal and Constitution,* 11 April 1990). The data strongly suggest that a basic part of the decline in black access to college in the Atlanta area is related to the weak academic preparation in city high schools, even for students who take the toughest courses that are offered. This is true not only for Atlanta. A 1990 study of the nation's largest metro areas showed that only one-fifth of the graduates of segregated high schools who enrolled in college in 1980 had received baccalaureates six years later (Camburn 1990).

IS INTEGRATION THE SOLUTION?

It is tempting to conclude that integration powerfully affects student achievement, since integrated schools perform so much better than schools with larger black populations. However, the data developed in this study are inadequate to support such a conclusion. These data average scores for all students in a school. Without separate test scores for blacks and whites within integrated schools, for example, we cannot study the effect of integration on the black students within the integrated school. These data show only that integrated schools had higher average test performance scores than segregated schools.

Nonetheless, these findings make it appropriate to review what two generations of research on school desegregation have shown. The most thorough recent review was commissioned by the Connecticut State Department of Education and carried out by Janet Scofield of the University of Pittsburgh (Scofield 1988). After reviewing hundreds of studies, she concluded that published studies were limited in scope and methods, with most focusing on narrow questions of academic achievement in the first year of integration. Despite these limitations, she found convincing evidence that desegregation had a modest positive effect on the achievements of black students and that this effect could be enhanced by proper implementation. She found significant evidence to support the proposition that beginning desegregation in the first grade strengthens the effects as does desegregating low-income children in predominantly middle-class suburban schools. The evidence was overwhelming that desegregation does not hurt the achievement of white children (Scofield 1988).

Research conducted in the 1980s suggests that the most dramatic impacts of desegregation were in areas other than achievement scores. Important work at Johns Hopkins shows that students attending desegregated schools were more likely to attend selective colleges, more likely to major in science and math-related fields, more likely to find employment in the growth sectors of the economy that require working in predominantly white settings, and more likely to live in integrated neighborhoods as adults (Scofield 1988; Braddock 1987). In other words, students attending integrated schools had a better chance of making it across the color line in metropolitan society on a number of dimensions. These findings bore out the patterns of poor access to college and jobs for city youths reported in the next two chapters. Integration does not end racial inequalities but, at least, it makes access to more competitive schools and preparation for a multiracial college, society, and job market possible.

Attrition

A basic ingredient in the recipe for a successful school is keeping students at their grade level and in school until graduation. Attrition is assessed by comparing enrollment figures for each grade level over a period of years to find out what percentage drop out.

Determining attrition rates in metro Atlanta proved to be a task of surprising difficulty. Overall rates for each city school were difficult enough to obtain, but the rates by race within the city and the suburbs were much harder to procure. As has been true in most areas studied by the Metropolitan Opportunity Project, the dropout rates reported by school officials had very little relationship to the real level of attrition in the schools. Such reports usually describe only the loss in a single school year, often omitting those who dropped out during the summer.

The important indicator of attrition is the relationship between the number of students graduating each year and the number that started high school four years earlier. Obtaining data on enrollment by grade, by race, by school, and by year in order to do the calculations involved not only assembling existing state and federal records but copying old hand-written documents from the Georgia State Archives.

The importance of reaching independent estimates of dropout rates should be evident from considering the rates traditionally reported by the Atlanta Public Schools. The school district, using a long-established definition, reported a dropout rate of 4.7 percent for the 1986–87 school year. The estimate produced in a working paper released by this project (Peskin 1987) was 39 percent, or eight times higher. Subsequently, the district, using a revised definition of "dropout," produced a revised estimate of 10.3 percent for the year and a longitudinal cohort analysis estimate of 26.5 percent, still only two-thirds of the Peskin estimate. This range of difference is by no means unique to Atlanta. Suburban districts also rarely report more than a small fraction of their true dropout rates. Obviously, when estimates of the student dropout rate vary by more than 800 percent from one calculation to another, analysts draw very different policy conclusions.

TRENDS IN ATTRITION

A significantly higher fraction of Atlanta-area high school students completed their high school educations in 1986 than was true of students enrolled a decade earlier. This improvement held true for every school district in the metropolitan area, city as well as suburban and for black as well as for white schools. In addition, the gap between the city schools and suburban districts narrowed over the course of the decade, an important accomplishment. Yet, students in city schools and majority-black schools still were less likely to graduate.

Because of incomplete data on totals of Atlanta-area high school graduates it is useful to examine the percentage of students who failed to reach twelfth grade as well as the percentage of students who failed to graduate. The twelfth-grade attrition rate (the percentage dropping out before the twelfth grade) is calculated by dividing the number of twelfth-graders in a given year by the number of ninth-graders entering high school four years earlier. This does not count substantial numbers who never start high school. Unfortunately, no data existed in Georgia which would have made it possible to follow individual students through their high school careers and thus accurately and conclusively determine how many dropped out of school. Attrition rates were the only way to compare dropout levels among districts during this period and offered the best approximation of the number of students dropping out of school.

The attrition rates here are not adjusted for the fact that some districts have more students transferring out than transferring in. They do not take into consideration demographic shifts or students who took longer than four years to complete their secondary educations (this should make little difference if the level is constant over time). While this method is far from perfect, it is the best available, and it is also used by the United States Department of Education in making state and regional comparisons.

On the metropolitan level, these data no doubt understate the true dropout rate. The enormous growth of the Atlanta metropolitan area means that there were many more school-age young people moving into the region than leaving it. Hence, some of those graduating each year were the product of net migration from other regions, not the success of local schools. If information were available to control statistically for migration, our calculated dropout rate would be slightly higher.

There were also migration effects within the metropolitan area. Since the Atlanta and Decatur public schools had a long-term trend of declining enrollment, a small portion of the dropout rate reported there was actually the product of net out-migration. If it were possible to study these cities' dropout rates more precisely, the figure would be slightly lower. Exactly the opposite is true for the rapidly growing suburban districts. In-migration makes their dropout rates appear slightly lower than they actually are.

These limitations are worrisome. Detailed studies in the Chicago Public Schools show, however, that the method used here produces much more accurate estimates than those traditionally reported by state and local administrators. One such study of student records in Chicago produced statistics very much closer to those developed from this kind of cohort analysis than to those that had previously been reported by school officials (Chicago Panel on Public School Finances 1985).

TWELFTH-GRADE ATTRITION

The data show that in 1985, the Atlanta city high schools had the highest twelfth-grade attrition rate of any of the six major school districts in the metropolitan area (29 percent), while Clayton County high schools had the lowest (18 percent). The small Marietta city and Decatur city districts both had much higher rates than the Atlanta city schools, but among the major districts, the range of attrition rates over the Atlanta region was less than 12 percent. By comparison, the range between twelfth-grade attrition rates in the same districts was 20 percent a decade earlier (see table 5.5).

While the differences among metropolitan Atlanta's school systems were becoming less pronounced, the narrowing of the gap between the

Table 5.5 Twelfth-Grade Attrition Rates (%)

System	1975	1985	Change
Atlanta	45.8	29.1	−16.7
DeKalb	25.7	23.1	−2.6
Fulton	27.7	27.0	−0.7
Gwinnett*	36.6	21.0	−15.5
Clayton	32.5	17.5	−25.0
Cobb	27.3	20.4	−6.9
Buford	45.0	28.9	−16.1
Marietta	40.6	39.1	−1.5
Decatur	47.4	42.2	−5.2

*1975 data missing, 1976 substituted.

city and suburban schools was significant. In 1975, Atlanta's attrition rate was 18 percent higher than the suburban rate. But the twelfth-grade attrition rate for Atlanta city schools declined by nearly 17 percent over the decade from 1975 to 1985, more than triple the 5 percent improvement in suburban schools, and by 1983 the gap between city and suburban twelfth-grade attrition rates had nearly disappeared before beginning to widen again in 1984 and 1985 (see fig. 5.5).

Suburban and city rates were probably even more similar than the statistics indicate since they do not take migration effects into consideration. While Atlanta city schools were steadily losing students over the decade from 1975 to 1985, many of the suburban districts were burgeoning. The suburbs as a whole increased their high school enrollments more than 19 percent from 1975 to 1985, while the city of Atlanta's high-school enrollment dropped 25 percent.

Contributing to the narrowing of the attrition gap were the lackluster performances of the two major suburban districts serving the greatest number of black students, Fulton and DeKalb Counties, as well as the city's substantial improvement. From 1975 to 1985 Fulton County's attrition rate decreased by only .7 percent, while DeKalb's decreased by 2.6 percent. By 1985, more than one-third of the students in each of these districts were black.

GRADUATION RATES

From 1977 to 1986, more than one-half million Georgia high school students failed to graduate. That figure averages out to 52,981 students a

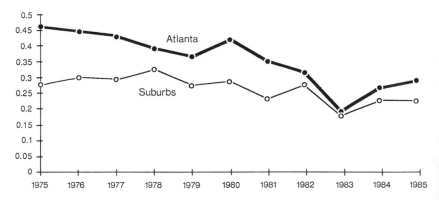

Figure 5.5. Twelfth-grade Attrition Rate for Atlanta City High Schools and Suburban Districts

year (Georgia Department of Education 1987, unpublished table). The percentage of Georgia ninth-graders who did not graduate from high school remained fairly consistent around the 38 percent mark, and as of 1986 it was 37 percent. Only four southern states—Louisiana, Florida, Mississippi, and South Carolina—had higher attrition rates than Georgia, and states such as Virginia and Arkansas had rates that were more than ten percentage points lower (Southern Regional Education Board, April 1987). This high statewide attrition rate was reflected in the metropolitan Atlanta high schools. A smaller percentage of city freshmen eventually received high school diplomas than did their suburban counterparts, with the exception of the small, poor, and heavily black Decatur system.

The graduation attrition rate in the Atlanta city schools in 1986 was significantly higher than in the suburbs (see table 5.6). All the suburban districts, except for the Decatur city schools, had graduation attrition rates well below the statewide rate, while Atlanta's was 2 percent higher.

According to the school district's own way of calculating dropouts, the dropout rate and the number of dropouts rose sharply after the adoption of tougher standards. The district reported about 5,200 dropouts, or 7 percent of total enrollment each year from 1982 to 1984. By the 1986–87 school year, however, the rate had reached 7,100 or 10 percent. The number of reported dropouts rose 36 percent between the 1982–83 school year and the 1986–87 year, even though the total enrollment was falling (Atlanta Public Schools, 25 April 1988).

The high school completion rate across Georgia dropped following the implementation of the new test requirements under the state education reform law. The graduation rate dropped from 65 percent in 1982, before the reform, to 61 percent in 1988 (*Chronicle of Higher Education*, 27 June 1990, A28).

Table 5.6 1986 Graduation Attrition Rates*

System	Rate (%)
Atlanta	39.3
DeKalb	31.8
Fulton	28.5
Gwinnett	29.0
Clayton	31.0
Cobb	27.3
Decatur	46.5
STATEWIDE	37.3

*Figures for Fulton County, Marietta, and Buford were not available.

The Atlanta Public Schools reported in 1988 that the number of graduates in the spring of that year was just 51 percent of the number of students enrolled in the ninth grade four years earlier. The school officials estimated that approximately one-half of the remainder had either transferred or were still in the system, leaving a cohort dropout rate of 25 percent. Looking back to the city's first-grade enrollment twelve years earlier, the report indicated that only 24 percent of that number had graduated and that an estimated 44 percent had dropped out. By another method of calculation, the district reported that 15 percent of its high school students left without graduating or transferring during that year (Atlanta Public Schools, 9 November 1988). That would amount to a net high school dropout rate over four years of approximately 48 percent.

Although a great deal of attention has been focused in recent years on dropouts in inner cities, one of the major findings of the metro Atlanta study, as well as a parallel study by the Metropolitan Opportunity Project in metropolitan Houston was that the suburbs had high dropout rates and were receiving little, if any, policy attention. Dropouts are generally seen by the public as a problem of little consequence in affluent systems. The data show, however, that the booming Cobb and Gwinnett County systems had rates of 27 and 29 percent respectively. These rates cannot be explained by social and economic or racial factors and suggest that a surprisingly large fraction of suburban youths faced a serious prospect of downward economic mobility.

RACE AND ATTRITION AT THE SCHOOL LEVEL

The difference between the graduation attrition rates for predominately black high schools (75–100 percent black) and predominately white (0–25 percent black) high schools was more pronounced than the difference between suburban and city rates. In 1986, the suburban-city difference was 9 percent, while the rate for predominately black schools was 12 percent higher than that for predominately white schools. More integrated schools (25–75 percent black) generally fell between these two extremes, but their recent graduation attrition rates have been closer to those of the predominately white schools.

The gap between black and white schools is, in part, just a reflection of the gap between suburban and city schools. The three Atlanta city high schools with fewer than 75 percent black students had graduation attrition rates of 23 to 28 percent, much lower than the Atlanta citywide rate of 39 percent. Overwhelmingly black schools fared the worst in preventing students from becoming dropouts.

Surprisingly, the more middle-class black suburban schools had graduation attrition rates that were even worse than those of their poorer inner-city counterparts (see table 5.7). Lakeshore High School in Fulton County, for example, was 99 percent black with only 21 percent of its students qualifying for free lunches, yet its graduate attrition rate reached 58 percent; in other words, students entering that school had less than a fifty-fifty chance of graduating from it four years later. On the average, the graduation attrition rate for these overwhelmingly black suburban schools was 4 percent higher than for city schools. Suburban schools that had increasing black student populations may have offered less remediation or support than city schools or they may have been caught up in more rigid tracking, leaving underachievers in the hands of teachers with even lower expectations than their counterparts in the city. Or it may have been that suburban districts were enforcing higher and more rigid graduation requirements or that students were lured away by the greater availability of jobs. The absence of sufficient black faculty and staff and the persistence of discrimination are other possible explanations. In any case, these dropout data suggest an urgent need for close scrutiny of suburban districts as they experience racial change.

As was true of the achievement data, the dropout statistics show that black families who leave the city but end up in all-black suburban school systems did not obtain the enhanced opportunities for their children that normally come with suburbanization. Atlanta-area suburban black dropouts, many of them the children of parents who struggled to work their way out of the inner-city ghetto, probably would not be able to match, let alone surpass, their parents' economic status.

Some of the problems affecting dropouts were reflections of more general social crises, such as the high level of teen pregnancies. Georgia had

Table 5.7 Graduate Attrition Rates for Black, White, and Integrated Schools, 1986

Type of Schools	Graduation Attrition Rate (%)	Black Population (%)
Black city	41.5	94.7
Black suburban	45.7	98.3
Integrated suburban	34.5	45.9
METRO AVERAGE	35.1	36.6

a particularly worrisome teen pregnancy rate, which ranked fifth in the United States. Sixty to 80 percent of teen mothers left school (Georgia Department of Human Resources 1987).

THE COMING SURGE IN DROPOUTS: GRADE RETENTION AS A STRATEGY

One of the surprising results of this analysis of the Atlanta public schools was that some of the most damaging conservative reforms were not imposed on Atlanta by the federal or state government but were, initially, adopted by the Atlanta school system itself in response to demands for tougher standards and an end to the practice of graduating functional illiterates. Superintendents who talked tough and promised to take decisive action to raise standards were seen very positively and Atlanta was only one of many cities which turned in this direction. Almost no one disagreed with the proposition that substantive standards should be raised and that students should know more when they graduate from an urban high school.

One of Superintendent Crim's basic reforms was the Pupil Progression Policy implemented in 1980 for the first grade and extending through the succeeding elementary grades in the next seven years. It was a precursor of a statewide policy implemented in the Quality Basic Education Act and gave many of Atlanta's students another set of requirements. The first year's program brought the failure of 17.5 percent of all Atlanta first-graders, compared to less than 4 percent through each of the next five grades. It was a major change. By the fourth year, the failure rates were 20 percent in grade one, 10 percent in grade two, 9 percent in grade three and 7 percent in grade four. The failure rate for boys was even higher (Atlanta Public Schools 1980–81, 35; 1984–85, 21). Students were facing repeated failure in the elementary grades. A student could finish grade school at a much older age than the rest of his class and be clearly labeled as a failure.

The state government carried the policy further, setting up thresholds where students had to pass tests or be retained in grade. The state policy, for example, had a minimum third-grade test score. In high school there was a basic skills test that high school students had to pass if they were to graduate. Perhaps the most controversial test was the one kindergarten children had to pass before entering first grade. Implemented in 1988, the test prevented 7 percent of Atlanta's students from beginning first grade in September. Georgia was the first state in the United States to impose a written entrance test for first grade (*Atlanta Constitution*, 27 May 1988, 1A, 15A). Negative reaction led to a more flexible system of evaluation for the second year (*Education Week*, 15 March 1989).

Although most of the reforms were popular, the policymakers and educators simply ignored a large body of research showing that they would not produce academic gains and would increase dropout rates. In other words, this was a policy with no probable educational benefits and large costs. The benefits were political and the costs were borne by at-risk students. The damage was psychological as well as educational, increasing the likelihood that at-risk students would drop out before receiving their diplomas; school districts were also hurt by the diversion of resources to repetitive years of education for many students. A 1989 meta-analysis (a systematic statistical analysis combining findings from many independent studies) of the effect of flunking students concluded after reviewing sixty-three studies that "on average, retained children are worse off than their promoted counterparts on both personal adjustment and academic outcomes." This was true across subject areas. The conclusions echoed findings of earlier research, dating back to the early years of the century (Holmes 1989, 17, 20, 27). Another study summarized evidence showing a systematic relationship between retention and dropping out. The effects were large. For black males in an Austin study, for example, flunking one grade "increases the risk of not finishing high school by 27 percentage points" (Grissom and Shepard 1989, 60–61). Kindergarten retention on a large scale was one of the innovations of the 1980s. A summary of twenty-one studies concluded that there were no educational or significant psychological benefits from repeating the grade and that there was some actual harm (Shepard 1989, 75–76).

When the Georgia governor and legislature decided to improve academic achievement by raising the requirements for obtaining a degree, they took a calculated risk. By raising the requirements and creating absolute thresholds for success at particular levels of schooling, they risked increasing the rate of students flunking and dropping out of school. Their hope, of course, was that this would not happen, that students would simply be given a very strong incentive to learn more, and that achievement would rise with few costs.

The statewide data for the 1980s, however, showed what appeared to be very significant costs. Reversing a pattern of increasing proportions of students finishing high school, the statistics for the 1980s show a decline. The high school completion rate was 65 percent in 1982, one of the nation's lowest. Six years later, after the Quality Basic Education Act, the completion rate had dropped to 61 percent (*Chronicle of Higher Education,* 27 June 1990, A28). As the educational demands of the labor market rose and the level of state spending on education rose rapidly, the state's proportion achieving the minimum necessary credentials fell further.

The negative consequences of the reforms will not be fully apparent for some time. The first-graders of September 1980 are the potential high school graduates of June 1993. Unless Atlanta is fundamentally unlike the other school districts studied over generations, there will probably be a very substantial increase in dropout rates, particularly for the large number of students held two grades or more behind their age level. Not only will they be much more likely to drop out, but they will also reach the legal age where they are permitted to drop out at a lower grade level, some leaving without ever enrolling in high school at all.

Attendance

If students do not attend school they cannot benefit from it. Schools in the Atlanta area reported high attendance levels. In metropolitan Atlanta good attendance correlated quite strongly with high test scores (.66) and negatively with dropping out ($-.28$). The range of average daily attendance in metropolitan Atlanta was not particularly wide—from 90.1 percent in the city to 94.5 percent in Buford—but the city rate was consistently lower.

Just as black and low-income students tended to score more poorly on standardized tests and dropped out of school more often than white and higher-income students, they also had poorer attendance records. The correlation between low income and poor attendance was quite strong in 1985 (.66), and the correlation between the percentage of white students and attendance also was positive, though not as strong (.38), and much weaker than the relationship between race and test scores.

The schools with the best attendance rates tended to be much wealthier and to have more white students than the schools with the worst attendance, but in 1985 the ten schools with the best attendance records were, on the average, 50.4 percent black, and two of them were located in the city. In some schools with substantial black enrollments, the administrators and parents had solved the attendance problem. However, nine of the ten schools with the worst attendance were located in the city, and they averaged 87 percent black enrollment. Students who are habitually absent from class are at a disadvantage, and in metropolitan Atlanta those schools most affected are poor and black.

Is Money the Answer?

Many believe that the most important factor in determining the success of a school system is how much money that system has to spend. In spite of a generation of research showing that the most important influences on achievement are family background, the background of the other students in the school, and the quality of the teachers, urban school leaders often insist that the reason that the suburban schools do better is that they spend much more money. Yet, in reality, the system with the most funding per student may be the least successful. The Atlanta city schools spent far more per student ($4,195) in 1985 than most of the other districts, yet they performed much worse in every category considered. Even when one's comparisons are restricted to "instructional costs" per pupil, Atlanta ranked second, behind the city of Marietta. In fact the amount spent on instructional costs shows a very negative correlation to standardized test scores ($-.70$) and a positive correlation to high attrition rates (0.90), as can be seen in table 5.8.

Merely raising the per-pupil expenditure is, obviously, no panacea for solving the problems of inequality of opportunity in schools. Even if there are clear benefits associated with compensatory programs—and primary school achievement evidence from federal Head Start and Chapter 1 suggested that there are—the gaps may be so large that money is simply insufficient to reverse the effects of demography and history (Koretz 1986, 1987). Truly massive expenditures may be necessary to reduce class size strongly enough to make a difference. It is possible, of course, that compensatory funds spent in different ways could have larger effects.

Table 5.8 1985–86 Cost per Pupil in Average Daily Attendance

System	Instructional Cost	Total Cost
Atlanta	$2104.37	$4195.29
Buford	1502.14	2624.05
Clayton	1632.42	2699.87
Cobb	1486.52	2555.00
Decatur	2049.47	3697.52
DeKalb	2010.62	3573.22
Fulton	1952.24	3529.62
Gwinnett	1491.01	2521.83
Marietta	2371.89	4254.49

Surely, spending more money does not *cause* lower achievement. Rather, the increased revenue available to schools with high concentrations of low-income and low-achieving students is simply insufficient to overcome current disadvantages, even when it helps. Family factors continue to be the most important influences on student achievement. And money does not necessarily affect the educational level of the other students or the quality of the teachers—the two other factors having high impact on achievement. Supplies, equipment, computers, class size, and almost everything else rank far below these three basic resources in predicting school effectiveness.

Former Superintendent Alonzo Crim's response to these data put the issue in perspective, asserting that we should think about spending in large city school districts in a different way. "Systems with high percentages of economically deprived students would be expected to spend more just to provide the basic foundation which more affluent students bring with them to school and which more affluent parents provide in resources to the school" (Crim, letter to author, 25 June 1988). This is a very important issue. Chapter 1 federal dollars and funds for physically and mentally handicapped students, both of which are found in disproportionately large amounts in city systems, provide for extraordinary expenditures just to accomplish the teaching of basic skills. Dollars targeted in that way may help but still may leave students behind their more privileged counterparts. This would not show that spending was without benefit but only that it was not sufficient to overcome disadvantages and create an equal opportunity school system. Much more radical differences in funding or an attack on the underlying structures of inequality, such as race and class segregation, may be necessary to achieve additional progress.

What these data do clearly show, however, is that the problem of equal school dollars, so long a goal of local black politics, was substantially solved, at least during this period. Unfortunately, however, it was not the real base of the inequality.

Magnet Schools and Choices for Poor Black Students

The structure of education within metropolitan Atlanta locked large numbers of low-income black children into schools offering the least competitive academic challenges and low graduation rates. If no changes can be made in the basic structure, it is very important to consider options possible within the Atlanta Public Schools. On the national level, the most actively discussed policy in the late 1980s was the expansion of student and family choice. President Bush's 1989 education policy, for example, placed primary emphasis on choice and magnet schools and many states were considering choice programs. A widely noted 1990 book argued that choice was the basic answer (Chubb and Moe 1990).

Like many contemporary urban school districts, Atlanta had a substantial system of magnet programs within its high schools. Atlanta's was unusual in that it had no desegregation goals. The approach began in the mid-1970s with the creation of an arts program. In the early 1980s it was expanded to include programs specializing in science and math, communications, international studies, and a variety of other subjects. In Atlanta, unlike many other cities, there were no entire schools devoted to special programs—no programs had as many as 500 students when the system was studied in 1988; they served 212 students on average.

All but one of the programs had special admission requirements, such as minimum required grades or test scores. Since the magnet programs were combined with the normal programs in the reporting of schoolwide data, and some were very new, it was very difficult to discover much about the specific backgrounds and performance characteristics of the students. Forty-one percent of the magnet students were in the magnet that happened to be in their neighborhood high school and the newer programs had even fewer transfers, statistics that may reflect weak recruitment and transportation systems.

The school district's own survey of students in 1987, however, showed that the magnet students were extremely positive about their experience and that both the magnet and nonmagnet students were almost unanimous in believing that elementary school children needed more information about magnet choices before high school. Seventy-eight percent of magnet students and 67 percent of students outside the programs agreed that "having the magnet program at this school improves the school for all students." Two-thirds of magnet students thought that the program had increased their "career opportunities," 93 percent said they had enjoyed the program, 91 percent saw it as a "major advantage," and three-fourths (77 percent) said it had "increased my chances of going to college" (Atlanta Public Schools, Rept. no. 5, vol. 22, 1988).

The science and math magnet programs may have strongly influenced both the socioeconomic composition and the academic achievement level of Mays High School, which stood apart from other city high schools. Research elsewhere has shown that magnet programs often increase race and class distinctions within school districts, particularly when they are

connected to screening procedures and lack free transportation to encourage transfers by low-income students and good information (Moore
and Davenport 1989). In such circumstances they tend to increase the
choices of the groups with the most education and the highest incomes
in the school district.

Some of these effects can be curtailed through strong policies making
information more widely available, prohibiting rigid screening, and assuring participants of free transportation. At the same time, magnet programs can hold middle-class children in public schools who would otherwise leave the system and, perhaps, the city. They can offer islands of
competitive, grade-level, college-preparatory education unavailable in
most city schools.

These programs entail trade-offs, but they need to be discussed. Perhaps Atlanta and the integrated suburbs should consider entire school
magnet programs funded with the support of the state government to
serve the entire Atlanta metropolitan area, as is being done in Little
Rock. Certainly the evidence in this chapter on the lack of equal opportunity for students in black high schools and the data on declining college
opportunities in the next chapter justifies exploring every possibility for
increasing their access to competitive schooling. Magnet schools offer
only a limited solution and have distinct dangers, but all choices are difficult within a structure of severe and increasing racial and economic isolation.

The Suburban Frontier of Racial Policy:
A New Court Order in DeKalb

Almost a decade after the last act of the Atlanta desegregation case, a
federal court surprised the metropolitan area by ordering development
of a new desegregation plan in the region's largest school district, DeKalb
County. This county was receiving one of the largest black suburban mi-
grations in the nation and had one of the most rapidly changing large
school districts. Many of the hopes of the next generation of the metro
area's black middle class now rested on the DeKalb schools.

Data in this chapter show that there were very serious reasons to be
concerned about the achievement levels and dropout rates in the county's
black schools. These schools were doing much worse than integrated high
schools with similar concentrations of low-income students. There were

serious racial problems as well. An *Atlanta Constitution* study of school records conducted during the summer of 1988 reported that among junior and senior high students, "DeKalb's black students this year were 3.6 times as likely to be expelled, assigned to alternative school or suspended more than ten days" as their white counterparts (*Atlanta Constitution*, 9 July 1988: A1).

The federal court ordered the district to move beyond its ineffective voluntary desegregation plan. On 10 October 1989, the U.S. Court of Appeals ordered suburban DeKalb County to take further steps to desegregate the large school district that then had 57 percent black students. One member of the three-judge court, Judge Robert S. Vance of Alabama, was killed two months later by a mail bomb. Vance had also participated in other recent school desegregation decisions (*Atlanta Journal and Constitution*, 24 October 1989, A5; *New York Times*, 26 December 1989.)

Although the district was transporting 55,000 of its 73,000 students to school, it was busing them to largely segregated schools. Two-thirds of the schools were not within 20 percent of racial balance and there were twenty-five schools that were less than 5 percent white. The school district leaders announced their intentions to rely on voluntary procedures, probably including a substantial expansion of magnet schools, in responding to the court order (*Atlanta Journal and Constitution*, 24 October 1989: A5). An *Atlanta Journal and Constitution* poll in the fall of 1989 showed that 60 percent of white parents threatened to leave the school district if the courts ordered mandatory busing. The district immediately appealed the case to the Supreme Court to block the order but the Supreme Court refused to issue a stay in late 1989 (*Education Week*, 13 December 1989: 20).

Given the rapid increase and high proportion of black students, it may well be that the DeKalb order was too late and covered too small a share of the metro area to make much of a difference in the spread of segregation. Among all of the nation's largest school districts, DeKalb's increase in percentage of black students between 1967 and 1986 was the second highest, rising from 5 percent in 1967 to 32 percent in 1980 and 47 percent in 1986 (Orfield and Monfort 1988, 10). Ironically, it may well be that DeKalb and its black middle class would have been the largest short-term beneficiaries of a metropolitan-wide desegregation plan that the county and Atlanta's black leaders fought a few years earlier.

The Next Round in Atlanta: A Second Black Superintendent

After nearly fifteen years of leadership, Alonzo Crim retired in mid-1988 and was succeeded by J. Jerome Harris, who had been superintendent of a community school district in Brooklyn. A booklet describing the new superintendent, authored by a black school board member, Robert Waymer, noted that he was not impressed by the record of black leadership in big cities:

Though being in control of the political structure in many cities, Blacks have yet to significantly improve education in any of these cities, Harris is quick to point out. . . . "Blacks are presently serving as superintendents in over a hundred school systems in the United States. It is not so much that Blacks gained control of these systems, but rather that Whites have abandoned them," Harris said. (Waymer 1988, 19)

In his "Strategic Vision" for reforming the school district, Harris observed that "many people have simply written off city schools as little more than human storehouses designed to keep young people off the streets (Waymer 1988, 21). He called it "the result of a piecemeal approach to education which now requires a unified comprehensive response." The response has to include early education, magnet programs, "clearly defined goals, and improved monitoring" (ibid., 22, 24), he said, sounding very much like Crim in his appeal for a "Community of Believers."

One of the basic problems in Atlanta Public Schools, he said, was "low expectations," the very problem the district had been mobilizing against for fifteen years. A basic need was to change an "intangible mindset." He promised results on test scores. Though they were inadequate, they were the "only barometer that I have to measure." He noted, "If test scores don't go up . . . the first thing you ought to do is to get rid of the superintendent" (Harris 1988). Overall, the school system showed an average gain of 3 percent in the number of students performing at national norms during Harris's first year. The reported gains in the "central focus schools" he targeted for special attention were higher (*Atlanta Constitution*, 2 June 1989: A1, A8).

In a 1988 speech to Leadership Atlanta, Harris stunned the audience by asserting that "a large part of the population get absolutely nothing from education" and that there was "a clear conspiracy that is designed to keep urban kids dumb and ignorant."

One of the basic reasons for the problems, he said, was the loss of middle-class families. "Our public education system," he said, "is in the process of being abandoned . . . by the white population and middle-class blacks." When they left, he argued, the schools lost their support. "If we don't find some way in Atlanta to attract back the white population and the middle-class black population then the school system is gone" (Harris 1988). Crim had made a similar comment responding to data showing the extreme segregation of Atlanta's students near the end of his term of office. "What perhaps is far more damaging in this resegregation of our cities is the fact that it's almost all poor. We do not have the social stratification that we even had at the height of segregation" (*Atlanta Constitution*, 1 October 1987: 11A).

Superintendent Harris was engaged in virtually open warfare with his board by 1990 and publicly attacked the board for lack of support. He was under attack for large expenditures on consultants and on his new African-American Infusion Program (*Atlanta Journal and Constitution*, 25 January 1990, 15 March 1990). The city's education organizations were increasingly critical. For example, Atlanta Association of Educators President Hinton Martin called Harris "an embarrassment to the system" (ibid., 16 March 1990).

The Atlanta School Board fired Superintendent J. Jerome Harris in July 1990, less than two years after he took office. The board announced that it had "concluded a change in leadership must be made" because of the absence of "the sense of teamwork which is necessary to achieve and sustain progress. . . ." (*Atlanta Journal and Constitution*, 10 July 1990). The firing came despite the reports that Atlanta had solved the problem of academic achievement. The system claimed, once again, to be above national norms.

Conclusion

The underlying economic and racial stratification of the Atlanta region is reflected in its schools with disturbing clarity. There is no evidence that the schools have the capacity, as presently organized, to provide genuine equal opportunity for young people trying to prepare for work or for college. The next chapter will show, in fact, a strong pattern of declining access to college for black youths. It is probably wrong to expect that schools, by themselves, can remedy the deepening racial separation and inequality written into the housing and job markets of the region. It was certainly wrong to think that this could be done within educational systems accepting racial and economic separation as a starting point for program development.

In the early 1960s Atlanta enjoyed the delusion that segregated schools had achieved racial and economic parity. Our findings suggest that much more is needed if the old system of unequal education, stratified by race and income, is to be changed in any significant way. The thesis that black politicians, conservative businessmen, and Atlanta's isolated low-income children had the same common long-term interests was wrong.

6

Declining Black Access to College

A pattern of declining minority access to college—surprising after more than a decade of progress—emerged across the country in the 1980s. The American Council of Education and the Census Bureau documented the general trend. The Metropolitan Opportunity Project went further, comparing minority applicants and enrollees with the college-eligible pool from which they came, in order to determine if declining enrollments merely paralleled population trends, or if the causes lay elsewhere. This procedure made clear that the decline did not mirror population trends and was even more dramatic than had been understood. The studies then went on to examine closely the nature of the changes in the different kinds of college and universities to determine where the losses were most critical.

The analysis of trends in metropolitan Atlanta focused on carefully tracing and comparing college enrollments of black and white high school graduates. The enrollment rate of each group was compared with its own previous level of college access. The study shows changes in high school graduation and in public and private college attendance rates throughout metropolitan Atlanta. It also discusses some of the policy changes associated with changes in access and completion.

There was little comfort in the Metropolitan Opportunity Project's findings anywhere in the United States on minority enrollment and degree attainment. There were declines in minority access in Atlanta, Chicago, Houston, Los Angeles, and Philadelphia, the five metropolitan areas studied. There were sharply increased racial imbalances in the four-year public universities, which became more selective and less accessible to minorities, and declining enrollments at the traditional black colleges,

149

with serious implications for the institutions as well as for the students. In every case there were precipitous declines for black males. And in the cities with substantial Hispanic populations, there were very serious losses for Hispanic students.

However, nowhere was the contrast between black and white, male and female access more striking than in Atlanta, home of the sprawling Atlanta University Center of black colleges. It was famous across the United States, but increasingly vulnerable to the underlying social and economic stratification of the Atlanta region and to student aid and college-cost crises of the 1980s.

In the 1970s a bachelor's degree seemed within reach of every high school graduate in metro Atlanta, but by the 1980s there were sharply rising numbers of black high school graduates with no realistic hope of obtaining one. At the same time, white access to higher education increased. These trends may well reflect not only the underlying social and economic stratification of Atlanta and changes in higher education policy, but also the widening racial income gap discussed in chapter three.

One of the great accomplishments of the 1965–75 period was the opening up of the dream of college as a real possibility for black youths. The proportion of blacks in the college population tripled. Colleges that had been for whites only opened their doors. But the evidence from our study, from the American Council on Education's analysis of national data, and from the ongoing work of the Metropolitan Opportunity Project elsewhere show that the college gates were closing again just as the future for those without college educations was becoming more limited.

The findings from metro Atlanta show that black students were behind in college access in the late 1970s and fell further behind in the 1980s. The gap between the number of black high school graduates and the number going on to college widened at all levels of higher education between 1975 and 1986, as did the gap between black and white college enrollees. In a great metropolitan area where a large proportion of the labor market, political institutions, and families would be affected by the cutoff of opportunity for black students, this was a basic threat to the future.

Social and Economic Consequences of Declining Access

The changes described in the following pages pose deep threats to future economic and social conditions in the black community and in the metropolitan community as a whole. Even with college educations, black men were more likely to be unemployed than white men. And at the other end of the spectrum, for those who did not finish high school the situation deteriorated severely. Labor force participation for young black male dropouts declined sharply, from 93 percent in 1960 to 81 percent in 1980 (U.S. Commission on Civil Rights 1986, 79, 154).

Among adult black men in 1985 the median income for high school dropouts was $10,800; for high school graduates without college it was $14,700, for college graduates $23,400 (U.S. Bureau of the Census, *Money Income*, 1988, table 35). Although the median income of black male college graduates was less than four-fifths that of their white counterparts, they earned 60 percent more than black high school graduates and 134 percent more than black dropouts (ibid.).

Thus declining access to higher education for black men contributed to their high unemployment rates, their overrepresentation in dead-end, low paying jobs, and their lack of readiness to take on family responsibilities. In his research on inner-city blacks, William J. Wilson found a connection between the sagging economic status of black men and the declining marriage rates of black women. It is understandable that in the absence of jobs and economic stability many black men were unwilling to assume the responsibility of a wife and family. By the same token, because of low wages, instability, and unemployment among black men, an increasing number of black women chose to remain single (Wilson 1987). These circumstances also contributed to other disproportionately black social and family phenomena, ranging from marital instability, single-parent families and illegitimate births, to street crime, drug addiction and child abuse.

A shocking proportion of Georgia's black men ended up in prison, where the state invested heavily in jailing them rather than developing their human capital. A 1989 study by *The Atlanta Constitution* showed that one black man in six was imprisoned during that period and that black men were much more likely than white men and women to be sent to jail for the same offense in most metropolitan Atlanta judicial districts. The Georgia prisons were so dangerously crowded in the late 1980s because of harsher sentencing practices that the governor was forced to release thousands of prisoners before the completion of their terms (*Atlanta Constitution*, 23 April 1989).

Education reduced unemployment and crime and greatly enhanced one's ability to support a family, especially in the recent shift of the urban economy from production to service industries, which eliminated many low-skill jobs for men. The number of jobs requiring less than a high school degree plunged by 9,000 in the Atlanta labor market from 1970 to 1984, a period in which John Kasarda found that 37,000 new jobs requiring some higher education were created in the region (Kasarda 1987).

Because black males were overrepresented in "smokestack" industries, the employment decline in this area proved especially deleterious. Georgia did experience a 27 percent growth rate in new jobs between 1980 and 1985, with 79 percent of them in the Atlanta metropolitan area, but these jobs required a higher level of training and education. The decline in smokestack jobs and increased requirements for new jobs created very serious employment problems for black men in metropolitan Atlanta despite the economic boom, and as the next chapter will show, there was very little job training available for black men lacking basic skills.

In the 1970s and 1980s the large number of baby boomers and educated white women entering the job market, along with educated newcomers from other parts of the country, permitted employers to set higher educational requirements. The bachelor's degree rapidly replaced the high school diploma as the minimum prerequisite for a job paying a wage adequate to support a family. If the current trend of declining access to college continues for black students, the absence of college degrees will constitute yet another barrier to mobility for black men and another factor in the poverty of black families. It is difficult to imagine any way in which the number of stable two-parent families could increase substantially without an increase in the education of black men.

From the perspective of the economic future of the metropolitan Atlanta region, the declining black access to college was a grim indicator. Since studies of the economics of education began in earnest, it has become apparent that much of the gain in productivity in the American economy has been directly related to the increase in education. A significant decline in educational opportunity for more than one-third of the region's population was a direct threat to the future economic growth of the region and to its social stability.

Georgia Higher Education and Federal Civil Rights Law

This analysis of college access is important not only because of the obvious social and economic significance of declining access but also because it is a very important example of the failure of the federal government to enforce the 1964 Civil Rights Act's prohibition against discrimination in institutions receiving federal funds. Georgia was one of the states covered by a 1973 court decision, *Adams v. Richardson*, that found the federal government under President Nixon guilty of intentional failure to enforce civil rights laws in higher education and ordered the development of plans for desegregation of separate black and white public colleges. Georgia devised various plans under successive court orders and federal regulations. When the last court order elapsed in 1985, none of the basic goals for black access had been achieved. On a number of important issues covered by the plan the state had actually moved backward. One of the first major civil rights decisions of the Bush administration, however, was to approve the state's performance and drop federal supervision of the Georgia plan. *The Atlanta Constitution* commented in early 1989:

The system has failed utterly to reduce the disparity in college going rates between whites and blacks, the gap rose from 16.8 percent in 1978 to 19.9 percent in 1985, the last year for which data are available. The system failed even in its modest goal of increasing black enrollments to 12.77 percent of the total. By 1985, the figure was 9.6 percent. (Editorial, 22 March 1989)

Nevertheless, a three-judge panel of the U.S. Court of Appeals for the District of Columbia dismissed the case a year later, ruling that civil rights groups could not sue the federal government to take steps against states or colleges that may be breaking the law. This ruling, by a court that became much more conservative as a result of Reagan administration judicial appointments, was a severe setback for black students and public black colleges throughout the South.

The Financial Aid Crisis

The other very large change in policy during the 1980s that should be kept in mind in studying these trends was the decline in the ability of colleges to offer full financial aid to low-income students. Reagan administration changes in financial aid policy meant that the government was offering students loans rather than grants at a time when college tuitions were rising faster than the cost of living; with fewer grants available, many students and their families were forced to rely more heavily on loans. Research on the access of low-income students to college had long pointed out the critical importance of grant assistance in making college affordable. The nation's basic source of need-based scholarships for low-income students, the federal Pell grants, rose much more slowly than the cost of a college education in the 1980s.

The Georgia public higher education system followed the typical national pattern in responding to the shortage of appropriations by forcing students to pay a larger share of total educational costs. In Georgia the tuition rose rapidly, more than doubling from 1982 to 1989 and rising about 15 percent each year from 1983 to 1985 (*Atlanta Constitution*, 11 April 1989: 6B).

The Georgia financial aid program for assisting students in college was small compared to many states and very little of the funds were awarded on the basis of student financial need. The Governor's Commission on Postsecondary Education concluded in 1982 that "currently only 20 percent of State aid is awarded on the basis of need." Much of the state money amounted to subsidies to non-needy students attending more costly private colleges. Part-time students were not eligible for aid (Georgia Governor's Commission on Postsecondary Education 1982, 8–10). A Southern Regional Education Board report in 1986 showed that Georgia ranked thirteenth among fifteen states in the region in the share of its financial aid that was awarded on the basis of need. Seventy-four percent was not awarded on the basis of need. (*New York Times*, 4 December 1986). Tuition in public colleges in Georgia rose 186 percent from 1978 to 1988, significantly more than the average in the South (Southern Regional Education Board 1989, 2).

It is particularly important to keep the costs of education and the workability of financial aid plans in mind not only when evaluating the declines in the public universities but also with regard to the drastic reverses in the black private colleges that served low-income Atlanta students.

This chapter examines the pattern of declining access to colleges for blacks in the 1980s, with emphasis on the severe decline for black men. These findings are divided into two parts: the first assesses the nature and extent of the decline; the second attempts to identify the barriers to access, especially for black men. These analyses make use of massive sets of data submitted by the state government to federal authorities and obtained by this project under the Freedom of Information Act. A final section examines the failure of the federal government to enforce civil rights law in Georgia's public colleges.

Declining Black Access to College

This study considered not only how many students were enrolled in college from 1975 to 1986 but how those enrollments compared to the changing percentages of minority and white high school graduates. The racial composition of the high school graduate population changed so rapidly during this period that this was the only way to reliably gauge what was happening. Whether an increase of 200 white students in higher education enrollment was a proportional loss or gain of access for whites depended on changes in their representation among the pool of high school graduates. The same was true for blacks.

The data from schools, colleges, the U.S. Department of Education, and the Georgia Department of Education showed that black college enrollments declined at both the four-year and two-year colleges and in both the public and private colleges as a percentage of black high school graduates. Fewer black high school graduates were going to college in 1986 than in the late 1970s. Not only were black students not making progress in closing the gap between themselves and their white peers, they were falling farther behind their own college-attendance rates in the 1970s. Their white peers, on the other hand, increased their college-attendance rates between 1978 and 1986. Even more serious is the finding that black students in Atlanta had larger declines in access than black students in any of the other metro regions studied by the Metropolitan Opportunity Project.

If one looks at the number of black students going on to college without considering increases in the number of black students graduating from high school, it looks as if there was a steady increase in the number of black students going to the four-year public colleges. In 1975 there were 2,501 black students enrolled and in 1986 there were 4,110. But if one looks at the same data and compares the percentage of black high school graduates with the percentage of black college enrollees, a completely different picture emerges (see fig. 6.1).

In 1980 black students made up 30.5 percent of the high school graduates, but only 12.1 percent of the enrollees at the four-year public colleges, producing a gap of 18.4 percentage points. In 1986 they made up 35.0 percent of the high school graduates but only 11.9 percent of the college enrollees, which produced a gap of 23.1 points. The gap had widened by 4.7 points.

At the four-year private institutions, the number of black students enrolled rose between 1975 and 1980 from 6,093 to 7,226 students, but then it fell steadily to 5,165 students in 1986. This was surprising because of the strong drawing power of the historically black colleges such as Clark, Morris Brown, Morehouse, and Spelman, in which blacks had previously enrolled heavily. The strength of this drawing power is indicated by the

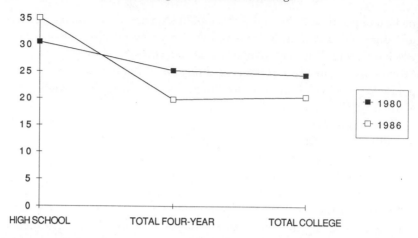

Figure 6.1. Percent of Black Higher Education Enrollment Compared to Percent of Black
High School Graduates

fact that in 1980 while black students made up 30.5 percent of the high
school graduates in metropolitan Atlanta, they constituted 51.8 percent
of the four-year private enrollment. It is true that two of the traditional
black colleges drew much of their enrollment from a national constitu-
ency, but declines also were obvious at those schools that drew largely
from the metro area. When the percentages of black high school graduates and of black college enrollees in the private colleges were compared
for 1980, college enrollment exceeded high school graduates by 21.3
points. In 1986 that figure had fallen to 7.3 points—a drop of 14.0 points
(see table 6.1).

The trend in total four-year enrollments showed that enrollment losses
at the private colleges outweighed gains in the public sector. The total
number of four-year enrollments rose from 8,594 in 1975 to 10,636 in
1980 but then fell steadily to 9,275 in 1986. This decline was even clearer
when the percentages of high school graduates and the percentages of
college enrollees were compared. In 1980 black students were 30.5 percent of the high school graduates and 25.2 percent of the four-year enrollees—resulting in a shortfall of 5.3 points. In 1986 they were 35.0 percent of the high school graduates but only 19.8% of the total four-year
enrollees, producing a shortfall of 15.2 points. The gap had widened by
9.9 points (see table 6.1).

At the two-year colleges there was a steady growth in the number of
black enrollees between 1975 and 1984 from 7,262 to 9,494, but then the

Table 6.1 Black Four-year College Enrollment Compared to Percentage of High School Graduates 1980–86

	1980			1984			1986		
	High School	College	Difference	High School	College	Difference	High School	College	Difference
Private	30.5	51.8	+21.3	35.0	50.4	−15.4	35.0	42.3	+7.3
Public	30.5	12.1	−18.4	35.0	11.5	−23.5	35.0	11.9	−23.1
TOTAL	30.5	25.2	−5.3	35.0	23.5	−11.5	35.0	19.8	−15.2

Table 6.2 Black Enrollment in Community Colleges in Metropolitan Atlanta, and Relationship to High School Population, 1980–86

	1980			1984			1986		
	High School	College	Difference	High School	College	Difference	High School	College	Difference
Black Percentage	30.5	21.9	−8.6	35.0	23.2	−11.8	35.0	22.0	−13.0
Total Enrollment		3,073			3,713			2,937	

number fell substantially to 7,449 students. When the available pool of black high school graduates was considered, however, one could see a steady drop in black enrollment from 1980 through 1986. In 1980 the shortfall was 8.6 points; in 1984, -11.8 points; and in 1986, -13.0 points— a total decline of 4.4 points (see table 6.2).

When two-year and four-year enrollments were combined to look at total black involvement in higher education, the number of students enrolled grew from 15,856 in 1975 to 19,925 in 1984, but then fell to 16,724 in 1986. As a percentage of black high school graduates, however, they steadily declined. In 1980, the gap was 6.1 points; in 1984 it was 11.5; and in 1986 it was 14.7.

These losses in black enrollment at all levels of the higher education system and in both the public and private sectors were very serious and were larger in Atlanta than in any of the other metro areas studied by the Metropolitan Opportunity Project (see fig. 6.2).

CHOICE OF COLLEGE

Another way of looking at access to higher education is to look at the colleges and universities most frequently attended by black and white students to see if there is a random distribution of students, or if there are differences by type of institution attended and admissions policies. Our research found important differences. A list of the eight colleges

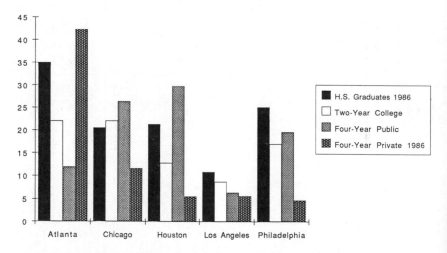

Figure 6.2. Percentages of Black Students in Each Institution Compared to High School Graduates, 1986

attended in the largest numbers by black students was made, along with a similar list for white students. When the lists were compared there were four schools in common and four that were completely different. Gender differences were not important. There was virtually no difference between the colleges attended by black men and women if Morehouse and Spelman, the region's elite black private colleges for men and women respectively, are viewed as closely related companion institutions. Nor were there any differences in the colleges attended by white men and women. But there were important racial differences.

Georgia State University and DeKalb Community College were the institutions black and white students shared most. Georgia State had the second largest number of both black and white students, while DeKalb had the fourth largest enrollment of both groups. The other two schools attended by both were Georgia Tech and Southern Tech. Beyond this, the colleges most frequently attended by blacks and whites were highly segregated both in 1975 and in 1986 despite the fact that the state of Georgia was under court order to desegregate its public higher education institutions (see table 6.3).

There was a small decrease in the amount of segregation between 1975 and 1986, but the fact remains that in 1986 five of the colleges attended in the largest numbers by white students were over 90 percent white and the other three had white enrollments between 80 and 89 percent. Three of the colleges attended in largest numbers by black students had black enrollments over 90 percent, a fourth was 88.1 percent black, and the remaining four were preponderantly white in enrollment with black students constituting between 6.7 percent and 19.2 percent. These data show a perpetuation of separateness which was unique among the five metro regions studied by the Metropolitan Opportunity Project and demonstrate that metro Atlanta continued to have an extremely segregated public higher education system.

BACHELOR DEGREE ATTAINMENT

Acquisition of a bachelor's degree is the goal of baccalaureate enrollment, but black enrollees were not as successful as white enrollees were in obtaining it. The number of bachelor's degrees awarded to white students rose steadily between 1975 and 1984, but dropped by 12 percent for black students after 1978. The twelve-percent decline for black students over six years was not the result of fewer bachelor degrees at the public colleges but at the private colleges. There was a modest increase in bachelor

Table 6.3 Colleges and Universities Attended in the Largest Numbers by Black and White Students in Metro Atlanta, 1975–86

Black	White
Morehouse/Spelman	Georgia Institute of Technology
Georgia State University	Georgia State University
Morris Brown College	Southern Tech
DeKalb Community College	DeKalb Community College
Atlanta Junior College	Emory University
Clark College	Clayton Community College
Georgia Institute of Technology	Kennesaw C.C./College
Southern Tech	Mercer University/Atlanta

Source: U.S. Department of Education HEGIS/IPEDS data tapes and Georgia State Department of Education.

degree attainment for black students at the public colleges, but it was overshadowed by a very large decline at the private institutions. This was a surprising finding because it reflected major declines in degree attainment at the traditionally black colleges.

During this period, blacks fell further behind at each stage in higher education. The disparity between high school graduates and college enrollees widened by 4.7 points at the public colleges, by 14 points at the private colleges, by 9.9 in total baccalaureate enrollment, by 4.4 points in two-year enrollment, and by 8.6 points in total higher education enrollment. Black students continued to attend heavily segregated colleges, and their bachelor degree attainment at the private colleges fell so heavily that it outweighed progress at the public colleges. How did this decline take place? How did black inequality grow? Our findings show that the single largest problem was that black men were not entering institutions of higher education in the numbers that they should have. The second part of this chapter looks at the problems of black men and college access in Georgia.

How Inequality Grew: The Situation of Black Men

The overall losses for black students were so substantial it was particularly important to determine whether the losses were shared equally by black men and women or were predominantly due to a drop in black male enrollment. The Metropolitan Opportunity Project was not able to obtain information on the percentages of black high school graduates that were male and female. The analysis therefore focused on changes in the number of college enrollees that were male and female without reference to the changing base of high school graduates. This put limits on the conclusions that could be drawn, but other evidence indicated that high school graduate data by gender would support rather than contradict the analysis by race alone and that the analysis of changes in numbers of blacks underestimated rather than overestimated gender differences.

Three findings were particularly important: (1) more black females than males were enrolled at nearly all levels in both public and private colleges in metro Atlanta; the sole exceptions were in two-year colleges in 1975 and in four-year private colleges in 1986; (2) female enrollment grew more at public institutions; and (3) the weakness and steady decline of black access in metro Atlanta was predominantly a black male problem (see figs. 6.3 and 6.4).

This study did not examine problems of black men in American society that have been studied elsewhere. Rather it examined the application, enrollment, and acceptance rates of black males in metro Atlanta and their progression and dropout rates while in college. It attempted to answer five questions: Did black men apply and were they accepted to college at the same rate as other groups? Did they spurn or were they rejected by bachelor degree granting institutions? Did two-year colleges meet their enrollment needs? What were the trends in attrition and graduation for black men?

This part of the research focused on twelve of the fifteen colleges in the Atlanta metropolitan area, excluding Agnes Scott and Spelman (the two female colleges that were included in the first part of the study) and DeKalb Community College (it did not enter the university system until 1986 and data was received too late for analysis). Ten of the twelve colleges were four-year institutions and two were junior colleges. Six were urban and six were suburban. Six were public and six were private. Three were traditionally black private colleges, namely, Clark (now part of Clark-Atlanta University), Morris Brown, and Morehouse.

The findings from this part of the research confirmed what had been suggested in the first part—that the institutions that had put college within reach of almost all students with a high school diploma a generation earlier were enrolling fewer black men. It can be hypothesized that these institutions were more receptive to an expanding pool of eligible black women, or that the more favorable labor market conditions for black women stimulated higher college attendance, or that there were national shifts in the attitudes of males and females toward college attendance that black men were responding to. There was in fact a national shift in which women were making up a rising share of college students among all racial groups. Yet none of these circumstances and hypotheses fully explain the research findings on what was happening to black men.

To comply with federal civil rights requirements, the state of Georgia was required to collect and report information about the various stages of access and retention of black men and women in the public higher edu-

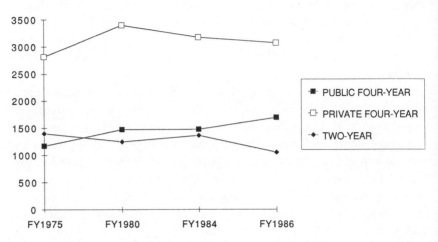

Figure 6.3. Male Black Enrollment in the Higher Education Institutions in Metropolitan Atlanta

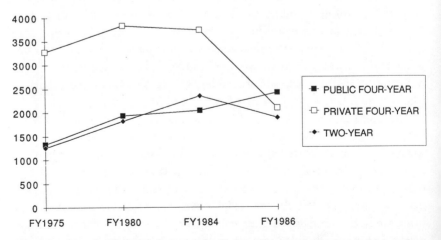

Figure 6.4. Female Black Enrollment in the Higher Education Institutions in Metropolitan Atlanta

cation institutions of the state. These data proved very valuable and are used extensively in this part of the research. The tables that follow show that black males were the least likely to apply, be accepted, or enroll in the public colleges in metro Atlanta. They also show that black males had increasing difficulty making academic progress from freshman year to graduation and that their dropout rates from college increased over the period of this study. All of this took place at the same time that Georgia's public higher education institutions were under federal civil rights pressure to increase their black enrollment.

APPLICATIONS AND ACCEPTANCES

It is important to begin with applications and acceptances: first at the two-year colleges, all of which were public; next at the public four-year institutions, and then at all public colleges, two-year and four-year. There was a large increase in the number and proportion of black male applications to the two-year colleges over the years of this study. In 1978 15.4 percent of all of the applications submitted to public higher education institutions by black men went to two-year institutions, but this had risen to 30.0 percent in 1986, an increase of 14.6 percentage points. By comparison, applications from black women increased by 9.8 percentage points, while those for white men and women increased 4.3 and 6.0 points respectively.

However, the acceptance rate of black men fell 39.8 percent between 1978 and 1985. In 1978, 88.8 percent of the black male applications were accepted; in 1984, 49.0 percent, and in 1986, 60.9 percent. In comparison with their peers, black males had a lower acceptance rate than any other group and the gap steadily widened through 1984. The imposition of academic standards for admission to the two-year colleges, including scores on the SAT exam, was the intervening variable after 1978 which affected all students, but also one that had a greater negative effect on the acceptance rate of black males than on any other group.

There were differences in the black male acceptance rate at urban and suburban two-year colleges. In the urban area, black men had 92.0 percent of their applications accepted in 1978, 43.9 percent in 1984, and 59.5% in 1986. The reverse was the case in the suburbs, where 53.3 percent were accepted in 1978 and 66.7 percent in 1986. The preponderant number of applications, however, was in the urban area, and therefore the declines affected a much larger number of black males.

At the four-year public institutions (Georgia State, Georgia Tech,

Southern Tech, and Kennesaw), the number of black male applications dropped substantially from 979 in 1978 to 696 in 1984 and then rose to 873 in 1986 for a net loss of 106 applications from a growing population. All of the loss came from declining enrollment at Georgia Tech, (− 350), which was offset partially (+ 244) by gains at Georgia State, Southern Tech, and Kennesaw.

Acceptance rates fluctuated. They fell from 45.9 to 37.7 percent between 1978 and 1980, then rose to 54.7 percent in 1984, and then declined to 53.8 percent in 1986. Although the basic trend was upward after 1980, at no point did they get much over fifty percent and the decline from 1984 to 1986 was significant though small (see table 6.4).

While black men had a higher application rate and a lower acceptance rate at the two-year colleges than any other group, at the four-year colleges they had a declining application rate after 1978 and a fluctuating acceptance rate which never rose much above fifty percent. Put together, fewer black men applied to the public two-year and four-year colleges than any other group. There was a small increase in their overall acceptance rate (3.1 percentage points), but it was out-of-state applicants whose acceptance rate increased rather than that of in-state black males, whose acceptance rate decreased.

ENROLLMENT RATES

Enrollment rates are not difficult to calculate, but they are difficult to interpret. Each institution reports the number of acceptances and the number of enrollments for a given academic year for each group of students. What is not known at the aggregate level is how many different institutions a student applied to and whether a refusal to enroll in a particular institution was a rejection of college or a choice to attend a different college. Individual-level data were not available to the Metropolitan

Table 6.4 Number of Applicants and Acceptance Rate for Black Males at the Public Four-Year Higher Education Institutions in Metro Atlanta

Year	No. of Applicants	No. Accepted	Acceptance Rate (%)
1978–79	979	449	45.9
1980–81	825	331	37.7
1982–83	702	327	46.6
1984–85	696	381	54.7
1986–87	873	470	53.8

Opportunity Project, therefore the data analyzed were aggregate data, and interpretations from them must recognize those limitations.

Black men who were accepted to the two-year and four-year public colleges in metro Atlanta had very low enrollment rates, in most cases the lowest of all their peers. At the four-year campuses, 48.8 percent of the black men accepted enrolled in 1978 and 49.4 percent in 1986. There was a brief gain between 1982 and 1984 when more than 60 percent of the accepted men enrolled, but that gain was short-lived (see table 6.5). In comparison with their peers, black men at these baccalaureate colleges had lower enrollment rates than any other groups in 1978 and from 1983 to 1986. Only in 1980 and 1982 were white male rates of enrollment lower.

At the two-year campuses, 72.2 percent of the black men accepted enrolled in 1978, 47.5 percent of those accepted enrolled in 1984, and a slightly better 53.7 percent of those accepted enrolled in 1986. Black men had a lower enrollment rate than any other group of students in 1978 and 1980. Beginning in 1984, however, black women had a lower enrollment rate and black men the second lowest, reflecting perhaps a heavier black female enrollment rate at the four-year campuses.

Black males, then, had the lowest total higher education enrollment rate in the public colleges of any group of students. There was only a 0.5 percent gain in their enrollment rate at the four-year campuses between 1978 and 1986, and there was a large net loss in enrollment at the two-year campuses. Overall, black men were the least likely to apply, to be accepted, or to enroll in the public colleges in metro Atlanta.

BLACK MEN AND THE PRIVATE COLLEGES

Similar application, acceptance, and enrollment data were not available for the private colleges because the Office for Civil Rights did not mandate it and the state of Georgia did not collect it. From the first part of

Table 6.5 Enrollment Rate for Black Male Recent High School Graduates Accepted to the Public Two-year and Four-year Higher Education Institutions in Metro Atlanta, 1978–86

Year	Two-Year (%)	Four-Year (%)
1978–79	72.2	48.8
1980–81	46.5	58.5
1984–85	47.5	62.7
1986–87	53.7	49.4

this chapter, however, it is clear that total black enrollment in the private four-year institutions fell as a percentage of high school graduates from 21.3 percent in 1980 to 7.3 percent in 1986. When those enrollment data were examined by gender, black male enrollment rose in the private colleges through 1980 from 2,818 to 3,396 students and then fell gradually to 3,071 in 1986. Black female enrollment also rose through 1980 from 3,275 to 3,830 students and then fell to 2,094 in 1986, a much steeper fall than for black men.

BLACK MALE ENROLLMENT AT THE
TRADITIONAL BLACK COLLEGES

Three of the private undergraduate colleges were black colleges (Clark, Morehouse, and Morris Brown) that played very important roles in opening the doors to college access and attainment of bachelor degrees for black men. It was particularly important to see whether and to what extent the drop in private enrollment was limited to the traditional white institutions or if it was also taking place at the traditional black colleges.

There was no loss of enrollment at Morehouse, which showed modest but steadily increasing enrollments for black men. The others did have enrollment losses: Morris Brown in 1978, 1980, and 1984, and Clark in 1984 and 1986. At Clark, black male enrollment fell by 35 percent from 612 in 1975 to 394 in 1986. At Morris Brown, there was a 45 percent loss from 731 in 1975 to 396 in 1984. In 1986, black male enrollment increased to 520, but this was still 211 students short of the male enrollment in 1975 (see table 6.6).

Another way of looking at black male enrollment at the traditionally black colleges was to ask what percentage of the total enrollment at these colleges were black males. This number decreased steadily from 1978 through 1986, from 68.2 percent in 1978 to 66.6 percent in 1980, to 63.4 percent in 1984, and to 62.4 percent in 1986 for a net loss of 5.8 percent-

Table 6.6 Black Male Enrollment at Traditionally Black Colleges in Metro Atlanta, 1975–86

Year	Clark		Morehouse		Morris Brown	
	No.	(%)	No.	(%)	No.	(%)
1975–76	612	35.5	1,378	98.3	731	48.1
1978–79	611	33.8	1,640	100.0	711	43.2
1980–81	709	33.7	1,907	97.7	626	39.0
1984–85	578	32.3	1,975	96.1	396	37.2
1986–87	394	32.0	2,058	97.0	520	32.0

age points. The same question was then asked about black male enrollments at Atlanta Junior College, which was overwhelmingly black.
There, enrollments dropped from a high of 686 black men in 1978 to 435
in 1984, rising by only fourteen students in 1986, while the percentage
of all enrollment that was black male fell from 46.7 percent in 1975 to
32.9 percent in 1984, rising slightly to 42.7 percent in 1986 for a net loss
of 4.0 percentage points.

Not only were black men the least likely to apply for college admission
and to be accepted in metro Atlanta, they were also the least likely to
enroll after being accepted in any college, public or private, traditionally
black or traditionally white, four-year or two-year.

ACADEMIC PROGRESS OF BLACK MALES WHO DID ENROLL

The ability to move forward from freshman through senior year in college
within a reasonable time frame is an important component of academic
success. While the time frame for many students has changed from four
years to five years or more, the time frame for minority students has often
been longer. This has had serious consequences for the ability to sustain
the costs of college, for morale, and for the ability to persist to completion.

The ability of black men in metro Atlanta to move forward academically decreased over the years of this study. As a net change from 1978 to
1986, the proportion of black men moving from freshman to sophomore
year within one academic year fell from 48.2 percent to 23.8 percent, a
drop of 24.4 percentage points. Their ability to move from sophomore
year to junior year fell almost as much—21.9 percentage points—from
60.5 percent to 38.6 percent. Between the junior year and the senior year
the decline was less, a drop of 13.2 points from 55.8 percent of the juniors
progressing to seniors in one academic year to 42.6 percent. Those who
did make it into the senior year in 1986 were, however, more likely to
graduate within one year than previously; the graduation rate within a
year of becoming a senior rose from 39.8 percent in 1978 to 51.7 percent
in 1986 (see table 6.7).

Difficulties in progressing in a timely fashion are directly related to
drop-out rates from college, and the drop-out rate for black men at the
public colleges increased at all levels except the senior year. In 1978, 27.3
percent of the black men who were freshmen dropped out, but this rose
to 41.2 percent by 1986. Their sophomore drop-out rate rose from 23.2
to 39.5 percent; their junior rate from 25.7 to 33.2 percent. The only
decrease in their drop-out rate was in the senior year when the rate fell

Table 6.7 Percentages of Black Males Enrolled in Public Four-year Higher Education
Institutions in Metro Atlanta Who Advanced to the Next Academic Level, 1978–86

Year	Fr./Soph.	Soph./Jr.	Jr./Sr.	Sr./Grad.	Total
1978–79	48.2	60.5	55.8	39.8	51.2
1980–81	38.5	42.3	49.1	23.9	39.0
1982–83	41.1	51.6	62.7	45.2	49.5
1985–86	26.3	38.6	46.5	33.7	34.0
1986–87	23.8	38.6	42.6	51.7	34.5

by half of one percentage point from 15.2 to 14.7 percent (see table 6.8). Among their peers, only black females had higher nonprogression and drop-out rates and that was only between the sophomore and junior years and the junior and senior years.

Black men had the hardest time progressing and graduating at Georgia State University, a level-one doctoral-granting university. They did a little better at Southern Tech and Kennesaw, which were level-two comprehensive colleges and universities, and a little better than that at Georgia Tech, a level-two research university. Their ability to progress better at level-two institutions was matched by their enrollment, for most of them were enrolled at level-two institutions, primarily in level-two comprehensive and liberal arts colleges.

INABILITY TO SUCCEED IN HIGHER EDUCATION

The failures of growing numbers of black men in metro Atlanta to reap the rewards of higher education perplexed researchers: Were black men spurning or being spurned by higher education? The fact that they submitted fewer applications overall indicates that higher education was not a high priority for them. The fact that fewer of their applications were accepted suggests that their preparation had been insufficient. Did the two-year colleges and the traditional black colleges meet their needs? Not really. Though more black men submitted applications to the two-year colleges, their applications were rejected in droves after academic standards were put in place for acceptance. Their enrollments fell at all of the traditional black colleges except Morehouse. The problems of black men were reflected in their declining application, acceptance, and enrollment rates, and in their difficulties in progressing to graduation.

Failure to Enforce Civil Rights in Georgia

The public colleges in Georgia were under federal court orders beginning in 1973 to make up for their deliberate past segregation by providing

Table 6.8 Black Male Drop-out Rates from the Four-year Public Higher Education
Institutions in Metro Atlanta, 1978–86

Year	Freshmen		Sophomores		Juniors		Seniors	
	No.	(%)	No.	(%)	No.	(%)	No.	(%)
1978–79	89	27.3	53	23.2	53	25.7	29	15.2
1978–79	76	29.6	53	30.3	42	25.5	65	47.0
1980–81	69	33.0	41	26.0	25	16.7	23	18.5
1985–86	219	40.0	123	40.2	104	30.2	95	28.0
1986–87	249	41.2	130	39.5	108	33.2	21	14.7

equal access for black students and by effectively desegregating their student bodies and faculties. The time frame for implementation of their desegregation plans fell within the period studied. One of their goals was to achieve a fair representation of the state's high school graduates, by race, in the colleges; in this, the state failed.

One of the basic civil rights problems in Georgia higher education was the state's tendency, as in the public schools, toward excessive reliance on tests. Unlike many states, Georgia required the SAT even for admission into two-year colleges. In the 1980s, it implemented a new and rigid test requirement to get into the junior year of college, triggering a battle.

The federal Office for Civil Rights received a complaint about the racial impact of the Regents test and spent a great deal of time investigating it. Governor Joe Frank Harris strongly defended the policy, saying it was "not negotiable" and was "grounds for us to go to court" (New York Times, 8 July 1983). Although it was clear that it would have a disproportionate effect on black students, the state university system decided to permit the test and to try to win assurances that special preparation would be made available at the black colleges. Since the test would affect black students in all public institutions and there were no public black colleges in metropolitan Atlanta, this did nothing to alleviate the negative effects on access to colleges in the region. It was, in effect, a decision to permit the state to enact a test policy that was bound to negatively impact the effectiveness of its own civil rights plan.

The conservative policy of Reagan and Bush administration civil rights officials toward higher education simply denied that the colleges had any responsibility to achieve results showing genuinely equal access, even in states with a history of more than a century of mandatory segregation and blatant inequalities in colleges. The assumption in earlier periods of civil rights enforcement was that governments openly discriminating for generations in their public institutions had the constitutional obligation to repair the damage caused by that discrimination. The Reagan administration, however, approved policies that had the clearly foreseeable effect of excluding black students. The federal officials said that the problem was really in the elementary and secondary schools, but they required no changes in the public school programs that prepared most blacks for college. In contrast to the civil rights groups, which believed that the law required a showing of actual progress toward equality, the Reagan and Bush administrations believed that the law could be satisfied if college authorities implemented a plan, even if it resulted in fewer blacks going on to college.

This federal policy orientation allowed key public institutions to be less supportive of black students. Universities came under cross pressures from the federal government for equity and from conservative politicians for tougher standards. As it turned out, the civil rights provisions in the plan were not enforced and the conservative policies tended to reduce minority access.

In Atlanta, as in each of the other big cities studied by the Metropolitan Opportunity Project, the basic impulse of the major urban public university in the 1980s was to bolster its public image by admitting a more selective student body and by turning increasingly toward research rather than teaching functions.

Georgia State University is a crucial institution for minority access to public higher education in metropolitan Atlanta. It is the only public, general-purpose university in Atlanta and is located in the heart of the city, only blocks from "Sweet Auburn," the traditional main street of black Atlanta where Martin Luther King's church and birthplace stand. (Georgia Tech [The Georgia Institute of Technology] is in the city but is more specialized.)

Joan Elifson, Georgia State University's assistant vice president for academic affairs, saw a difficult situation of declining access for inner-city students, one created to a substantial degree by state policies. An increasingly rigid set of tests and deadlines limited access to college, limited what the college could do to help poorly prepared students, and made test scores more important than the judgment of the professors.

The Regents Test controlling progression to the junior year in the state's colleges, according to Elifson, had a "deadly impact" on students from weak inner-city high schools enrolled in weak junior colleges. The Atlanta Junior College, which was the only readily accessible campus for many local students, taught mostly students below grade level.

Most of the black students who got into Georgia State University came in through a compensatory program called "developmental studies," created as part of the state university system's desegregation plan. About two-fifths of GSU freshmen were in developmental studies, which meant that they had to take special remedial courses in math, reading, and/or composition. Most had to take courses in two or three of the fields. GSU decided to set its minimum requirements for admission and for getting out of developmental studies considerably higher than the statewide standards. GSU also raised its minimum admissions scores on the SAT by fifty points in 1986, excluding about one-fifth of the black applicants on the grounds that they would probably not graduate anyway.

The state university system also had decided by 1987 to require another year of high school algebra for admission to the university. This was another standard that doubtless had the greatest deterrent effect on black students wanting to attend GSU or another state campus.

Those working on the program, said Elifson, felt "overregulated at that point and the faculty [were] very frustrated." They felt that "their judgment [was] not counted for much." There were "entrance tests, exit tests, and limits on the time a student [could] stay in the program." Federal civil rights officials, however, raised no objections.

Indeed, even as Georgia institutions moved backward, federal officials congratulated them for their success. In its final review, in 1988, the U.S. Office for Civil Rights simply left out all evidence of failure. The OCR, in its letter to Governor Joe Frank Harris, said that all that remained to be done was the completion of a few specific commitments aimed primarily at strengthening three historically black campuses. There was no indication that the state had fallen short and a specific statement that the state's success should not be judged by whether or not its plans had succeeded (Daniels to Joe Frank Harris, 9 February 1988). The OCR acted in the final months of the Reagan administration to accept the assurances of the Georgia governor that those remaining steps would be taken, praising the state for its "cooperation" (Daniels to Harris, 30 August 1988).

Summary and Conclusions

The colleges of metropolitan Atlanta reflected and perpetuated the region's deeply rooted inequalities of race, income, and education. As higher education became more crucial to individual success, colleges became less accessible to blacks, and external pressure for civil rights compliance disappeared. And as blacks moved backward, white access increased.

Enrollment and graduation declines, especially at public four-year colleges and traditionally black institutions, closely paralleled and may have been attributable to erosions in financial aid, minority recruitment, and remedial programs in the 1980s. Declining enrollments at financially troubled, traditionally black institutions could cause lasting problems, if they resulted in fewer college berths for black high school graduates in the future. The colleges serving local, at-risk populations were themselves most vulnerable to financial aid and government policy changes.

Private black colleges, like their white counterparts, were badly caught up in the cost cycle of the 1980s, which led to very rapid tuition increases. With soaring costs, frozen federal scholarship levels, overwhelmingly low-income student populations, and strong resistance to huge loan indebtedness from families with tiny cash incomes, the schools which were most accessible to low-income blacks faced an impossible bind. A final straw was the threat to their eligibility for future student loans.

Thus, the situation of black men in the colleges and universities of metropolitan Atlanta, never very good, became worse. Yet in an economy well into the postindustrial transition, in which new urban jobs were overwhelmingly low-paying service or high-skilled white-collar jobs, college training was critical to the success of these men and to the families that would not be formed or sustained if they failed to secure decent jobs. Their prospects for doing so withered.

Blacks were a growing share of the high school graduates in metro Atlanta between 1975 and 1986, but a decreasing proportion of the college enrollees. Black students were not just falling behind white students but also falling behind previous levels of black college attendance in the region.

In comparison with other metropolitan regions, the negative racial gap in college enrollments as a percentage of high school graduates grew wider in metro Atlanta. The differences were substantial.

Broad national forces were obviously at work in the colleges of the metropolitan Atlanta area, but there were also special local conditions that widened the racial gap here more rapidly, producing increased access to college for whites as black access declined. The national forces included a policy of nonenforcement of civil rights in the 1980s and a major deterioration in the capacity of the financial aid system to support low-income students through college.

The increase of white access to college was doubtless related to the extraordinary economic growth and income increases in the white sections of the metropolitan area. Whites were overwhelmingly located in suburban school districts with high schools that could prepare their students for college. The state developed two major new campuses, Southern Tech and Kennesaw—both of which were situated in outlying, overwhelmingly white parts of suburbia—easily accessible to white students. The substantial widening of the income gap between whites and blacks from the late 1970s into the 1980s, discussed in chapter three, doubtless affected the college-going disparity.

On the higher education front, some state and institutional policies in the public institutions probably contributed to these patterns. Georgia State University, located immediately adjacent to the black community, tightened its admissions standards and limited its remedial programs, thereby reducing its accessibility to black students and their chances for success on campus. The state of Georgia, unlike others under study, required an admission test, not just a high school diploma, to get into a community college. Unlike the other states studied in the Metropolitan Opportunity Project, Georgia also adopted a Regents Test as a requirement for admission to the upper division of its university system. This test had a disproportionately negative impact on blacks and limited the number who would be permitted to pursue bachelor's degrees. Each of these tests doubtless excluded some students who would have received degrees. Georgia compounded the effects of growing income differences and inadequate scholarship aid when it raised tuition much faster than the cost of living in the 1980s.

Nothing was more central to the dream of contemporary American families than that their children would be able to go to college and obtain the degree that opens the way to most of the interesting and well-paying jobs in the American economy. Metropolitan Atlanta had claimed a leadership role in the economic and social development of a new South freed from the divisions and the human waste of segregation, with justifiable pride in the gains of Atlanta-area blacks from the mid-1960s to the late 1970s. These gains gave substance to the most pivotal of these aspirations by funneling more blacks into the regional pool of college-trained youths from which the next generation of skilled workers and political leaders would be drawn. But the college-going trends of the 1980s are cause for alarm, posing a clear and present danger to the economic, social, and political future of the region.

7

Job Training

When many people are out of work, the issues of jobs and training can dominate politics. A job with a decent income is the key to many forms of opportunity in the society for both the worker and his family. In a society where a job is the basic source of status and the only way to support a family at a decent standard of living, joblessness is an ultimate fear. And this fear was fanned, in the early 1980s, by high unemployment in much of the country, especially among blacks, for whom the unemployment rate has long been at least twice the rate for whites.

The basic political responses have been to promise either to expand the economy, thus increasing the demand for workers, or to establish new training programs to increase the "human capital" jobless people have to offer in the labor market. Conservatives, who tend to see few structural barriers in the labor markets, rely primarily on economic growth. This was very clear in Reagan's "supply-side economics," which provided the rationale for economic policies based on steep reductions in services such as job training and subsidized housing accompanied by large tax cuts for high-income households. Liberals, on the other hand, recognize the need for growth but tend to see serious inequalities and imperfections in the labor markets and to invest more heavily in enhancing human capital through education and training. They favor direct regulation of problems such as job discrimination.

Atlanta provides a good test of the value of the supply-side approach and the effect of general economic growth for young black workers in the 1980s. In Atlanta, the economy was rapidly expanding in the 1980s and it seemed reasonable to hope that the growth would provide better opportunities and more equity for black workers.

The best way to lower overall joblessness, of course, is to increase the number of jobs. Some argue that with a large enough economic expansion, racial disparities would diminish. In *The Truly Disadvantaged*, William J. Wilson concluded that the basic solution to the problem of inner-city black disadvantage was a "tight labor market." This analysis from a socialist perspective ironically parallels the conservative position with its emphases on the primacy of economic factors and on downplaying the need for racially specific strategies.

Atlanta provides an excellent test of such theories. It has had the kind of economic expansion in the 1980s that most metropolitan areas could only dream about. The region was viewed with the greatest favor by firms considering expansion. The city's black leadership was strongly oriented toward business expansion and implicitly accepted the Wilson argument. If the problem of black joblessness could be solved by dramatic growth and a positive economic climate, if there were educational and training gaps that could be closed by a forceful black mayor and an influential black business establishment, it should have happened in Atlanta.

Educational preparation for the labor market was, of course, highly unequal as described in the chapters on high schools and colleges. Almost two in five city students became dropouts in the mid-1980s, and there were vast numbers of older dropouts in the city's labor force. This chapter asks how well the only substantial Reagan-era job training program, the Job Training Partnership Act, worked in metropolitan Atlanta. The city administration, which ran the local program in cooperation with business leadership, was led by black politicians sympathetic to the goals of job training and affirmative action. If JTPA did not work in contemporary Atlanta under nearly ideal overall labor market conditions, it is essential to ask why.

The Job Training Partnership Act of 1982 was the first major legislative triumph of the Reagan New Federalism policy, which set about reducing federal authority in domestic programs, cutting funds, and increasing the power of state governments and private business. The JTPA law was cosponsored by future Vice President Dan Quayle and was very strongly praised by President Bush in his 1988 campaign as an outstanding success.

During the late 1960s, when overall unemployment was very low, there had been intense federal focus on reducing poverty and reaching the hard-core unemployed that emphasized dealing with the special problems of disadvantaged workers. During the 1970s, as the country experienced successive recessions and high levels of overall joblessness, job training expanded and a large public service employment program was implemented. This program focused heavily on highly disadvantaged workers after the 1978 Carter administration amendments. In the 1980s, however, the idea of government as employer of last resort was abandoned and the basic emphasis was shifted to a much smaller business-oriented program driven by the two goals of low costs and high placement rates. This focus rapidly changed the nature of job training.

The program implemented conservative beliefs in the market and in small government. It said that businessmen should control training policy and that policy should aim to satisfy businesses. Anything that produced a cheap placement was considered efficient and a success. In its enthusiastic pursuit of acceptance by business, however, it risked a new kind of abuse: subsidizing business without accomplishing any clear public purpose. The JTPA law built in massive protections against abuse of federal funds by people being trained, but virtually none against abuses by businesses.

There were a number of perfectly legal ways in which businesses could have recruitment and training costs and even part of wages subsidized for taking workers screened by JTPA, even if they were the same kind of workers those businesses had always hired. At the same time, training agencies could be paid large fees for placing workers in entry-level jobs that required very little training and seldom provided lasting work.

A basic reason for the selection of metropolitan Atlanta for this study was that it was one of the fastest growing job markets in the country and an ideal setting for a business-oriented job training program. Diverse industries created a broad spectrum of jobs and job requirements. Black political leadership in the government and in many other city institutions created a disincentive for discrimination, at least in the city. The city's contracting policies encouraged black businesses.

Atlanta's history of weak and discriminatory education meant that there was a vast pool of people without basic skills in urgent need of training. The jobs and the need were there, but federal and state policies restricted the program. The emphasis on control by businessmen and on job-related rather than basic-skills training meant that the program often functioned as a subsidized source of workers prepared for a simple low-paying job. The standards created a disincentive for providing long-term training to the hard-core unemployed, and the lack of living-expense stipends meant that the very poor could not afford to be trained unless they were women on Aid to Families with Dependent Children. It was much easier to meet the program goals by training mostly women and placing city participants in traditionally black occupations than by trying to change that pattern by teaching them new skills or trying to find better jobs in the mushrooming labor markets of the white suburbs.

Minority male dropouts, though their futures were likely to be dismal if they did not obtain educations, were a threat under JTPA rules because they were expensive to train and less likely to find jobs when trained because of discrimination. They had no money to live on while receiving long-term training. The barriers to obtaining the basic-skills or high-school-equivalency training were overpowering.

JTPA had no public employment program to provide jobs to those who could not be placed after training. A few months after President Ronald Reagan was elected, the Public Service Employment program that had given jobs to 800 low income Atlantans was shut down and many of those displaced were unable to find work (*Atlanta Constitution* reprint, "Black and Poor in Atlanta," October 1981: 8).

The metropolitan area clearly needed job training. A major study of metropolitan Atlanta, conducted by the National Alliance of Business with assistance from the U.S. Labor Department, showed very serious problems for both employees and the economic future of the region if job skills were not upgraded. The report, *Atlanta 2000*, concluded that 39 percent of the region's "total adult population lack the skills to get a job or to perform one adequately." The report predicted 463,000 additional jobs and 282,000 replacement jobs in the metro region by the turn of the century, an increase much in excess of expected population growth. The new jobs, however, were going to have high educational requirements. "The average new job will require fourteen years of formal education, with many requiring sixteen or more" (National Alliance of Business 1988, 3). The future promised a good market for workers with skills but growing isolation for those who could not obtain them. It was clear that private business was not going to solve these problems. The National Alliance of Business survey of the area's largest employers showed that nine-tenths offered no basic remedial education and training for their employees and that private employers were training "less than 1 percent of those in need" (ibid.).

The survey found many firms having problems and spending large amounts of money hiring workers but operating without effective personnel plans. For example, some posted jobs on bulletin boards and did not advertise in city newspapers. The most common kind of recruitment of new workers was from acceptance of walk-in applications, followed by college visits, and then ads in newspapers. On average, the total cost of recruiting and hiring one new worker was estimated to be $3,575 (Dealy 1987, 70–79). Obviously, the outreach, screening, and training functions of JTPA could be of great value.

More than three-fourths of the large employers hired no one without a high school diploma. More than 15 percent of the firms said that they were "generally not satisfied with the quality and educational develop-ment of their new hires." Most of the problems were encountered in the field of sales and customer-relations staff. The most common field for the most employees needed was clerical, followed by professional. They es-timated that 88 percent of their jobs required at least high school and 52 percent at least some college.

The Job Training Partnership Act gave states a high degree of flexibil-ity to tailor job training programs to state needs. Georgia, like many other states, made little use of this flexibility. Georgia accepted the Rea-gan administration goal—of high placements at the least cost—as its own. Atlanta officials concurred.

Thus, Atlanta's job training program placed its participants largely in semiskilled and unskilled entry-level jobs in the low-wage service sector. It trained people who were unable to enroll in other types of training in community colleges or private technical schools. But it had little to offer dropouts, the group most in need of a second chance and the most ex-pensive to train.

The city of Atlanta's JTPA program offered virtually no remedial train-ing, which turned it into what was basically an employment referral and training agency for private businesses seeking low-wage, entry-level la-bor, often in traditionally black jobs. The heavy emphasis in the JTPA legislation on job placement with private business helps to explain why JTPA conformed to existing racial job patterns. An earlier study of job training programs in the 1960s found similar patterns in the South (Kahn 1966).

The federal job training program was set up to operate through four local Service Delivery Areas (SDAs) in the Atlanta labor market. The city of Atlanta operated the largest program during the 1985–86 program year, with 2,702 participants or 57 percent of the metropolitan total. The North Suburban SDA (officially called the Metro Atlanta SDA) was the second largest, followed by DeKalb and then Clayton, one of the smallest SDAs in the entire country. The basic problem with this structure was that it separated the concentrations of poor people from the concentrations of job growth.

Major State Policy Decisions

Early state policy decisions and local circumstances shaped the character of job training in these four Service Delivery Areas. Eligibility for the largest training component of the Act, Title IIA, was limited to those living below the poverty level or to those receiving public aid. The federal government established a set of seven performance standards to maximize the number of job placements at a minimal cost. The critical measures were the percentage of those finishing the training placed in jobs, the cost per placement, and the wage at placement. The others were the entered-employment rate for welfare recipients, the percentage of youths who successfully completed training, the number of youths who received employment, and the cost for each youth who successfully completed training.

The states could have required additional performance standards or provided exceptions to the federal rules, but most did not. States were handicapped by fiscal cutbacks by Congress. In its first year, the JTPA budget allocation was 69 percent less than the training and employment budget had been at the height of the Comprehensive Employment and Training Act (CETA) program in 1978 (Orfield and Slessarev 1986).

Georgia took a generally passive role in administering JTPA. Governor Joe Frank Harris's administration saw job training as part of economic development and saw the role of the state as one of "monitoring the pass-through of federal funds to localities," not one of setting training standards (Maclachlan 1987, 6) The economic development emphasis was not one of developing systemic local economic plans but one of helping "individual employer activities," assuming that whatever the business did, the result was beneficial. "Service to employers is what the Georgia Department of Labor now sees as its mission" (ibid., 8). It was almost a perfect state counterpart of the view of the proper relationship between government and business that was central to the Reagan administration policy.

Thus, there was tremendous pressure on local program administrators to set up training programs that maximized the number of job placements at the lowest cost possible. Agencies could not spend more than 15 percent of local allocations on support services, such as the cost of transportation, meals, and day care.

Georgia officials heavily emphasized the goals of high placement at low cost. Administrators restricted training to no more than six months and avoided training that was not directly related to a specific job. This obviously discouraged high school completion programs. Preference was given to customized training classes where participants were taught job skills that matched the exact needs of companies that had agreed in advance to hire a certain number of JTPA trainees. Several of the Atlanta SDAs contracted with Prosync, a contractor which specialized in such training.

Brief training for a specific job was unlikely to teach transferable skills useful in the trainee's future. The federal funds simply paid one company to do the exact minimum training desired for certain jobs by another company, lowering the employer's costs and allowing the local job training agency to claim credit for the placements. Within the system's closed frame of reference, everything looked fine.

The state government put pressure on Atlanta by issuing year-end rankings of local programs across the state, which stirred up the competitive instincts of the businessmen running the local programs. Incentive funds were given to programs ranking the highest. The result tended to "drive down program length and costs to such an extent that the more difficult to serve . . . cannot be served" (Maclachlan 1987, 19–20).

By the 1987 program year, the Atlanta program had focused so intently on these standards that it received the "Governor's Cup" for having the best placement and cost statistics in the state. It also received a national Labor Department award. Its statistics through early 1989 showed a high level of placement with training costs per person one-third cheaper than the state goal (*PIC Perspective*, Spring 1989: 1–2). In other words, very little money was spent training and placing each person in the program.

One of the problems with the performance-contracting system in Atlanta, according to a local study, was that it tended to drive out organizations that worked with highly disadvantaged workers, including very prominent black groups. Of the three black community organizations that had previously done a great deal of job training, "one, the Atlanta Urban League, has opted not to contract for JTPA because of a reluctance to enter a performance-based contract; another, the Atlanta OIC, is funded at low levels . . . and the third, Economic Opportunity Atlanta, receives primarily summer youth program contracts" (Maclachlan 1987, 10).

DIVIDING THE LABOR MARKET

Governors were authorized by the act to establish the boundaries of local Service Delivery Areas for job training and were encouraged to make them contiguous with local labor markets. The act, however, also granted a local government with a population of more than 200,000 authority to establish its own separate agency. In a large labor market such as metro Atlanta's, a municipality of 200,000 would, of course, cover only a small part of the market.

Initially, Georgia's governor proposed that the entire seven-county metropolitan Atlanta area be designated as a single Service Delivery Area so as to include the entire labor market. This plan was also favored by the region's business leaders, many of whom had branch offices in several counties. "There was heavy-duty pressure from the governor and the local business community to have a metro PIC [Private Industry Council]." The plan fell through when several local politicians objected (Montgomery interview, 5 March 1987; Weissman interview, 30 August 1986).

Andrew Young, Atlanta's mayor, opposed the establishment of a metro PIC because he did not believe the city would get adequate funding if it were part of a larger SDA. The city wanted control because of a tradition of local job training programs "dating back to the 1960s when local, community-based organizations received funding directly from the federal government under War on Poverty and manpower programs." The city's CETA program had been important in building links between the first black mayor, Maynard Jackson, and community organizations which received the training contracts. Jackson used CETA to "extend jobs and training opportunities to the black community in addition to giving jobs to administrators and training contracts to community-based organizations." It was not surprising that the city political leaders wanted to keep control and that they were suspicious of the suburbs (Maclachlan 1987, 4). The data in this chapter suggest, however, that the interests of the political leaders may not have been the same as the interests of poor blacks without jobs.

Following Mayor Young's decision, the chairman of the DeKalb County Board of Commissioners, Manuel J. Maloof, then decided that suburban DeKalb County should also be a separate SDA. Clayton County decided it wanted its own tiny SDA. The remaining suburban areas of metropolitan Atlanta were then consolidated into what we call the North Suburban SDA (its official name is Metropolitan Atlanta SDA). The North Suburban SDA contained the major suburban job-growth areas on the northern perimeter of metro Atlanta, including Cobb and Gwinnett Counties and several newly urbanizing outlying counties.

Black political power in the city, in this instance, served to detach the part of the labor market with most of the area's poor from the regions with the most jobs. The separate DeKalb SDA isolated the main area of black suburbanization from the areas of the most economic growth.

The decision to set up four SDAs was followed by a series of negotiations in which cooperative agreements were worked out between them. Theoretically, participants would be allowed to cross over into any of the SDAs to enter training. However, the federal law allowed for only "limited exceptions" to the general requirement that eligible individuals be served by the SDA in which they lived. The cooperative agreement provided few exceptions. In 1984, that meant that the North Suburban SDA could serve no more than fifty-one people from outside that SDA (Cooperative Agreement, 1 July 1984). There was no workable mechanism to encourage even such miniscule transfers. Effects of housing segregation were written into the job training system.

The state said little to the SDAs about who they ought to be serving and provided little assistance to the city. Atlanta City SDA Director Wynn Montgomery, who had served as assistant director of the city's CETA program, expressed disappointment at the state's attitude, saying, "I view them [state officials] as less helpful than the feds" (Montgomery interview, 5 March 1987). The state also took a passive role with regard to civil rights and relationships with public schools.

One of the most significant changes in the administration of job training under JTPA was the strong policy role it assigned to the Private Industry Councils (PICs). The law put the program under the control of PICs dominated by business members, who had to constitute at least 51 percent of the council. Most SDA administrators saw this as a plus that would enhance the image of job training in the eyes of private employers who would then be more willing to cooperate with the program (Kusmik interview, 5 March 1987). And Atlanta's PIC was said to be the strongest, with representatives from some of the area's largest corporations, including the Coca-Cola Company, Delta Air Lines, Lockheed-Georgia, the Georgia Power Company, Equifax, the Marriott Corporation, and the Trust Company Bank. An early chairman of the Atlanta PIC later became chair of the National Alliance of Business, perhaps the most important of the pro-JTPA lobbies in Washington.

The increased private sector involvement also discouraged political interference, according to Jinx O'Neil, a state JTPA administrator (O'Neil interview, 4 March 1987). Politicians had more influence under CETA. The Atlanta PIC laid down two requirements when it offered the city a contract to run JTPA: the city council would no longer have the power to approve contracts, and the director would not be a political appointee.

Atlanta, like several other cities studied in the Metropolitan Opportunity Project, had struggled with corruption under CETA. A local researcher, Professor Gretchen Maclachlan, concluded that the program had been "beset with charges of mismanagement and payroll irregularities," which led to eleven indictments. Though this involved a small share of the funds, it had seriously damaged the program (Maclachlan, May 1978b, 24).

"Under CETA all contracts went through City Council," said Director Montgomery, "so I had to spend lots of time explaining contracts to the council, I saw a lot more political influence there. We would get calls from City Council members saying 'I have a friend who needs a job,' and we would bring them in if they were eligible" (Montgomery interview, 5 March 1987). There was a similar shift away from political control in DeKalb County (Kurmik interview, 5 March 1987). JTPA did not have the public service jobs that made CETA a tempting patronage target.

Even though the PICs helped improve the image of job training within the business community, their members have not been very helpful in placing participants in their own companies. The large corporations that sit on the Atlanta city PIC were not usually major employers of JTPA participants. The PIC's main role was in program design and publicity (Montgomery interview, 5 March 1987).

Who Gets into Training?

Local administrators reported that because of the economic boom there was far more employer demand for trained workers than there were people enrolling in JTPA in the mid-1980s. All four SDAs had problems with low enrollments, with the worst rates being in suburban areas. Officials in the booming North Suburban SDA reported receiving five times as many job inquiries from businesses about the program as they had people to place in jobs (Garrett interview, 4 March 1987). According to Wynn Montgomery, city training agencies were "desperate to get trainees" (Montgomery interview, 5 March 1987).

The low enrollments, however, were not the result of an insufficient number of eligible people. According to the 1980 census, there were 214,517 people in the metropolitan Atlanta area living below the poverty level. Only three percent of that population was enrolled in JTPA in the 1985–86 program year. 1985 Bureau of Labor Statistics data showed 59,000 unemployed in the metropolitan area and hundreds of thousands of additional "discouraged workers" who had stopped looking for work.

Montgomery attributed the low enrollments (in comparison with CETA) to the lack of support services and the stricter paperwork requirements for applicants under JTPA. Additionally, some enrollees would have earned less at placement than they were receiving in welfare and related benefits. "We regularly have people who realize they would be worse off financially after they finish training" (Montgomery interview, 5 March 1987).

The Reagan administration blocked a raise in the minimum wage throughout its two terms in office, meaning that more and more entry-level workers could work full time and still be below the poverty line. The state of Georgia paid very low welfare benefits ($208 a month for a family of three in 1985), plus Food Stamps and Medicaid assistance. Many entry-level jobs provided no medical coverage.

Few men, however, received welfare payments since the main welfare program, Aid to Families with Dependent Children (AFDC), served almost exclusively women who were single parents. Georgia had no state-wide general assistance program for poor men and provided no income for them to live on while being trained. Many were too poor to be able to afford to be trained for any length of time under JTPA.

WORKFARE

Like many states, Georgia experimented with workfare in an attempt to encourage AFDC recipients to take training and find jobs. In 1989, it was still experimenting in a few counties with a version it called PEACH (Positive Employment and Community Help), which sought to ease the transition from the welfare rolls to full employment by providing four months of medical coverage to enrollees after they had started their new jobs (*Atlanta Constitution*, 11 July 1988: 1). Unfortunately, as in many previous experiments, the women who received such training were substantially less likely to be employed or to remain employed after training in low-paying jobs made less practical by the absence of health benefits or childcare. Fifty-six percent of those trained were placed in jobs but only about one-third (38.1 percent) were working after three months (*PIC Perspective*, Spring 1989: 2). The tendency of workfare programs was to falsely diagnose the problem of welfare mothers as laziness and to fail to provide sufficient training and support to permit the women to hold onto those jobs in the face of childrearing problems. The result has often been to divert funds from training people more likely to remain at work and to coerce women through a difficult and, ultimately, embittering process.

WHO WAS TRAINED?

The various local programs enrolled different proportions of blacks and women. Across the four SDAs, women made up roughly two-thirds of the enrollments (see table 7.1). In 1985, young men made up the smallest percentage of total enrollments. The same group that was declining in the colleges was not making it into job training.

Atlanta ran an almost entirely black (98 percent) JTPA program. Enrollment of young black men in the year-round classroom training program was 27 percent below their representation in the city's disadvantaged population. Adult black men were underrepresented by 21 percent.

Black women's participation was almost half again their share of the disadvantaged population. Even in a city run by black men, the JTPA program failed to effectively reach jobless black men (see table 7.2).

In the North Suburban SDA, young men were the least likely to participate in the basic program. Young black women constituted 3 percent of the poverty population yet made up 21 percent of enrollments.

The data on eligible populations is difficult to interpret in prosperous suburbs, since a large fraction of those counted as "poor" in the census are only temporarily poor as a result of divorce or illness, a fact that may help account for the underrepresentation of poor whites in JTPA. Blacks are much more likely to face long-term poverty.

In DeKalb County, young men were again the least likely participants. Black women constituted over one-half of all enrollments while white women accounted for only one-tenth in this area of rapid black suburbanization. White adults made up 37 percent of the poverty population yet only 12 percent of enrollees.

Across all four SDAs, only a small percentage of all young black applicants enrolled in the classroom skills training. White youths, though applying in much smaller numbers, were much more likely to receive such training. The majority of black applicants participated in the Summer Youth Program (Title IIB), which was mainly a work experience program where they received modest wages, but usually no training. The fact that there was at least temporary income may have made this program more attractive (see table 7.3).

In the city, one-twelfth of young black male applicants enrolled in training classes. Almost three-fourths (72 percent) enrolled in the Summer Youth program, which offered little training; this program grew out of efforts to prevent riots in the 1960s by putting inner-city youngsters to

Table 7.1 Disadvantaged Population and Enrollments for Title IIA (%)

Characteristics	Disadvantaged	Enrollments
City of Atlanta		
white male youth	3	0
black male youth	11	8
white female youth	2	0
black female youth	13	23
white male adult	5	1
black male adult	19	15
white female adult	8	2
black female adult	37	49
North Suburban		
white male youth	8	4
black male youth	2	4
white female youth	8	12
black female youth	3	21
white male adult	24	7
black male adult	5	6
white female adult	36	21
black female adult	10	22
DeKalb County		
white male youth	8	2
black male youth	5	9
white female youth	8	2
black female youth	7	14
white male adult	15	4
black male adult	11	16
white female adult	22	8
black female adult	19	41
Clayton County		
white male youth	9	10
black male youth	0	3
white female youth	13	17
black female youth	3	6
white male adult	24	8
black male adult	3	2
white female adult	3	38
black female adult	7	15

Source: EEO tables from Georgia JTPA Management Information System (MIS), 1985.

work. In all the SDAs, young white female applicants were the most likely to enroll in the basic substantive (Title IIA) training programs.

Whites were more likely to be in a program that could improve their long-term work assets. An average of 47 percent of young white women went into the classroom training component as compared to an average

Table 7.2 Percentage of Participants Enrolled in Major Training Program by SDA

Characteristics	Atlanta		N. Suburban		DeKalb		Clayton	
	IIA	IIB	IIA	IIB	IIA	IIB	IIA	IIB
white male	38	62	28	72	40	60	43	57
black male	10	90	16	84	19	81	13	87
white female	67	33	46	54	48	52	66	34
black female	17	83	41	59	23	77	21	79

Source: Georgia JTPA EEO data, 1985.

of 11 percent of young black men in JTPA. White male and female youths were more than twice as likely to enroll in skills training as blacks.

The high percentage of black participants suggests that across the metropolitan area JTPA was largely perceived as being a black program, and thus very few whites applied. Job opportunities of course, were also more abundant in white areas, so there was less need. Blacks were much more likely to be unemployed. In 1985, the white unemployment rate was 3.1 percent while the black rate was 9.9 percent (Georgia Department of Labor 1986, table 23).

Even in areas where whites constituted the majority of the eligible population, blacks were significantly overrepresented in the applicant pool. The Atlanta area CETA program had also been overwhelmingly black (98 percent black in its last year). According to Jinx O'Neil from the state office, "Whites don't want JTPA. In DeKalb County, which is primarily white, the whites would rather go to the local junior college that recently became part of the state university system" (O'Neil interview, 4 March 1987). Wynn Montgomery, Atlanta's director, also felt the program was viewed as being a black program. It operated primarily in the black part of a segmented labor market.

Table 7.3 Percentage of Youth Applicants Enrolled in Title IIA and IIB

Characteristics	Atlanta		N. Suburban		DeKalb		Clayton	
	IIA	IIB	IIA	IIB	IIA	IIB	IIA	IIB
white male youth	29	47	22	56	29	42	37	49
black male youth	8	72	13	73	10	42	12	84
white female youth	53	26	37	43	34	37	65	34
black female youth	14	69	34	50	12	42	19	70

Source: Georgia JTPA EEO data, 1985.

Types of Training

State officials' strict adherence to federal goals led local program administrators to seek out short-term, low-cost training. In the Atlanta, North Suburban, and Clayton SDAs this usually consisted of classroom training of less than six months. Classroom training involved either remedial instruction in math and reading or skills training.

Remedial education is essential if disadvantaged youths and adults are to attain any employment beyond low-skilled, entry-level positions. Studies indicate that although fewer participants in remedial programs obtain immediate employment, their new skills are more likely to result in higher salaries and lasting gains. Researchers report the "single most important screening device used by employers is education credentials" (Magnum and Walsh 1978). A dropout receiving a GED high school equivalency certificate becomes far more employable.

On-the-Job Training (OJT) put participants to work immediately and reimbursed their employers for up to 50 percent of their wages while they were enrolled in JTPA. Customized OJT training could be tailored to the needs of individual companies, and many JTPA administrators concentrated their advertising campaigns on promoting the savings in wages and training costs to companies using customized training programs.

In the Atlanta, North Suburban, and Clayton SDAs classroom occupational skills training accounted for roughly two-thirds of all training available. Atlanta had the most with 69 percent, more than one-third of it customized for specific companies. The largest of these customized programs at the time of this study was for the Marriott Marquis, a large new downtown hotel.

There was very little remedial training within the Atlanta metropolitan area, with the exception of DeKalb County. The city of Atlanta had only ten people enrolled in remedial education while Clayton County had none. In contrast, DeKalb County had 184 people in the remedial training component of their program.

The programs focused almost entirely on training that would result in immediate job placements. According to Nancy Bross at the state Department of Labor, "Many people at the state and local level feel that job training resources should only be used for literacy training and remediation as a last resort. Their strong preference is that remediation be provided by the education system and linked to job training through coordination agreements" (Bross letter, 23 June 1987).

Yet, many of those eligible for JTPA were the very people who were unable to learn these basic skills in the regular educational system and for whom the lack of such skills would become the major barrier to long-term employment. The fact that almost two-fifths of Atlanta students failed to complete high school means that there was an enormous unmet need for remedial training. Very few older high school dropouts ever return to high school where they might be humiliated in classes with much younger students. The city's JTPA program offered them even less than the programs in the suburbs. Assuming that the schools would fill the gap was absurd.

Remedial training could be paid for with either regular training funds or with the educational set-aside (8 percent of all JTPA funds). The funds for the educational set-aside were purposely not tied to performance standards so SDAs could use them to fund types of training that might not produce fast, low-cost placements. They were supposed to stimulate cooperation with the schools. In Georgia, however, local administrators were not required by state policy to use this money to provide basic skills training by working with the schools. In the 1986–87 program year, only one-fifth of the 8 percent educational set-aside was used for remedial education statewide.

The picture was worse in Atlanta. In the 1985–86 program year, the city spent none of its educational set-aside on remedial education and in the following year, 1986–87, the city spent only 9 percent of the set-aside on remediation by providing one remedial class for thirty students. JTPA enrolled another ten students in city public school remedial programs without reimbursing the school district (McCluskey interview, 28 May 1987). JTPA provided no significant second chance for dropouts.

The city had a long-standing problem of connecting education and job training, in spite of the obvious importance of the issue of low-income students with poor employment prospects. Large city school bureaucracies tend to be unresponsive and difficult to coordinate with any other agency, no matter how consequential the task may be. A local 1980 analysis of the implementation of the Carter administration's ambitious youth training programs observed that the Atlanta in-school program was the "least innovative" in the region, that the school officials had not been seriously involved, that work experience and academic credit were not coordinated, and that the agreements were late in being negotiated (Maclachlan 1980, 7). The pattern continued under JTPA.

The mix of other types of training varied throughout the region.

DeKalb had 13 percent of its trainees in On-the-Job Training while the rest had no more than 5 percent. DeKalb also had the largest portion of its training slots set aside for job search preparation.

In the 1985–86 program year, the city of Atlanta had an additional 869 participants enrolled in short, two-week employment preparation classes. These classes were intended to serve as an orientation program prior to placing people in occupational skills training. However, 44 percent of these participants left the program without receiving any substantive training.

Rob Snow of Georgia State University commented that the local JTPA program would "take a person with intermittent employment in the tertiary sector and get them another job in the tertiary sector" with little wage mobility. His colleague, John Hutcheson, agreed, adding that the program was "training people for jobs that don't require training" and was really not training but a subsidy to the businesses. The program "made it so the private business could fill high turnover-rate jobs (Snow and Hutcheson interviews, 2 July 1987).

What Happened to Those Trained?

There were significant differences in jobs found and earnings received after training. The distribution of types of training chosen by each SDA affected both the likelihood of finding a job and entry-level wages.

Among the forms of training offered, the greatest success in finding jobs was for those receiving customized training or On-the-Job Training (OJT). Only about one-tenth of the trainees in each SDA, however, were in those programs. Table 7.4 shows that in Atlanta only 6 percent of placements were in OJT and 1 percent in customized training in the year studied. Part of the reason for the higher placement rates in those programs, of course, was employer screening, which diminished their value for highly disadvantaged workers. Most of the OJT training was subsidized start-up work in manufacturing located predominately in the suburbs.

Program administrators said they were placing increasing emphasis on customized training that screened and trained entry-level workers to employers' specifications. These training courses normally consisted of two weeks of intensive pre-employment training, after which participants were placed in probationary jobs with companies. There was a high demand for customized training among employers. The North Suburban SDA had three customized training contracts with four large hotels who were taking youths at $4.50 to $5.00 per hour. Screening and training entry-level hotel workers cut corporate costs, but did not necessarily

Table 7.4 Percentage Placed in Jobs by Type of Training

| Type of Training[1] | Percentage of Participants | | | |
	Atlanta	N. Suburban	DeKalb	Clayton
occupational skills	69	62	41	61
remedial	0[2]	4	15	0
individual referral	5	11	1	2
customized training[3]	1	9	3	0
On-the-Job	6	4	13	5
job search	11	5	17	1

Source: Georgia JTPA Program Status Summary, 1985–86.

[1] Categories are based on the program codes assigned to each contract by the state. Program types with only a few participants have been eliminated from the table, therefore columns do not sum to 100 percent. These include work experience, exemplary youth, youth competency.

[2] Atlanta had two participants in remedial education.

[3] The customized training category is undercounted due to inconsistent coding.

change either the number or the kinds of workers who would be hired. Nor did it guarantee long-term work.

All four metropolitan Atlanta SDAs made few placements in the public sector, even though the number of available jobs in the Atlanta region had grown significantly during the last fifteen years. Because of negative associations with JTPA's predecessor, CETA, administrators avoided the public sector. Nancy Bross of the state JTPA staff said that public sector placement "has not been a major program focus" (Bross interview, 19 June 1987). Yet, in the last two decades the public sector hired blacks and women in far greater percentages and for more responsible jobs than did private industry. One-fifth of all black employees in the metro area worked for government agencies in 1988 (Georgia Department of Labor 1989). Not placing people in government jobs eliminated a major source of better-paying jobs in a sector of the economy that had years of experience integrating job training graduates into its work force. The idea that a job placement in a fast-food shop was inherently superior to working for a public library or street repair crew was a reflection of the program's conservative ideology.

Relying on employer preferences, JTPA did not challenge racial or sexual stereotypes in the labor market. There were few job placements in the construction industry, another sector that has shown considerable job growth over the last fifteen years. Placement in construction jobs has often been difficult and controversial because of hiring and training practices in the industry. Construction jobs were well-paid positions that would have been attractive to many men. In 1988, however, whites were still 44 percent more likely than blacks to work on construction jobs (Georgia Department of Labor 1989, table 25).

After years of JTPA, blacks were still substantially underrepresented in 1988 in construction and in the rapidly growing finance, insurance, and real estate sectors of metropolitan Atlanta and very substantially overrepresented in government employment. Among the area's civilian labor force, 6.5 percent of whites but only 4.5 percent of blacks worked on construction jobs; 6.0 percent of blacks but 8.9 percent of whites were in the finance, insurance, and real estate sectors and blacks were almost twice as likely as whites to find their jobs in the governmental sector— 20.4 percent as compared to 11.5 percent (Georgia Department of Labor 1988, table 27).

City training programs placed few people with employers in the high-growth northern suburbs. All SDAs mentioned the lack of public transportation as a major obstacle to placing participants in jobs throughout the metropolitan area. Even the North Suburban program sometimes sent its own trainees back to work in the city of Atlanta. They had many difficulties making placements in booming areas where there is often no way to get to work, even from within the county, by public transportation (Garrett interview, 4 March 1987). Outer suburbs in other metro areas studied by the Metropolitan Opportunity Project often reported similar problems, some noting that it was even impossible to get to the job training site unless the trainee had a reliable car.

The DeKalb job training director also reported problems with transportation. The area of rapid job growth in DeKalb County was located at the northern end of the county, adjacent to Gwinnett County. The northeastern DeKalb area experienced a 304 percent increase in jobs between 1970 and 1985. Yet, the trainees could not reach those jobs because few bus lines ran from the southern end of the county, where the majority of the blacks and the poor lived, to the northern end of the county where the jobs were.

"The lack of transportation restricts blacks from moving into jobs in the northern counties," said Gloria Kusmik, director of the DeKalb SDA. "The politicians in those counties don't want MARTA [Atlanta's mass transit system] because it is perceived as bringing blacks in. Gwinnett County has refused to join MARTA, yet the people who live there use MARTA by driving to stations in DeKalb County and then going downtown" (Kusmik interview, 5 March 1987).

David Chesnut, chairman of MARTA's board of directors, said in 1986 that a regional transit system was a long way off and that "the reason is 90 percent a racial issue." Chesnut was disturbed to hear young suburban professionals talk about creating an organization they called "NNIG—No Niggers in Gwinnett" (*Atlanta Constitution,* 3 June 1987). The MARTA acronym was sometimes described cynically as standing for "Moving Africans Rapidly Through Atlanta." U.S. Transportation Secretary Samuel Skinner spoke out on the problem in a 1989 Atlanta speech, saying it was "manifestly unfair and totally irresponsible" to isolate low-income workers in cities without transportation to jobs. Cobb County created a small mass transit system permitting movement across the county line in 1989, and it was handling up to 1,000 reverse commuters per day in early 1990. Gwinnett still had no system. By 1990, more people were commuting out on the MARTA system than were coming downtown to work (*Atlanta Journal and Constitution,* 14 March 1990).

A job training program alone cannot overcome the growing geographic separation between the poor and the areas of high job growth. Job training cannot place people in jobs that are geographically unreachable. This is one of the costs of a system of residential segregation reinforced by program fragmentation.

ARE THERE EQUAL REWARDS FOR TRAINING?

The entry-level wages of trainees getting jobs vary by region and by type of training. With a handful of exceptions, trainees had beginning wages below $6.00 per hour (see table 7.5).

Most job placements from classroom skills training were in low-wage occupations requiring minimal skills. The North Suburban SDA offered the greatest diversity in the types of classroom training available. In contrast, the DeKalb and Clayton SDAs offered training in a limited range of occupations.

Table 7.5 Wages of Participants in Each Training Program by SDA

	Entry Wage[1]			
Type of Training	Atlanta	N. Suburban	DeKalb	Clayton
occupational skills	$5.32	$5.46	$4.99	$5.18
remedial	NA	$6.50[2]	$4.65	NA
individual referral	$5.64	$4.37	$5.16	NA
customized training	$4.75	$5.39	$5.09	NA
On-the-Job	$5.66	$5.03	$5.25	$7.58
job search	$5.19	$3.98	$4.50	NA

Source: Georgia JTPA Program Status Summary, 1985–86.

[1] Wages listed are average of those programs with a reported wage rate.

[2] N. Suburban placed nine people in jobs out of its remedial programs.

The largest single category in three of the SDAs was clerical training, a predominantly female category with expanding opportunities in the service sector. A 1987 survey of major employers showed that this was the major hiring category (National Alliance of Business 1988). In DeKalb and Clayton Counties, over two-thirds of the training slots were in clerical occupations. DeKalb trainees were first enrolled in a basic typing class, then sent on to more advanced classes in data entry or word processing. In the 1986 program year, 223 studied beginning typing and 81 percent finished. Thirty-three people or 18 percent of those finishing got jobs immediately, and another 63 percent transferred into other programs.

Much of DeKalb's classroom training, including the classes in typing and building maintenance, was contracted out to the DeKalb Vocational School, which provided inexpensive clerical classes at a cost of approximately $800 per person.

In Atlanta, the largest class of occupational skills training in 1986 was for hotel work, involving 42 percent of all participants. The Atlanta SDA trained more than 500 people in the 1985–1986 program year for various hotel jobs. It also trained people for clerical, custodial, food preparation, and retail sales jobs. A small number of participants trained for manufacturing jobs at Lockheed (Montgomery interview, 5 March 1987). An additional 294 people enrolled in customized classroom training.

Atlanta trained 276 people for the Marriott Marquis, a new hotel in downtown Atlanta, prior to its opening. According to Dee Parks, the director of human resources at the Marquis, "The participants were mostly placed in housekeeping positions. People were also given jobs in cold-food preparation, utilities, as assistant cooks, and some front desk work" (Parks interview, 26 May 1987). The city of Atlanta's own records indicate that 56 of the 223 participants (25 percent) got jobs in housekeeping (Montgomery letter, 30 June 1987).

The Marriott Marquis had approached the city's job training administrators and expressed an interest in using JTPA to hire unskilled workers for their new hotel. The JTPA staff was very enthusiastic since it offered the possibility of a large number of low-cost, high-placement jobs. Atlanta Director Wynn Montgomery said, "In terms of the numbers we have to produce it did some good things for us." Although the Atlanta PIC was initially opposed to the project "because it didn't want 250 people placed in the hotel industry," it finally approved the program (ibid.). When asked whether he felt the Marquis had hired people they wouldn't have hired otherwise, Montgomery reported that the hotel had provided information showing that the personnel they hired through JTPA had less hotel work experience than those hired off the street and that a larger share had been on welfare or were long-term unemployed. The state's own data showed that 87 percent reported they had jobs with Marriott when they left training and 76 percent were still working there after three months. The job training office of this black-controlled city government financed a hotel to train black women as maids and then reported great success in job training.

The logic of the JTPA system, along with the continuing strong gender segregation of jobs, produced very strong incentives for training black women for traditional, low-wage jobs with little mobility. The kinds of entry-level jobs being created in large numbers within the inner city were predominantly clerical and service related. Typing and housekeeping could be taught in relatively brief periods with limited budgets. Employers in those occupations were used to hiring black women. It was much less risky to meet JTPA requirements by going with the conventions of the labor market than by trying to change them.

Classroom training for manufacturing jobs, a very desirable form of work for low-skill workers, accounted for over one-fourth of the training slots in the North Suburban SDA, but for only 1 percent in Atlanta and 6 percent in DeKalb. These key mobility jobs and the training programs that led to them were concentrated in the outlying white suburbs. This was where new manufacturing jobs were concentrated. Jobs of this sort had been exactly what had permitted mobility for urban ethnic groups with relatively weak educational backgrounds in earlier generations (Lieberson 1980).

The North Suburban SDA had 114 participants in its Lockheed training program who were preparing for work in a major aircraft factory in the suburbs while the city of Atlanta had less than one-sixth as many. JTPA did the initial personnel screening for Lockheed by testing applicants' reading and math skills. Those who were referred to Lockheed by the SDAs were then screened again by the company.

The North Suburban SDA also conducted classes on circuit-board assembly in Gwinnett County, which fed into the Rockwell Company located there. It also had a few clerical classes tied to local banks, and 12 percent of its classroom training slots were in warehousing. These classes had high placement rates at good wages, mostly in Gwinnett County (Garrett interview, 4 March 1987).

Although clerical opportunities were expanding rapidly, the large clerical training programs had some of the lowest placement rates. DeKalb

devoted 79 percent of its occupational skills training slots to clerical training and placed 64 percent of those in its advanced classes. In the northern
suburbs, the clerical placement rate was 83 percent.

Hotel job training averaged a job placement rate of 76 percent in the
SDAs in which it was offered. The service sector had an average rate of
78 percent.

Manufacturing training had the lowest average placement rate of 68
percent. The city of Atlanta placed less than half of the thirteen people
who completed its structural assembly training class for Lockheed. Of
those enrolled in the North Suburban SDA's Lockheed training program,
almost two-thirds of those completing the program were actually placed
in jobs. Because the suburban program trained so many more for Lockheed, almost nine-tenths of those who actually got Lockheed jobs were
from the suburbs.

The two main suburban SDAs placed people in jobs that, on the average, paid 6 percent more than those in the city of Atlanta. Some found
relatively high-paying manufacturing jobs. DeKalb placed fifteen people
trained in electronics at $7.09 an hour. The forty-nine people placed at
Lockheed by the North Suburban SDA received entry wages of $7.52.
The other occupational training program that led to relatively high-wage
jobs was bartending, which paid $5.88 to the people who obtained jobs
in the city and $6.44 to those placed by the North Suburban SDA.

Participants in Atlanta's clerical programs received the highest clerical
entry wages of any of the four SDAs. A small number of participants in
the word processing classes did best, with Atlanta placing ten people at
$5.68 per hour. Data entry jobs averaged below $5.00 an hour.

Participant Characteristics

At least two-thirds of the participants in all programs, except On-the-Job
Training, were females. High school dropouts and the long-term unemployed were seriously underrepresented in the city of Atlanta.

The overwhelming majority of classroom participants in Atlanta and
DeKalb were black, but most were white in the North Suburban SDA,
which had the highest entry-level wage rates through access to higher
paying manufacturing jobs.

IS THERE A SECOND CHANCE FOR DROPOUTS?

One of the most important questions about job training is whether or not
it functions to offer a real second chance to the vast number of high school

dropouts in the region. High school dropouts made up only 15 percent of the participants enrolled in Atlanta's occupational classroom training, the smallest percentage of any of the four SDAs. Although the city had the highest dropout rate, its programs were the least responsive.

Research on JTPA in Illinois also found a trend of declining service to high school dropouts, as have national studies of JTPA. In Illinois, the percentages of high school dropouts in training programs had declined by 50 percent since CETA's high point in 1978 (Orfield and Slessarev 1986, chap. 6). Most CETA data for Georgia no longer exists, but our interviews indicated the same was true of Georgia (Montgomery interview, 5 March 1987). Under the special Youth Employment projects of the Carter administration, for example, a study reported statistics showing extensive provisions for Atlanta dropouts. During the 1978 fiscal year one-fourth (24 percent) of the participants in the YETP programs and nearly two-thirds (64 percent) of those in the out-of-school YCCIP program were dropouts (Maclachlan, November 1978c, 2). Much less was done in the 1980s.

The DeKalb County SDA, whose director reported training "very few dropouts," served more than the Atlanta SDA. Wynn Montgomery, the Atlanta SDA director, agreed that opportunities for people without high school diplomas had declined since CETA. "In CETA we always tried to find programs for people below a sixth grade education. Now the test scores have gone up, probably because of the performance standards." Montgomery added that all training agencies under JTPA contracts did supplemental screening in addition to the tests administered at the SDA's intake center. "The contractors are all requesting higher educational levels in the contracts" (Montgomery interview, 5 March 1987). People with more education were easier to place in jobs and meant the program faced less risk of losing a training contract. Serious training became almost nonexistent for Atlanta's dropouts.

Atlanta primarily trained recently unemployed people still in the labor force. Two of the other SDAs drew roughly one-third of their classroom participants from discouraged workers not in the labor force. The city programs reached very few of the people who were severely isolated from the job market.

Most of the city's OJT trainees were women. Administrators noted that the lack of support services probably resulted in enrolling women with fewer children than under CETA.

None of the local JTPA administrators know why so few men are enrolled in the program. Several said that they had tried to attract more men by starting up male-oriented training classes in building maintenance and warehousing but nonetheless attracted few male applicants. Some mentioned the lack of living-expense funds.

Whites seldom applied for job training in Atlanta. The city's Summer Youth Program had almost no whites. The racial division worked against poor whites who could not afford the costs of community college or private skills training. It hurt blacks because the training system was well linked only to jobs traditionally reserved for blacks.

Compared to occupational skills training, an even higher percentage of participants in remedial training were women, including substantial portions of AFDC recipients. The city of Atlanta and North Suburban SDAs had few youths in remedial skills training programs. In Atlanta, the remedial program was tiny and there were only four high school dropouts among the ten participants.

A much greater percentage of men were enrolled in OJT, the only year-round training program that provided an income while participants learned. Over two-thirds of DeKalb County's OJT trainees were males. In Atlanta, men constituted only 22 percent of the participants in remedial programs, and 29 percent of the classroom training participants, but 40 percent of the OJT participants. (The much greater male participation in OJT was also found in the Illinois JTPA program, where men outnumbered women two-to-one [Orfield and Slessarev 1986]. Given the absence of living stipends for men in JTPA, On-the-Job Training, which provided a salary, was the only kind of training many poor men could afford.

Most of the OJT slots were in manufacturing, where men were more likely to be hired than women. In contrast, most of the classroom training was for traditionally female clerical jobs. The OJT slots had among the highest job-placement rates once training was completed.

OJT participants were generally the most "job-ready," that is, people who would have had the easiest time finding jobs on their own. On-the-Job Training and customized training were the programs most heavily geared to the private sector.

Youth Training

Youth participation within metropolitan Atlanta's JTPA program was a critical issue for the region's future labor force. Research on job training shows that training makes the most difference for young people with little previous experience in the work force (Levitan and Johnston 1975; Mallar et al. 1978). The JTPA law required that SDAs spend 40 percent of their training dollars on youths. Yet, JTPA initially did not seek to develop specifically youth-oriented programs. Youths were simply placed into regular training programs along with adults. In the 1985–86 program year, there were few special youth programs that did not require job placement. The "exemplary youth" programs, which allow for successful training outcomes such as competency in work maturity, basic education, and job specific skills were only available for fourteen- and fifteen-year-olds in the Atlanta area and involved classes in school-to-work transition, pre-employment skills, or try-out employment.

The North Suburban SDA had the most diversified mix of programs. Atlanta had the highest concentration of its youth participants in classroom training, but only three young people in remedial training in the entire city.

State officials had a very limited vision of youth programs and looked only at placement statistics, not basic skills development. When the Atlanta SDA designed a youth competency program that included remediation, the state insisted that the basic education component be job-related. Unable to agree with state officials, the Atlanta program decided not to fund remedial training (Montgomery letter, 30 June 1987). In fact, the state criticized the Atlanta Board of Education for including GED preparation in its youth competency program (Montgomery interview, 5 March 1987), even though the high school equivalency degree is a vital asset in seeking employment or higher education.

The North Suburban SDA only began its youth competency program in the last quarter of the 1985 program year, yet it had placed 12 percent of its youth participants in that program by the end of the year. DeKalb, which had no youth competency program in 1985, instituted one aimed at handicapped youth during the 1986 program year.

The State Board of Education emphasized its Quality Basic Education reforms upgrading academic achievement, which JTPA administrators feel has led to a downplaying of vocational education. By increasing academic requirements and tests for high school graduation, the reform left students without space in their course schedules for vocational training. This was a general trend across the United States in the 1980s. For students not going to college, it made high school more difficult and cut the possibility for job-related training.

State JTPA leaders think local school systems have become less receptive to establishing JTPA programs such as work experience for in-school youth. In a sense, the conservative reforms in the high schools, which downgrade vocational training, produce direct conflicts with the conservative reforms in job training. These in turn provide much less service for dropouts and assume that the schools can take care of much more of the training.

Youths finishing training and getting jobs were generally paid less than adults. With the exception of OJT in Atlanta, none of the youth programs' wages exceeded $5.25 per hour, and the majority were under $5.00 an hour.

YOUTH OCCUPATIONAL SKILLS TRAINING

Patterns of enrollment, job placement, and entry-level wages were significantly different for youths than for adults. Both the Atlanta and the North Suburban SDAs placed over half of their youths receiving occupational skills training in either clerical or retail sales training. Atlanta had almost one-fourth of its youth participants in training for the hotel industry.

Atlanta made heavy use of retail sales training in programs for youths. The DeKalb and Clayton SDAs placed over half of their youth participants in clerical training. Youths made up 97 percent of all retail trainees in Atlanta and 100 percent in the North Suburban area. This category includes fast-food jobs ("McJobs") that involve few skills and little training. They are easy to train for and easy placements, thus they make the JTPA system look good. The youth retail sales training programs in the city of Atlanta and the North Suburban SDAs had the highest entered employment rates.

In the North Suburban SDA, almost two-thirds of all youth participants received training in the service occupations. In DeKalb, however, close to one-half of all youths were trained for manufacturing occupations. In the Atlanta SDA, 23 percent of the participants in the special Marriott Marquis training program were youths.

Manufacturing jobs offered youths the highest entry-level wages in all three of the SDAs that provided youth training. The Northern suburbs had the highest youth wages in the service, hotel, and manufacturing categories, and Atlanta offered the highest clerical wages for youths.

YOUTH PARTICIPANT CHARACTERISTICS

As was true of adults, females made up over two-thirds of the youths participating in occupational skills training in all four SDAs. All the occupational skills participants in DeKalb were black, and 95 percent of them were female. Ninety-five percent of the classroom participants in Atlanta were black. Only 16 percent of Atlanta's youth occupational skills participants were high school dropouts, considerably below the percentages for the other SDAs. Almost one-half of Atlanta's young occupational skills participants had been unemployed for less than fifteen weeks. Atlanta's youth programs were not reaching the hard-core unemployed youths in the city, but drew most trainees from the small segment of urban black youths who already had some work experience.

Very few youths were enrolled in remedial education: the city had three enrollees and the northern suburbs had sixteen. DeKalb served forty youths in its remedial program, by far the largest in the metropolitan area. All told, JTPA provided remedial education for seventy-nine young people in all of metropolitan Atlanta in the 1985–86 program year; this, in an area with thousands of new dropouts every year.

SUMMER YOUTH PROGRAM

The city of Atlanta had a total of 2,064 youths enrolled in its Summer Youth Program in 1986, the largest among the four SDAs. The great majority of participants received limited work experience in public sector jobs for low wages.

The city of Atlanta, in contrast to some other big cities, had difficulties finding youths to enroll, meeting only three-fourths of its planned summer enrollments. The total was also less than one-half the average enrollment in the CETA summer youth program from 1975 to 1981, though spreading poverty among city families meant that many more were eligible. Most summer youth participants were fourteen and fifteen years old; the city's policy limited the program to this group. The city's program was not used to give work experience or training to dropouts but concentrated on younger students.

Beginning in 1987, the federal government mandated that summer youth programs put a greater emphasis on remediation than on work experience. In response, the SDAs began setting up summer programs that combined skills training with remediation. In Atlanta, an earlier effort was called Project Alert, and it served 167 fourteen-to-sixteen-year olds during the summer of 1985. Evaluation showed some significant, if limited, educational gains, particularly in information about work and completion of some high school credits (Jonas 1985).

Atlanta's summer program for older youths was a small, unsubsidized private-sector summer program aimed mainly at youths between eigh-

teen and twenty-one years of age, employing JTPA screening and orientation assistance. In the summer of 1986, it enrolled 196 young people
even though the SDA had received six times as many job offers as it had
participants available to take the jobs.

The city's Private Industry Council recommended ending the targeting of this summer program toward those with serious training needs. Its
report concluded that "you can't get an employer to hire the hard-core
unemployed even if we could get them into the program" (Montgomery
interview, 5 March 1987). It then suggested that the SDA concentrate on
a middle group of young people who want to find jobs but don't know
where to look. The report recommended opening up the private sector
jobs to all young people who were not poor (Montgomery letter, 30 June
1987). The state JTPA administrators agreed to this proposal since no
public resources were being put into the program. The SDA was not
reaching the hard-core unemployed youths and moved further away from
that goal and even closer to placements very much like those that would
have occurred without a program.

DO THE JOBS LAST?

Georgia was one of the first states in the country in institute a follow-up
study of all participants ninety days after they had been placed in a job.
Across the state, 80 percent of those placed in jobs were still employed
in some way at thirteen weeks. In the 1985–86 program year, 63 percent
were still working in the job of their original placement. In other words,
almost two-fifths of placements lasted less than three months.

The northern suburbs had the strongest thirteen-week retention rates
for adults, the highest average wage, and their participants worked an
average of nine out of the thirteen weeks after completing training. It was
the only SDA in which the adults averaged a full forty-hour work week
after the thirteenth week. The same favorable conditions that meant a
wider range of training opportunities and better placement at better
wages helped hold workers on the job. In other areas, workers were earning less and working fewer hours and were less likely to hold their jobs.

Youths were much less likely to remain at their original jobs. Most
youths in DeKalb and Clayton Counties were not at the same job after
thirteen weeks, nor did they average forty hours per week in any SDA.
JTPA placed many in what turned out to be marginal, short-term, part-
time jobs with high turnover rates. What appeared to be high placements
at low cost often actually involved spending many hundreds of dollars per

young person to get a part-time job that would have been available without training and which lasted less than three months. Narrowly focused customized training providing no basic skills gains made little sense if those specific jobs lasted only a few weeks.

Conclusions

Even within a booming regional economy that was experiencing job growth in all major occupational categories, the national job training program of the 1980s prepared only a small fraction of eligible Atlanta-area people for only a narrow range of jobs. The program functioned under severe constraints, some of which were intrinsic to its policies, others of which were due to the regional dynamics of segregation and uneven economic growth patterns. State authority over the program only intensified its concentration on less needy trainees and superficial training. Black power in the city did not challenge business domination of the program but did help fragment the labor market. In some important respects, such as service for dropouts, the city's program was worse than those in the suburbs.

Job training alone could not provide broad labor market access for minorities locked in inner-city neighborhoods far away from the primary job growth centers. The program reflected the fact that housing and educational isolation and white prejudice had confined many blacks to the secondary labor market—of low-skill, low-wage jobs with few benefits and little possibility of advancement. Inadequate skills contributed to low wages and unemployment, but federal requirements for quick, low-cost job placement blocked the needed basic-skills training.

Job training administrators showed that they could indeed operate a program that produced high job-placement rates while spending far less than earlier programs, but they paid a price to meet these new "bottom-line" criteria. Administrators had to choose low-cost, short-term training classes that served few severely disadvantaged workers. Achieving apparent success meant wasting the chance of having a long-term impact on those most in need.

Participants were trained for a narrow range of relatively low-skill jobs rather than for the wide range of jobs being created. The decision to orient all job placement toward the private sector closed off many possibilities in local, state, and national government—areas traditionally more willing to hire blacks.

Atlanta limited services for the hard-core unemployed even more than the suburbs did. Our studies of Chicago and Los Angeles show higher levels of service and more remedial training, though neither could offer the kind of training that had been available under CETA. Despite its much better economy, Atlanta served an even smaller percentage of high school dropouts than the city of Chicago. On several levels, the Atlanta suburbs provided more appropriate services for highly disadvantaged workers. City job trainers did not work effectively with the city's troubled public schools. The program reflected and subsidized normal practices in the labor market.

JTPA policies created recruitment problems. The pool of enrollees declined as local administrators and contractors became more selective and excluded people with the lowest skill levels and as strict documentation requirements created still other barriers. Weakened links to local educational institutions and community-based organizations made it more difficult to reach and provide worthwhile services for those with the greatest need.

Administrators did find more support from businesses for JTPA than for CETA. It appeared, however, that many businesses were attracted to JTPA as a means of having their normal personnel recruitment and training costs subsidized by the federal government. It is unclear to what extent businesses hired people through JTPA whom they would not otherwise have hired. JTPA did very little to change the distribution of opportunities for work or income in a metropolitan economy experiencing extraordinary growth and creating vast wealth.

8

The Lessons of Atlanta: An Agenda for Urban Racial Equality in the 1990s

After decades of attack on the social policies adopted during the five years of the Great Society, it is time to run the tally on the policies adopted during nearly two decades of conservative political domination. Conservatives have been remarkably effective in blaming social problems on a few years of liberal domination in the mid-1960s, while downplaying their own much longer control of the federal administration, many state and local governments, and their growing influence in other institutions. This book examines the conservative proposition that the market would solve problems of inequality by race given abundant economic growth and reasonable access by minority leaders to local political power. The data from metropolitan Atlanta show that the market did not solve the problems. In fact, conservative policies have deepened the inequality of opportunity.

Analyses of the housing, schools, colleges, job training, and employment patterns of the region document the shrinking of black opportunity in the 1980s. The stories of families giving up their dreams amidst the prosperity and exuberant economic growth of the period show some of the human costs. This chapter reviews the basic assumptions of the conservative program, summarizes our findings, and suggests an agenda for reopening paths out of the ghetto and into the mainstream of society.

The Conservative Program

The federal and state policy changes successfully implemented by conservatives entailed a total redefinition of the problem of racial inequality. Throughout government and in the management of many major institu-

tions, the belief that further governmental action for racial equality was
necessary simply disappeared. Although the issue of civil rights had been
at the very top of public concerns in the polls briefly in the mid-1960s, it
went to the very bottom by the early 1970s, and surveys showed that
whites believed the problems had been solved. Almost three-fourths of
the whites surveyed in 1989, for example, believed that opportunities
had improved for blacks during the Reagan era (*USA Today*, 22 September 1989: 1).

Within a few years the perception of the late 1960s that America faced
a fundamental racial crisis was replaced by the belief that everything reasonable had been done and that, in fact, policies had often gone so far as
to be unfair to whites. Conservatives argued that the policies were even
hurting the intended beneficiaries and that minorities would be better
off if welfare programs and policies such as affirmative action and school
desegregation were abandoned. Officials holding these views took charge
of the major social policy and civil rights agencies of the federal government.

Within a few years, the liberal belief that white institutions were fundamentally responsible for urban racial inequality, set forth in the 1968
Kerner Commission report, gave way to a totally different dominant
understanding. The black community was seen as responsible for its own
problems.

Assumptions that the remaining problems stemmed from deficient minority aspirations, culture, and family structure dominated the federal
executive branch in the 1980s, giving great prominence to such neoconservative researchers as Thomas Sowell, Charles Murray, and Glenn
Loury, who argued that the civil rights and social policies of the past had
led to welfare dependency. Soft-headed liberalism was seen as responsible for destroying black families and black aspirations. By the mid-
1980s, tremendous interest had developed in efforts to describe the path-
ologies of the ghetto underclass and to develop coercive solutions for
them. Welfare reform, for example, focused on pressuring mothers of
young children to work, not on raising the level of payments. In Georgia
in 1987, for example, the maximum AFDC payment for a family of three
was only one-third of the poverty-line income level (*Atlanta Constitution*,
19 May 1988).

Problems of the welfare system, teen pregnancy, juvenile crime and
drug addiction were dealt with through punitive measures and advocacy
of better values. Welfare was made less desirable by cutting the real level

of benefits and imposing work and training requirements. Teen pregnancy was attacked by reducing benefits and health care while advocating chastity. Crime was to be reduced by increasing the severity and frequency of sentences for convictions and building more prisons. Drug abuse was to be stopped by stepped-up law enforcement and by public relations campaigns against drug use.

The basic idea was that if social policy became tough enough, social decay would stop and poor black people would behave more like the white middle class. If they did, the policies assumed, they would have the same opportunities whites had. A key assumption in the entire argument was that discrimination was no longer structural but only a secondary problem that could be dealt with by taking action against those few individuals who discriminated.

Similar approaches were adopted in the schools, colleges, and job training institutions. Since large numbers of inner-city students were failing to meet the standards for graduation, the problem was assumed to be permissiveness and the standards were raised. Diplomas were withheld from students unless they completed more course requirements and passed more standardized tests. Colleges decided they could upgrade the quality of their student bodies by substantially raising admission requirements, sometimes requiring courses not even available at many inner-city high schools (Orfield and Mitzel 1984). It was assumed that the schools would respond by providing them.

Public universities moved to phase out their remedial programs and their special admissions and outreach efforts for minority students, assuming either that the problem of declining minority admissions would eventually be eliminated by the tougher high school graduation requirements or that the two-year colleges could pick up the slack (ibid.). New policies were often adopted without discussion of their racial consequences or analysis of the capacity of the institution serving minority youths to make the necessary changes. Test requirements were raised.

Tuition and financial aid policies were changed so that it was impossible for many low-income students to attend college unless they obtained federally insured student loans from banks, loans that were huge compared to their families' incomes and net worth. The new policies assumed that low-income families would take out such loans, despite evidence to the contrary. When many former students at black colleges and technical schools were unable to repay these loans, the government announced plans to prohibit future students of those institutions from receiving federally guaranteed loans, with the stated purpose of forcing the poor and their colleges to be more responsible.

In other words, after making it impossible for many black students to attend without taking out loans that would be difficult to repay, the government policy would continue to punish those who came after them.

Moreover, financial packages for minority students assumed that they would have substantial summer earnings, making no distinction between students living in jobless ghettos and those living in the job-rich suburbs.

There were similar policy changes in job training. The idea of paying a stipend for young people not on AFDC to live on while they received training, an important feature of the old training programs, was rejected and funds for day care, counseling, and other support services were radically reduced in its successor, the Job Training Partnership Act (JTPA). These were seen as frills. Training time was sharply curtailed and training of the hard-core unemployed deemphasized. Businessmen were put in charge.

Trainers were punished rather than rewarded for trying to train those lacking basic skills. If their placement rates were not high enough, and their costs were not low enough, the training organization would lose its contract. Naturally, the training organizations that survived were those which excluded the people who were hard to train in favor of those who were job-ready.

By the late 1980s some of the consequences of a generation of profoundly conservative policies were apparent. Nearly twenty years after fair housing laws made discrimination illegal, for example, the average family had moved at least three times and great numbers had moved into metro Atlanta from somewhere else; but there was more profound isolation of ghetto residents, and poverty was up sharply in the inner city.

After a generation of real accomplishment in raising the academic achievement of the most disadvantaged groups, the federal government reduced both funds and targeting. Across the country, in spite of the issuance of the "A Nation at Risk" report in 1983 and reforms in almost all of the states, there were no national educational gains in the 1980s according to the National Assessment of Educational Progress. Education Secretary Lauro Cavazos concluded that the "haphazard and piecemeal" reforms had not raised the "dreadfully inadequate" scores for reading and writing (*Education Week*, 17 January 1990: 1, 21).

After nearly two decades of learning through experience what was needed for more effective job training and public employment policy, the federal government adopted an approach in 1982 that did just the opposite. By 1990 even the U.S. Department of Labor was conceding the need for substantial revisions in the Job Training Partnership Act, which had been hailed in the 1988 presidential campaign as a central achievement of the Reagan administration, particularly by its author, Vice-President Dan Quayle.

During the 1980s these conservative trends reached their apogee. In a rare and sweeping ideological turnaround, both the civil rights policies aimed at ending racial separation and the substantive policies aimed at ameliorating ghetto conditions and building bridges of opportunity to mainstream society were reversed suddenly in 1981. Liberal policies holding back the market and individual initiative gave way to a fullblown reliance on toughness, market forces, and local initiatives. The effects on opportunity in metropolitan Atlanta are spelled out in terrifying detail in this book.

The Abandonment of Civil Rights

One assumption that permeated all areas of policy in the federal executive branch in the 1980s was that civil rights enforcement was no longer needed. Under the Reagan administration, there was no serious enforcement against civil rights violations by schools, colleges, or job training institutions. Instead, civil rights agencies slashed data collection, investigations, and public release of information. The U.S. Civil Rights Commission, the Justice Department's Civil Rights Division, and other key agencies were put under the authority of officials who attacked the goals of the nation's major black and Hispanic organizations. Civil rights research funding was reduced or eliminated in federal agencies. Some research was commissioned to provide ammunition for the Justice Department's attack on previously established school desegregation orders.

Although the laws were still on the books, the basic attitude was to minimize enforcement. Nothing was done. In the job training program enacted in 1982, civil rights regulations were never even issued in spite of the 1964 Civil Rights Act's prohibition against discrimination in federal programs. In higher education there were no sanctions against colleges. In fact, the Justice Department successfully urged the Supreme Court, in the *Grove City College* case, to narrow its interpretation of the sex discrimination and civil rights law. Then, citing the *Grove City* decision to justify its inaction in other civil rights cases, it simultaneously opposed Congressional attempts to strengthen the law. Congress finally enacted the 1988 Civil Rights Restoration Act over the President's veto, but the administration continued on the same course of nonenforcement.

Under the Reagan administration none of the basic elements of an effective civil rights policy were in place in educational and job training programs. To make matters worse, the administration often placed civil rights agencies under the leadership of harsh critics of civil rights, officials who used their authority and public positions to resist civil rights enforcement by the federal courts. In a concerted effort to alter the direction of the federal courts, President Reagan named most sitting federal judges by the end of his term through a process of unprecedented ideological screening. This effort, which culminated in massive battles over Supreme Court nominations, was intended to change the whole context within which issues of social change were debated in a way that would endure long after the Reagan administration.

Change in civil rights enforcement policy not only affected the operation of institutions but also reduced the possibility that the courts would challenge the residential and educational segregation on which so much of the self-perpetuating inequality was based. The basic conservative policy was acceptance of the ghetto system as natural and denunciation of policies intended to challenge or end the color line—such as busing, dispersion of subsidized housing, and tough fair-housing enforcement—as unworkable and unfair to whites. During the Nixon, Ford, and Reagan presidencies, the basic policy of the federal government was to preserve the racial status quo in metropolitan areas.

As the federal government withdrew from civil rights enforcement, the policies of state governments became much more important. As the state of Georgia took over job training, the education block grant, and other programs, civil rights enforcement disappeared as a serious goal. No significant mechanisms for finding or correcting racial discrimination were implemented.

High School Inequality

There was both intense segregation of black students in the high schools of metropolitan Atlanta and a powerful and continuing relationship between race and income. These in turn were very strongly related to academic achievement and to dropout rates. In other words, minority schools were almost always low-income schools and were very likely to have low achievement scores and high dropout rates. White schools, on the other hand, were almost certain to have few low-income students and to do better on all measures of school success. This was true in spite of the strong and nationally publicized leadership of School Superintendent

Alonzo Crim, a black, Harvard-educated intellectual who considered no child "ineducable."

Metropolitan Atlanta high school students became more segregated in the 1970s and 1980s both by race and income. The data showed clear trends toward increased isolation of inner-city students from the black middle class as well as from whites generally. Although the suburban black schools were less isolated and far less poor than those in the city, a new crop of severely disadvantaged and low-achieving black schools emerged. By 1986 just over half of the region's black students were enrolled in schools outside of Atlanta. Even some of the middle-class, segregated suburban schools had low achievement scores.

Civil rights organizations had shared the dream of transforming the segregated and unequal schools of Atlanta into integrated schools offering black students access to better opportunities. The strongly conservative federal district judges in Atlanta, however, moved slowly and left segregation largely intact until 1971. By that time, the city schools were overwhelmingly black, and black leaders worked out a bargain to forego desegregation in exchange for black control of the local school district. Later, when a poorly financed American Civil Liberties Union lawsuit attempted to merge city and suburban school districts, it failed. The only Democratic president since the 1960s, Jimmy Carter, was governor at the time and a supporter of the compromise which ended the pursuit of integrated education in Atlanta. As president, the man he singled out to be his attorney general was Griffin Bell—the judge who approved the ruling.

A number of the most prominent neoconservative critics of school desegregation testified in federal court against a desegregation plan that would have bussed children across city-suburban lines, arguing that segregation was natural and that any attempt to change it would be counterproductive. Under black leadership, the Atlanta schools tried to implement much of the conservative agenda of self-reliance, intense focus on basic skills, and flunking students who did not meet minimum test scores. By the mid-1980s, the city schools had become virtually irrelevant to metropolitan Atlanta's whites, 98 percent of whom were in suburban schools, and the city schools were rapidly losing the remaining black middle-class students.

For years, reports of high achievement levels by Atlanta students helped make the compromise seem successful. According to the city school district's statistics, the district had performed the remarkable feat of bringing a school district composed largely of highly disadvantaged students above the national norms in just a few years. The city's school district also reported few students dropping out of school, gleaning favorable publicity for itself across the United States.

Much of this accomplishment was more apparent than real. Although the city schools did make progress with dropouts between the early 1970s and the early 1980s, both the test scores and the dropout data were presented to the public for years in an extremely misleading form. Even if Atlanta city schools could have been shown to be performing modestly better than inner-city schools elsewhere our study found city high schools inferior to suburban white schools in the metropolitan area by every measure, and the large majority of the city students were below national norms on achievement tests. In the upper grades, the gaps were extremely large after fifteen years of the neighborhood-school, basic-skills educational strategy favored by the Reagan administration. This did not mean that the strategy was a harmful one but only that the inequalities were deeply rooted in community conditions. There was no reason to believe that a bootstrap approach could work or even that it was in the power of the schools to provide genuinely equal opportunity in the context of profound and deepening racial inequalities.

The Atlanta area schools were among the most segregated in the nation at the start of the period under study, and they became more segregated even as extremely rapid black suburbanization took place. Suburbanization did not bring the same opportunities for blacks as it had for whites.

Georgia, like almost all other states, enacted a package of important educational reforms in the 1980s. The Georgia law, the Quality Basic Education Act (QBE), raised high school graduation requirements and imposed new test requirements that reflected conservative assumptions about what was necessary to motivate low-income students. The Atlanta Public Schools had earlier adopted punitive, test-oriented policies of retaining large numbers of students in grades for more than one year to try to coerce learning. Both sets of policies reflected the conservative assumptions dominant in the public policy of the period.

In the early 1980s, however, dropout rates began to rise again and the gap between suburban and city rates increased. The teacher test mandated by the law took teaching credentials from a substantial number of black teachers in Atlanta—although many returned to Atlanta classrooms as substitutes. A very large proportion of Atlanta students were not in the grade normally attended by children of their age because of the retention policies, a trend almost certain to produce further increases in dropout rates as they reach high school (Shepard and Smith 1989). The basic character of the reforms has been to punish victims of inequality without doing anything to change the structural forces in which inequality is rooted. The assumption is that progress can be achieved by threats.

The school reforms did lead to a better understanding of the problem. Publication of more accurate achievement data, required by the reform law, showed Atlanta's much-vaunted claims to be without foundation. In fact, Georgia pushed the test craze to an extreme, excluding a large number of children from first grade on the basis of standardized tests. But no substantial resources were targeted for inner-city schools and nothing was done to provide inner-city students with the opportunity to attend the region's more successful schools.

Liberal reforms, such as compensatory education, desegregation, and Head Start were often denounced as failures by conservatives because they did not end educational inequality in a few years. The best recent evidence, however, shows real long-term benefits from those reforms, particularly for young southern blacks (National Assessment of Educational Progress 1985; Koretz 1987). And our findings in both the high schools and colleges suggest that the conservative "reforms" made a bad situation worse in key respects.

College Access

There was an across-the-board slippage of access to college in the metropolitan area for young blacks, most dramatically for males and inner-city residents. Access rose for whites. Contrary to our expectations, the decline during the period studied was most drastic in historically black institutions that primarily served the local black community, particularly at Morris Brown College. The public higher education institutions declined in black enrollment faster than the private white institutions. Atlanta Junior College (now Atlanta Metropolitan College), the one low-cost, public two-year college available to inner-city students, experienced a sharp plunge in enrollment.

Young black men were less likely by the mid-1980s to be admitted to college and much less likely to make regular progress through college if they got in. Given the obvious importance of college training for employment, income, and access to the most desirable jobs and to leadership positions in society, the consequences will damage the men, their families, and the community. There has been no significant policy initiative to address this crisis, although private efforts at a few black colleges showed some progress in the late 1980s.

FINANCIAL AID AND REMEDIAL PROGRAMS

National research shows that tuition levels and financial aid have large effects on the black college-attendance rate. The failure of the federal government to adequately increase Pell grants for low-income students as the costs of college have risen and the strong tendency of colleges to rely more on tuition increases and less on public funds has meant a rapidly growing gap between college costs and available assistance for many students. Georgia has many low-income young people and has substantially raised its tuitions, more than doubling costs between 1982 and 1989 (*Atlanta Constitution*, 11 April 1989: 1). The lack of general support and research funding for colleges has also shifted a growing share of total college costs to the students.

This increasing gap between aid and costs, which has to be filled by income from jobs, family support, and student loans tends to work against black students in several ways. Black family wealth in the United States averages at a level less than one-eleventh the resources of white families, and few have large assets, such as equities in substantial homes, to draw against. This book shows a recent decline in black homeownership in metropolitan Atlanta and shows blacks living in homes of much lesser value. Many live in communities with few opportunities for good part-time and summer jobs. Many have divided families, which complicates the completion of paperwork and financial disclosure forms. Many black families have no reserves to draw on and the ability of their children to obtain higher education depends on public policy.

Another very important policy change is simple but basic. State government is now investing less in programs designed to let young blacks know that they really can go to college and to help them survive if they get in. The most important public university in the area, Georgia State University in downtown Atlanta, cut back its special admissions and strictly limited the duration of student remediation, no matter how needy a student might be or how much basic intelligence he might have. Such limitations tend to punish inner-city high school graduates for the bad educations they have been given.

Two key community- and parent-related differences between white and urban black students are information and encouragement. Whites are much more likely to be in the middle class and to grow up in families where information about colleges, saving for college, and preparation for college tests is discussed. In low-income neighborhoods with few adult college graduates, students must rely more on school and college personnel for information and they typically receive much less. Students and families need not only information but also active encouragement to try college, and they need technical help with financial aid, particularly now that financial aid is less able to cover soaring college costs.

When students get to college, those who have weak high school backgrounds, no support systems at home, and personal and financial problems need special counseling and support to avoid being knocked out of school. These programs have been reduced or eliminated in many cases.

THE IMPACT OF MILITARY RECRUITMENT

Military recruitment practices may contribute to the college-attendance rate of young black men. The armed forces' advertising campaigns persuade many eligible men that they will be able to learn a skill in the service and receive support to go to college later. This promise may be particularly enticing to young black men, who make up a disproportionate share of the enlistees, far more than their share of the high school graduate population. (More than nine-tenths of the recruits are high school graduates.) Black male high school graduates, who form the college-eligible population, are much more likely than similar white males to enlist in the military (Jaynes and Williams 1989, p. 71). The promise of scholarships after service is more enticing, particularly to those who do not know how much less probable it is to complete college in one's late twenties. Significantly, military recruiters are often very active in schools where college recruiters are not.

We need to understand how and why the choices of young black men diverge from those of young whites in the Atlanta metropolitan area. It is important that they be offered the full range of choices and information about the likely consequences of their decisions.

CIVIL RIGHTS ENFORCEMENT

The public colleges of the metropolitan Atlanta area were under a court order for fifteen years to increase their minority enrollment. The university system that runs all public colleges in Georgia negotiated a plan with the federal government with goals for progress at each institution. None of the institutions have achieved their goals and most have been running backward in recent years. Yet the federal Office for Civil Rights took no action to enforce the agreements or federal civil rights law under the

Reagan administration, and one of the early acts of the Bush administration was to free the university system from the obligation of meeting its goals.

The reform movement of the 1980s has also affected Georgia higher education. Standards for college entrance were raised. Georgia continues to employ a rising junior test that makes it impossible for a good many students to reach the upper division of their colleges. The negative effects of this test on black students were anticipated and the use of the test challenged by civil rights advocates; the federal government refused to act although it was a public policy that had the clearly foreseeable effect of making things worse for blacks in state universities in a state with a history of de jure segregation and obligations under the 1964 Civil Rights Act.

The state's teacher certification test (TCT) is having negative effects on teacher training programs in a number of black institutions in the state. The disproportionate number of blacks failing the test and the fact that graduates of predominantly black institutions' teacher training programs experienced serious problems discouraged blacks from considering teaching as a career and undermined the programs at those colleges. The effort to raise standards was not accompanied by either major new resources for the education schools or by strong pressure on the white schools to increase their black enrollments in teacher training. A number of key institutions, including the area's most important general purpose public institution, Georgia State University, raised standards in ways that reduced the number of black students enrolled.

Each of these policies was designed, of course, to address real problems and we have found no direct evidence of racial animus. Some teacher training institutions were inadequate, some remedial students were admitted without any real chance of success, and all college faculties want better-prepared students. It is a good thing to try to raise the standards of achievement in educational institutions, but doing this by raising barriers and ignoring the racial inequalities in the process only increases those inequalities. The net effect on minority access is strongly negative unless there are large new programs implemented to make sure that black students will be able to clear the rising barriers. Neither the state nor the federal government had policies requiring such programs.

Job Training Programs

In a metropolitan area with a high dropout rate and a very rapidly changing and expanding labor market in which most decent jobs demand at least a high school education, job training has obvious importance for those otherwise doomed to marginal employment. Each young person who falls through the large cracks in the educational system experiences a tremendous loss of potential income and ability to support a family unless he or she acquires basic skills and gets started on a job which offers some hope for mobility. Neighborhoods where most people lack skills and decent jobs face massive social and economic problems. Young blacks without diplomas, basic skills, or good work histories living far from areas where new jobs are being created face the worst problems. Within the city of Atlanta at least one-third of the young people face all of these burdens. If they are not reconnected with the normal economy, they will find a less socially acceptable way to survive.

Job training should offer another chance. Research shows that the greatest long-term benefits accrue when basic skills are provided to those who have none. This study found a drastic decline in government job training resources and almost no basic skills training for inner-city dropouts. Only about one-sixth of the trainees in the city program were dropouts; that is fewer than any other inner city studied by the Metropolitan Opportunity Project and below the national average. The program in the inner city concentrated its resources on training black women with high school degrees for traditional low-wage, dead-end, entry-level jobs, a substantial number of them as hotel maids. There was very little serious-long-term training and no effective linkage between the job training institutions and the public school systems. The division of the metropolitan area into separate job training areas, done at the instigation of Atlanta's mayor, served to separate the poor blacks needing training from the areas needing workers. There was no civil rights enforcement within the federal job training program.

Housing and the Changing Color Line

Location is a key element of opportunity in contemporary metropolitan Atlanta, and the supply of housing grew very rapidly from the mid-1970s to the mid-1980s, permitting the black community to expand far beyond its previous boundaries. But the pattern of segregation has also expanded far into the suburbs. The black middle class, a generation after its white counterpart, has largely left the city, but in a different direction. It has been moving south while the white middle class, the money, and the booming job markets have been concentrated along the northern perimeter highway and beyond.

After a period of expanded opportunities for homeownership in the

1970s, spurred in part by white flight from the city, blacks faced shrinking opportunities in the 1980s. And this was not primarily because of income differences. Even compared with whites with the same income and family situation, the opportunity of black households to own their own homes was declining. *The Atlanta Journal and Constitution* won the Pulitzer Prize in 1989 for its investigation proving that mortgage lenders made very little capital available in black neighborhoods.

For blacks concentrated in the rental market, things got even worse. The boom in the economy drove up the competition for housing and the housing cost burden of those whose incomes had not kept pace. Blacks with incomes above the poverty level were paying more for housing of worse quality than that occupied by poor whites and were doing so in neighborhoods served by less effective public schools and which offered fewer job opportunities. Renters do not accumulate housing wealth and have very little opportunity to live in the communities served by the most competitive schools because of suburban land use policies excluding affordable rental housing.

Renters below the poverty line faced the most drastic problems. Those unable to obtain subsidized housing—and there was no significant new construction of subsidized family housing in the rapidly growing Atlanta area—faced impossible cost burdens that may worsen as competition for the limited supply of low-cost rental housing intensifies. The maximum AFDC payment for a female-headed family with two children in Georgia in 1985 was $208 a month, hardly enough to subsist in a booming metropolis (U.S. House Ways & Means Committee 1989, 546). Families below the poverty level were forced to spend more than two-thirds of their cash incomes for housing costs by the early 1980s. Such families had no housing choices and no ability to meet those costs and provide other basic essentials for their children.

Those who were able to reduce their financial problems by finding subsidized housing found it concentrated in areas without connections to the mainstream society. A black mother moving into one of Atlanta's major housing projects cut her housing costs, but only at the price of raising her children in intense isolation from middle-class life in neighborhoods served by some of the area's worst schools.

Isolation, Crime, and Fear

Low-income blacks were not only confined to neighborhoods with inadequate schools and jobs, but they often became virtual prisoners in their homes because of the risk of crime. A 1981 survey showed deep fears. For example, 53 percent of low-income blacks said that they would be "afraid to walk within a mile of home at night" (*Atlanta Constitution* staff 1981, "Black and Poor," 17).

FBI reports showed that the city had the nation's highest rate of violent crime in 1988—up 23 percent in a single year. Atlanta's rate was twice that of Washington, D.C., and much higher than Chicago or New York's (*New York Times*, 27 April 1989). Atlanta led the country on this measure again in 1989, well ahead of Miami, which was in second place. Violent crime increased 13 percent that year (*Atlanta Journal*, 9 April 1990). While disputing the statistics, Mayor Maynard Jackson's office pointed out that crime prevention had been his leading campaign issue and the "central issue" of his first months in office. The Mayor was supporting a staff increase of nearly one-third in the police force (ibid.). Just between 1988 and 1989, drug prosecutions increased 150 percent in Fulton County (*Atlanta Journal and Constitution*, 17 January, 15 March, and 26 March 1990).

Things were worst where the poor were most concentrated and isolated. Residents in Atlanta Housing Authority projects called on the governor to declare a "state of emergency" and send in the national guard to act. There had been more than fifty people killed in drug-related violence in the projects in a year. There were massive police sweeps in early 1990, but the additional effort was only temporary (*Atlanta Journal and Constitution*, 17 January 1990).

The problem was not likely to yield to laws requiring longer imprisonment. The state's prison population soared by 58 percent from 1978 to 1988 under the impetus of conservative law and order policies. By the end of the decade, the state was involved in a $150 million prison construction program, was holding 4,000 state prisoners in inadequate county jails, was planning to release thousands of prisoners early, and was seeking more alternative solutions. State Department of Corrections Commissioner David Evans observed: "We're never going to build our way out of the problem" (*Atlanta Constitution*, 23 April 1989). The state had been following a policy of putting large numbers of young people, including a very high fraction of young black men, in prison, but crime continued to soar. One problem was that most prisoners and all juveniles serve their term and are released after a few years, but there were no major programs to get the growing numbers of ex-offenders to work and back into the society. The state's overflowing prisons were turning convicts free before completion of their sentences to avoid building still more facilities. By early 1990, however, about one-sixth of those released the previous year had already been caught and sent back for new offenses (*Atlanta Journal and Constitution*, 3 April 1990).

The Atlanta experience strongly suggests that the conservative theory of deterrence through rigid mandatory sentencing without rehabilitation was not working. Hundreds of millions of dollars were committed to this theory in Georgia and most other states in the 1970s and 1980s. There was no serious evaluation by state government of its efficacy and the responsible officials now have little confidence in the basic assumptions. Strict and punitive imprisonment without policies for rehabilitation, reemployment, and strong parole supervision constantly pump back into the most depressed parts of the urban economy and society large numbers of people with advanced training in crime, networks of criminal connections, and virtually no marketable talents or possible employment in the private economy that would enable them to support themselves and their children.

Recognizing the Racial Dimensions of Urban Problems

There is a self-perpetuating and deepening cycle of inequality that maintains segregated and fundamentally different societies within metropolitan Atlanta for blacks and whites. Even under economic conditions so favorable that most American cities have no real hope of equalling them, many young blacks were shut out. Assumptions that a prosperous free market and a less coercive government would close the gap have not been fulfilled. Nor have suggestions that a planned economy with low overall unemployment would solve black problems.

The Atlanta experience shows that it is essential to confront the issue of racial discrimination directly, as the color line remained an extremely powerful force in distributing opportunity and destroying aspirations. Young blacks did not have equal preparation or opportunity at any stage of life.

Beginning Again

It is much easier to describe problems than to prescribe changes. There is no way of being certain about the impact of a new policy. There is often a kind of bias in policy discussions that limits possibilities to what has already been tried. If a tentative, short-lived version of a social reform failed to produce results, we may assume that the approach was worth-less, rather than that it must be tried in a more intensive way for a longer time. Neither proposition, of course, is necessarily true. Atlanta has seen no serious efforts to attack the urban color line; leaders of both races as well as federal and state authorities have tacitly accepted racial separation on an ever expanding scale on the assumption that fairness could be achieved, somehow, in the absence of integration. They assumed that separate could be equal in contemporary metropolitan America, even though there is no evidence that this has ever been true in any American city.

Nationally, the late 1960s through the early 1970s was a period of ex-periments with job training, but the results may be unduly pessimistic because it was a period of declining economic growth with an expanding work force swelled by the simultaneous impact of the postwar baby boom generation coming of age and the flood of women into the workforce. A series of recessions in the 1970s and the worst recession in fifty years in 1981–82 all meant that market conditions were very poor for the absorp-tion of the most marginal sector of the labor market: young, poorly edu-cated blacks and Hispanics living in areas a long way from the outer sub-urbs where most of the new jobs were being created. Educational and training programs are least effective when labor market conditions are difficult.

Conditions will be more favorable in the 1990s when a drastically smaller cohort of young people entering the labor force will create highly favorable circumstances and a very tight market for entry-level workers if the economy is relatively healthy. Under these radically different cir-cumstances, the economic value of training for the most disadvantaged workers would be higher.

What Must Be Done?
REVIVING CIVIL RIGHTS

Restoration of civil rights enforcement is a fundamental goal for all pro-grams. Reversing deep and worsening racial inequalities requires inves-tigation of discrimination and a vigorous response where it is found.

Federal civil rights enforcement has been rendered meaningless in the 1980s. Civil rights agencies overseeing housing, schools, colleges, job training, and employment agencies should require those receiving fed-eral funds to develop and implement plans to assure equal access for minorities and to let underrepresented groups know about opportunities.

They should aggressively monitor and punish any clear discrimination by individuals or institutions. The state of Georgia has no significant civil rights enforcement and the city of Atlanta has no capacity to reach the large issues of state policy or the discrimination that occurs in the suburbs, where most of the opportunities are located.

The first imperative is the appointment of federal civil rights officials and judges who are familiar with civil rights laws (especially the 1988 fair housing law), who support their enforcement, and who are receptive to evidence of discrimination. Staffs decimated by Reagan-era cuts and demoralized by ideological purges need to be rebuilt.

Federal agencies providing dollars to public schools, colleges, and job training institutions must be redirected and rigorously monitored to insure that minorities are not excluded. Federal agencies should fully enforce outstanding court orders, compliance agreements, and consent decrees to which the government is a party. The 1988 action by the Justice Department advocating dissolution of existing school desegregation orders in various parts of Georgia and the 1989 decision by the Education Department to ignore the failure of the state's higher education desegregation plans were shocking examples of negative federal leadership.

Federal leadership will not, of course, be decisive. Atlanta needs strong private advocacy organizations, with research capability, to work on a metropolitan scale on such serious issues as housing segregation and lack of access to suburban jobs.

More positive approaches are also critical. Under the Nixon administration Congress enacted the Emergency School Aid Act, which provided federal aid to school districts undergoing desegregation and helped in achieving the necessary educational changes and improved race relations. This program was repealed in the first Reagan budget. Under Presidents Ford and Carter, local governments were required to prepare Housing Opportunity Plans that set out methods for helping lower-income families move into their communities as a condition for receiving federal community development aid. That requirement was also ended. Since 1964 there have been federal grants to support preparation, recruitment, and retention of minority college students, but they have served only a very small fraction of those potentially eligible. All of those efforts need to be revived. Institutions should be recognized and rewarded for progress toward equal opportunity and full integration.

Litigation could also become a more effective agent for change, despite the ideological shift in the federal judiciary under Reagan, if advocates of black rights have adequate financing and appropriate targets are sought. The DeKalb County school desegregation order in 1989 shows the continuing possibilities of raising unpopular issues through the judicial forum even in a highly conservative era. In a number of other cities, the inner-city school board has joined with civil rights organizations to sue its state government to obtain resources needed to repair some of the damage caused by separate and unequal schools. The state of Arkansas settled such a case with Little Rock in early 1989. When challenges to even limited gains arise, such as the lawsuit against minority set-aside contracts in early 1989, civil rights policies need skilled and powerful defense. There has been no coordinated program of civil rights litigation in the Atlanta area at any point during the past several decades. As the metropolitan scale of the racial inequalities becomes apparent, this is badly needed.

A METROPOLITAN APPROACH

Young blacks in a metropolitan area where economic conditions are among the best in America face a growing racial gap in all the institutions studied. Young black males are especially at risk in education and job training. If these problems are to be addressed, there must be policies that explicitly recognize the racial dimension of the problem, that affect many different institutions in the public and private sectors, and that are carried out on a metropolitan scale.

During the last generation metropolitan Atlanta has been through a massive economic transformation in which the suburbs have clearly become dominant. Racial issues, however, have received very little attention, even in the inner city. The city's black political leadership has acquiesced in the preservation of segregation in the public schools, the largest major urban race issue that has been brought into the federal courts in Atlanta. There has been no significant initiative of any sort to desegregate housing in the rapidly growing suburbs or to increase blacks' access to a reasonable share of the newly created jobs.

Racial equality has not happened spontaneously and does not appear when blacks take over inner-city institutions. It needs to be monitored and planned for, like any other basic urban goal such as transportation or pollution control. It is wrong to think that middle-class blacks who rise in politics or in governmental and educational bureaucracies in the city will necessarily take care of the interests of poor blacks. While they tend to be sympathetic, some are under pressure to keep poor blacks concentrated in certain areas; some have even tried to make political hay out of conservative notions. Under black control, the Atlanta school system accepted segregation and, through the use of highly misleading test results, reported that the segregated system was working.

Atlanta is rapidly evolving into an inner city with similarities to Washington, D.C., a community with black leadership but peopled by poor blacks and affluent whites, each participating in an economy requiring highly trained workers. In the suburbs, where more black children and all but a tiny fraction of young whites are growing up, segregation is spreading rapidly. The largest school system in the metropolitan area, DeKalb County's, is now majority black and experiencing rapid racial transition. There has been no planning for the integration of schools or housing, and civil rights groups pressing for change in the courts have been stymied by lack of funds.

Public agencies, including the Atlanta Regional Commission, regional educational organizations, transit agencies, and the state job training office need to systematically monitor and report on services to and achievements of blacks and whites in the metropolitan areas and to devise plans for opening up opportunities across racial lines. Private efforts are needed as well—by research centers at universities, by civil rights organizations, and by business leadership—to prepare specific agendas for greater opportunity in each sector of life in the region. If public agencies continue to ignore the issues, private philanthropy should finance investigations and civil rights litigation as this may be the only way to force some of the vital issues of black rights to the point of decision.

POVERTY AND INCOME INEQUALITY

At the root of many of the racial inequalities in metropolitan Atlanta are tremendous differences between black and white families in income and wealth. These differences reflect the present-day consequences of discrimination, exclusion, and unequal education in the past. The 1986 data for the entire country show that black families' median income was only 57 percent of the white level, down from a high of 62 percent in 1975. And 31 percent of all blacks in the United States lived in poverty, three times the white level (*Focus*, October 1987: 4, 8). The Annual Housing Survey data on incomes in metropolitan Atlanta between the mid-1970s and early 1980s shows that the racial gap in income increased in metro Atlanta and that black families had an average income only 54 percent of the white level. The gap between city and suburban incomes was becoming wider.

The racial income gap is a basic reason why there is such strong concern about inequalities in education and training programs intended to make opportunity more equal. We need policies to make these programs more equal and to break through the color line separating black and white communities.

Poverty works together with the housing market and with the operation of various major institutions so that those who have the least get the worst housing in the most dangerous neighborhoods and have to move often because they cannot keep up with rent and utility payments. With the worst housing come the worst schools and the most devastating social climate for children to grow up in: high schools where few students are expected to do serious post-high-school work and many are expected to be involved in crime or teen pregnancy. The poorest ghettos are virtually untouched by the metropolitan job boom. Every teenager knows of dedicated, religious, hard-working people who endure long bus rides to be maids in other people's homes and who work full time for poverty-level wages with no benefits or retirement plans; of adults with high school degrees working at minimum-wage, dead-end, fast-food jobs who make less in a week than a street hustler can make in a few hours. There are few intact families; almost everyone who has real prospects for their children has left.

Even those middle-class blacks who come into poor ghetto communities every day as teachers, policemen, and welfare workers may have intensely negative attitudes toward inner-city people. Seldom, for example, does a black teacher entrust her own children to an inner-city school.

The conservative movement of the 1980s ushered in a set of tax cuts for the middle and upper classes and benefits cuts for the poor that made an already skewed income distribution substantially more unequal and then discouraged any serious political debate over those policies. Tax policies increased the share of income going to the wealthiest two-tenths of the population between 1977 and the late 1980s (*Washington Post Weekly Edition*, 23 November 1987; U.S. Congressional Budget Office 1988, 28–38). These growing inequalities, very apparent in metropolitan Atlanta, have obvious racial implications. To believe that the educational and training institutions can create more equal opportunity while we implement policies transferring more income from the poor to the rich is absurd. This trend must be reversed.

There were other policies designed to make the poor poorer. The failure to raise the minimum wage from 1981 to 1989 meant a sharp drop in real income for millions of people working at or just above that frozen level. The real value of AFDC payments fell by more than one-third nationally between 1970 and 1989. The monthly AFDC payment in 1989 for a family of three in Georgia was $270 a month (U.S. House Ways & Means Committee 1989, 546–47). The severe reductions of medical care and food stamp eligibility for the working poor, the radical cuts in housing subsidies, and the rent increases for subsidized tenants all made a precarious situation significantly worse (Palmer and Sawhill 1984). As more poor children grow up without basic health care, without secure housing, and without money for decent clothes or school supplies, there are obvious impacts on family hopes and on success in schooling. So long as the black jobless rate is twice the rate for whites, and far higher for young blacks, it introduces an enormous, pervasive bias into the operation of all institutions.

Blacks in metropolitan Atlanta would benefit from a wide range of policies designed to alleviate poverty or improve the life choices of poor people. Vital services—including health coverage, day care, and college scholarships—would help the working poor, who have been hurt severely by the anti-poor as well as the anti-black policy changes of the 1980s. Civil rights enforcement is not enough. Any attempt to make a real difference in the inner city would have to include resources for the provision of affordable housing, transportation to job sites and special schools, upgrading of school offerings, substantial support for higher education, and a very different kind of job training.

EDUCATION AND JOB TRAINING

Undoing the deeply rooted inequities woven into many aspects of life and many institutions will require strong and persistent efforts on many fronts. Even if all discrimination were eliminated, the inequalities would be self-perpetuating. If a notice were sent around one of Atlanta's housing projects, for example, that any resident could have free tuition at Georgia Tech, a few miles away, the impact the following fall would probably be negligible because the students living there would not have received the necessary math and science backgrounds in their schools. It is very important to think about the key policies that might begin to produce a change.

COLLEGE ACCESS

Although this book shows extremely discouraging patterns of downward mobility for Atlanta area black students during the 1980s, it also contains clear evidence of the impact of earlier very positive trends. There were extraordinary advances in black access to college from the mid-1960s to the high point in the mid-1970s. Since that time the proportion of blacks in the college-age population has increased greatly, a higher fraction are graduating from high school, and black scores on college entrance exams have improved considerably. If the colleges had not changed their admissions, testing, and financial aid policies, minority access would be increasing rather than shrinking. There seems to be a relatively simple first step toward a solution—reinstating policies and programs that gave poor blacks a chance.

Some of these changes are going to be costly, primarily for financial aid and remediation. Black access was at its peak when federal and state aid were best able to cover the cost of going to college. As Georgia college costs have soared, aid has fallen far behind. Rationing education by price in an area where white family income is almost twice as high as it is for black families means rationing education by race.

The university system and individual campuses have also changed their policies, particularly through entrance requirements and the required test for the upper division, in ways that have reduced black access. State systems of higher education must not be operated on the preposterous assumption that the state has provided a fair system of secondary education.

Each campus needs a plan and the university system needs statewide goals and monitoring. If it was possible to make progress earlier in spite of a much smaller pool of college-ready black students, it can be done again. The federal government should require the submission of multi-year plans to move each college toward better representation of the overall college-eligible population. Lacking federal action, there should be serious consideration of a private suit by civil rights groups against the state university system. So long as a college meets its negotiated goals it should be left with minimal reporting requirements. Colleges are much more comfortable designing methods which suit their own communities than they are facing detailed external decisions. When a college falls seriously behind, it should make changes or face a full-scale compliance review by federal civil rights officials. Federal funds should be cut when reviews show failure to meet commitments.

It is most important to make sure that more of the black high school graduates are ready for college and seriously consider their options for attending college. To be ready, they must be told honestly throughout school what is needed to go to college, be offered real college-prep courses taught at competitive levels, and have strong counseling. In inner-city high schools where there are so few college-bound students that serious precollegiate training cannot be offered, students intending to go to college should be advised to transfer.

Atlanta students now have only limited opportunities to transfer to more demanding magnet schools. These choices should be expanded and there should be a serious effort to obtain access to available spaces in suburban high schools. Lawsuits by the St. Louis, Little Rock, Milwaukee, and Indianapolis school boards have won such access for substantial numbers of black inner-city students to suburban high schools, with the state government paying the bills. The Atlanta school board should consider this option.

Colleges should inform high schools and parents when their students have not been adequately trained. The state government should reconsider its teacher test requirement, which is shrinking the pool of minority teachers in a state with a very large number of black students. The colleges with the best teacher training programs should be required to establish firm goals for increasing the enrollment and graduation of black teachers, counselors, and administrators to offset the loss of certified black professionals elsewhere.

Colleges could also help expand the pool of blacks fully ready for college through early identification of students with college potential in disadvantaged schools and communities. This has been done successfully on a small scale for twenty-five years under the Upward Bound program, which has demonstrated that students with college potential exist in every inner-city community. Students identified in the late elementary or early high school grades should be provided with special summer and weekend instruction in basic pre-collegiate skills. Many campuses across the United States have successfully run small programs of this sort for years.

Special efforts need to be made to reach young black men, to persuade them that serious dedication to study is an important and legitimate thing, and to show them that it has a high payoff. Many young men in the ghetto have no father at home and are strongly influenced by a peer group which ridicules studying and where the norm is dropping out of school and anti-social behavior. Young men in this setting need targeted efforts to legitimize study and to put them in contact with successful adults. In areas such as Atlanta with predominantly black colleges and powerful black leadership, there are many resources to draw on. The

Atlanta organization, One Hundred Black Men, provides one model of positive community involvement. The last wave of reform in college access, in the late 1960s and early 1970s, was much more successful in increasing admissions than in getting black students through college. Our research shows that retention remains a very severe problem in metropolitan Atlanta. Resources for pre-college remedial work, counseling, peer tutoring, emergency loans, and other forms of assistance to help students survive the transition to a much more demanding environment—more readily available on private black campuses than on public ones—are critical.

JOB TRAINING PROGRAMS

The existing federally funded job training programs in metropolitan Atlanta have spent most of their money on superficial training of high school graduates who are not severely disadvantaged and who would probably find work anyway. The most fundamental need is to change the system's focus from one of producing good statistics on high placements at low costs to one of helping those least able to find work to obtain the basic skills and experience that will qualify them for a job. Atlanta area training programs need more effective outreach and support services. They need to build stronger ties with the public schools for dropout prevention and for more effectively linking school performance to summer jobs and eventual full-time employment. The summer job program needs a much stronger educational component.

New performance standards should be developed by state and local officials to address the most severe barriers to employment, including dropouts, people with very low test scores, and ex-offenders. There should be modest living stipends, contingent on regular attendance and progress in training, for young workers who cannot otherwise afford to learn basic skills.

Data should be regularly collected and published on types of training by race and sex. Statistics indicating unequal treatment should be investigated by civil rights officials.

And in order for these programs to be effective, training should be targeted to jobs that provide a reasonable entry-level wage and an opportunity for moving up to a solid income. If these jobs are being created mostly in the suburbs, state, city, and suburban officials should work with job discrimination agencies for the placement of inner-city black workers rather than recruiting whites from other regions.

No employer should be permitted to leave behind a heavily minority work force in an inner city, to move with governmental subsidies to an outer suburban all-white area, and to then use the lack of local black residents as a defense against affirmative action requirements.

It was probably a mistake for the city of Atlanta to insist on separate job training agencies rather than one covering the metropolitan labor market. Business leaders recommended a unified approach in the beginning. In this instance, what would have best served their long-term needs would probably have been best as well for low-income, jobless minority youths. There should be a merged agency or, at least, very active sharing of job training slots and job listings. The well-known difficulties of any inter-agency coordination argue strongly for a single agency with an aggressive policy of connecting workers in need with suburban employers with unfilled jobs. The state government should work to facilitate this effort.

The fundamental mismatch between burgeoning suburban jobs and concentrated inner-city poverty is a root problem for poor blacks in the city. In the future, it may well become a basic problem for businesses in the outlying locations where entry-level workers may soon become scarce. Transportation and affordable suburban housing are long-term ways to obtain suburban jobs. Suburban officials and corporations should be asked to locate large concentrations of jobs where they can be linked through mass transit to the inner city. Even the best education and training systems cannot prepare workers for jobs that are physically inaccessible.

There should also be summer jobs funded by the JTPA summer youth program with strong educational components for low-income city students making satisfactory progress in school. For students with severe basic skills problems who are unable to function in a normal high school, there should be an expanded Job Corps or the establishment of a new program like the American Conservation Corps passed by Congress but vetoed by the President in 1985. Some young people need a radical change in environment and a highly structured program to turn their lives around. Job Corps has the best track record of any federal job training program. When even the most vigorous placement efforts cannot obtain work for a trainee, the government should become the employer of last resort under a carefully targeted and limited public employment program.

PUBLIC JOBS

One solution to the problems of poverty and unemployment that was not even seriously discussed in the 1980s in Atlanta was the one most favored by local blacks. When asked what was the key to helping the poor, middle-class metro Atlanta whites favored education by a large margin. Both low-income and higher-income blacks, however, gave highest priority to government jobs, as did low-income whites. Low-income blacks favored government jobs or jobs in private business over education by a three-to-one margin. Obviously, they felt that jobs were essential to changing their status, and they were not confident that either education or the private market were able to solve their problems (*Atlanta Constitution* staff 1981, "Black and Poor," 28).

The white belief that education would solve the problem of black joblessness was belied by the fact that black unemployment grew as black high school completion rates increased. Throughout the 1980s job training programs were run as if there were adequate numbers of jobs available in all parts of the area; that assumption may need reconsideration in light of the employment and placement data in this book.

HIGH SCHOOLS

The data in this study show profound and persisting differences in schooling by race and income, especially with regard to dropouts. Almost two-fifths of city students are lost before graduation and the recent trend is upward. There may well be a link between policy decisions raising standards for high school completion and the recent rise in dropouts. There is abundant research showing that Atlanta's policy of flunking many students and retaining them in grade for a second or third year is powerfully linked to higher dropout rates.

There should be a full-scale evaluation of the impact of reforms in the Atlanta Public Schools and in the Quality Basic Education Act (QBE) on the dropout rate. If the policies have increased the dropout rate and not significantly increased achievement, they should be reversed.

There must be a large-scale commitment to "at-risk" high schools, focusing on school-work coordination, college preparation and counseling, and instruction evaluation, as well as dropout prevention.

High schools should make very strong efforts to retain young minority men and to break the social pressures leading to dropouts. There should be a similarly urgent effort to prevent women who become pregnant as teenagers from simply checking out. Schools should be evaluated and rewarded for accomplishments in these fields as they are now for achievement scores.

Another very important way to diminish the effects of inner-city isolation is to develop policies explicitly intended to give low-income children experiences in middle-class settings. This is, of course, a principal goal of school desegregation and one of the most important consequences of housing desegregation, particularly of policies that permit low-income families to live in middle-class areas.

If there were not the very close association between race and poverty and unequal education documented for metropolitan Atlanta, there would be far less reason to be concerned about the consequences of segregation. If blacks and whites had similar incomes and family educational backgrounds, there would be no reason to expect sharply unequal schools or any serious concerted campaign to transfer from one kind of school to another. In fact, however, educational and residential segregation by race, superimposed on a system of fundamental economic inequality by race, means that when students are not only kept separate in schools but that the schools are not connected to opportunities in the mainstream society, basic change is needed.

Racial desegregation, particularly on a city-suburban basis, could put significant numbers of low-income young people in predominantly middle-class schools. Low-income black children who cross the color line usually also cross the class line and find themselves growing up in a setting with many more middle-class fellow students than those that remain in the all-black schools.

School desegregation is the only available way to break out of the self-perpetuating cycle of racial isolation on a significant scale in the foreseeable future. It has many limits, of course, including the fact that the child returns from the middle-class school to the poor family and neighborhood each night and spends most of his time in an environment that conflicts with rather than reinforces the school.

Large-scale housing desegregation would have an even greater effect, but is much more difficult to achieve. There is, however, significant evidence to show that desegregation in predominantly middle-class settings from the beginning of schooling can have an effect on academic achievement, on college attendance and success, on employment, and on adult functioning in an interracial setting. These are very important effects and the extreme segregation of black children in metropolitan Atlanta denies them this opportunity.

Atlanta city officials should seek ways to open up opportunities for education across racial and class lines. Within the suburbs where the racial future is still very much in the balance, black and white leaders within each suburban district and in the metropolitan Atlanta region as a whole need to make it a priority to work for stable school desegregation.

Housing is an absolutely central issue because nothing else so strongly determines the family's situation in the overall community. Without being able to afford housing where the family can stay securely, there is no basic stability in a family's life and no consistent lasting relationship with institutions, friends, and community. Housing determines access to schooling, safety, friends for the children, and the ability to get to work in a reasonable time. Without stable housing, for example, schooling may be constantly disrupted in a way that makes it almost impossible for the child or the school to succeed.

Until incomes rise greatly in metropolitan Atlanta, there will be an enormous unfilled need for subsidized housing. This has always been a federal function in terms of financing and regulating the operation of the housing and a local function in terms of selecting sites (with federal approval), renting to tenants, and maintaining the units. Atlanta's massive and turbulent urbanization is occurring in a period when the major resources for creating new subsidized housing for families have been eliminated and civil rights regulation of scattered-site housing has disappeared. Low-income families in metropolitan Atlanta, a very disproportionate number of whom are black, badly need subsidized housing near the job centers. If it is to be accessible to blacks, that construction must be accompanied by strict civil rights regulation on the location and tenant selection policies.

Almost twenty years after the passage of the federal fair housing law it is apparent that the law has had a major effect on the social structure of the Atlanta metropolitan area and on the economic stratification and suburbanization within the black community, but almost no impact on the overall severity of racial segregation in the metropolitan area. Under fair housing, the black middle class has found it much easier to expand outward and the boundaries of the black residential areas have expanded very rapidly, well into parts of suburbia. Nothing has been done, however, to produce significant lasting residential integration, and there is almost no organized effort for housing integration.

Research elsewhere has shown that stable integration is far more possible than it was in the past and that it has strong benefits in terms of jobs, education, and investment, but that it rarely occurs by accident. Between 1963 and 1990, for example, the percent of whites who said that they would move out if a black family moved in next door fell from 45 percent to 5 percent. (Gallup Poll in *Minneapolis Star-Tribune*, 13 June 1990, 18a). There are so many powerful forces in the housing market and in peoples' expectations that ghetto expansion is the overwhelmingly likely outcome in the absence of skillful and concerted efforts to maintain integration. A vital part of the strategy for equal opportunity in Atlanta should be integrated housing.

LEADERSHIP

Reversing the backward trends of the 1980s will require, at the outset, clear recognition that racial problems have been getting worse, that this threatens the entire community, and that institutions must reach the people who have been excluded. There must be leaders willing to raise large, uncomfortable issues about the need for basic racial change in the metropolitan area. Things are not working out well, and opportunities for young blacks are shrinking in ways that suggest that hard questions have to be faced. Even on less controversial issues, the preparation of at-risk youths for post-secondary schooling and jobs requires special efforts by many people if cycles are to be broken. Leaders must help them understand why and reward successful performance.

The shared sense that the nation as a whole faced a fundamental legal, social, and moral crisis played a vital part in the movement of the last generation toward equal opportunity. That sense has been lost in the 1980s. The clear evidence is that the door to opportunity has been closing for young blacks in metropolitan America and that commitments must be revived and new policies forged to reopen that door. The problems are deep and will require a new vision of a city without rigid color barriers and with many institutions working to make opportunity a reality rather than a tarnished slogan for black Atlantans.

References

Abbott, Carl. 1981. *The new urban America: Growth and politics in Sunbelt cities.* Chapel Hill: University of North Carolina Press.

Abney, Glenn F., and John D. Hutcheson, Jr. 1981. Race, representation, and trust: Changes in attitude after the election of a black mayor. *Public Opinion Quarterly* 45, no. 91: 91–101.

American Council on Education, Office of Minority Concerns. 1986. *Minorities in higher education.* Fifth Annual Status Report. Washington: American Council on Education.

———. 1987. Sixth Annual Status Report. Washington: American Council on Education.

———. 1988. Seventh Annual Status Report. Washington: American Council on Education.

———. 1989. Eighth Annual Status Report. Washington: American Council on Education.

Atlanta Constitution staff. 1981. Black and poor in Atlanta. Reprint of articles appearing 18–27 October.

Atlanta Department of Community Development. 1986. *Housing conditions and affordability for the city of Atlanta and its neighborhoods.* March.

Atlanta Junior College. 1980. Student Development Services Annual Report (1979–80). Office of Student Services, August.

———. 1985. Student development services annual report (1984–85). Office of Student Services, October.

———. 1987. Institutional retention study (1986–87). Office of Student Services, 26 April.

Atlanta Private Industry Council. Spring 1989. *PIC Perspective.*

Atlanta Public Schools. 1981. Statistical Report: School Year 1980–81.

———. 1985. Statistical Report: School Year 1984–85.

———. 1986. *Achievement testing.* Program of the Atlanta Public Schools. Rept. 4, vol. 21, February 1987.

———. 1988. Application for Dropout Demonstration Project, 25 April.

———. 1988. Report no. 5, vol. 22, 9 November.

Atlanta Regional Comission. 1983. *County and city data book.*

————. 1986a. *Age, race, sex.* Update '85.

————. 1986b. *Employment.* Update '85.

————. 1986c. *Household income.* Update '85.

————. 1987. *1986 population and housing estimates for the Atlanta region.*

Bane, Mary Jo, and Paul Jargowsky. 1988. Urban poverty areas: Basic questions concerning prevalence, growth, and dynamics. Prepared for Committee on National Urban Policy, National Academy of Sciences, Washington, D.C., February.

Berry, Brian J. L. 1985. Islands of renewal in seas of decay. In *The new urban reality,* edited by Paul E. Peterson, 69–96. Washington: Brookings Institution.

Birnbaum, H., and R. Weston. 1974. Homeownership and wealth: Position of black and white Americans. *Review of Income and Wealth* 20: 103–18.

Bluestone, Barry, William Murphy, and Mary Stevenson. 1973. *Low wages and the working poor: Policy papers.* Policy Papers in Human Resources and Industrial Relations. Ann Arbor: Institute of Labor and Industrial Relations.

Boston, Thomas Daniel. 1988. *Race, class, and conservatism.* Winchester: MA: Unwin Hyman.

Braddock, Jomills, II. 1987. The impact of segregated school experiences on college and major field choices of black high school graduates. Paper prepared for the National Conference on School Desegregation Research, Chicago.

Bronstein, Scott. 1989. City-funded apartment study finds racial bias. *The Atlanta Journal and Constitution,* 14 May 1989, p. 1A.

Bross, Nancy. 1987a. Interview with Georgia Job Training Partnership staff, 19 June.

————. 1987b. Letter to Gary Orfield, 23 June.

Camburn, Eric M. 1990. College completion among students from high schools located in large metropolitan areas. *American Journal of Education* 98 (August): 551–69.

Chicago Panel on Public School Finances. 1985. Dropouts from the Chicago public schools: An analysis of the classes of 1982–1983–1984. Chicago: Chicago Panel on Public School Finances.

Chicago Urban League. 1990. *The geography of opportunity: A report on the status of African Americans in the Chicago area economy.* Chicago: Chicago Urban League, March.

Chubb, John E., and Terry M. Moe. 1990. *Politics, markets, and America's schools.* Washington: Brookings Institution.

Citizens Commission on Civil Rights. 1989. *One nation indivisible: The civil rights challenge for the 1990s.* Washington: Citizens Commission on Civil Rights.

Clendinen, Dudley. 1986. Urban education that really works. *New York Times,* Education section, 13 April: 68–71.

Cooperative Agreement. 1984. Cooperative Agreement signed by metropolitan Atlanta JTPA Service Delivery Areas on 1 July.

Crain, Robert L. 1986. The long-term effects of desegregation: Results from a true experiment. Paper prepared for the National Conference on School Desegregation Research, Chicago (September).

————, and Carol Sachs Weisman. 1972. *Discrimination, personality and achievement: A survey of Northern blacks.* New York: Seminar Press.

Crim, Alonzo. 1983. *Community of believers.* Atlanta: Altanta Public Schools (March).

————. 1988. A community of believers creates a community of achievers. *Educational Record* (Fall 1987–Winter 1988): 44–49.

Crouse, James, and Dale Trusheim. 1988. *The case against the SAT.* Chicago: University of Chicago Press.

Daniels, LeGree, Assistant Secretary of Education. 1988. Letter to Georgia Governor Joe Frank Harris, 9 February and 30 August.

Dardin, Joe. 1987. Choosing neighbors and neighborhoods: The role of race in housing preference. In *Divided Neighbors,* edited by Gary Tobin, 15–42. Newbury Park, CA: Sage Publications.

DBS Corporation. 1982. *Comparison of exposure rates and desegregation indices: Years 1970 and 1980.* Washington, D.C.: Report submitted to the Department of Education, Office for Civil Rights (August).

————. 1987. *1986 elementary and secondary school Civil Rights survey, national summaries.* Report to Office for Civil Rights, U.S. Dept. of Education (December).

————. n.d. *1986 elementary and secondary school Civil Rights survey: National and state summary of projected data.* Computer printouts.

Dealy, William A. Jr. 1987. *Atlanta 2000.* Atlanta: National Alliance of Business.

Dedman, Bill. 1988. *The color of money: Home mortgage lending practices discriminate against blacks.* Reprint of series in *Atlanta Journal and Constitution,* 1–4 May and 13 May 1988.

Dimond, Paul R. 1985. *Beyond busing: Inside the challenge to urban segregation.* Ann Arbor: University of Michigan Press.

Farley, Reynolds, and Robert Wilger. 1987. *Recent changes in residential segregation of blacks from whites: An analysis of 203 metropolises.* Report no. 15. Washington, D.C.: National Academy of Sciences, May.

Flint, Barbara J. 1977. Zoning and residential segregation: A social and physical history, 1910–40. Ph.D. diss., University of Chicago.

Fossett, James W. 1987. The downside of housing booms: Low-income housing in Atlanta 1970–1986. Chicago: Metropolitan Opportunity Project. Working paper no. 9. University of Chicago, October.

————, and Gary Orfield. 1987. Market failure and federal policy: Low-income housing in Chicago 1970–1983. In *Divided neighborhoods,* edited by Gary Tobin, 158–80. Newbury Park, CA: Sage Publications.

Freeney, Sabrina. 1987. Interview with author at the Atlanta Bureau of Planning, 2 July.

Garrett, Jim. 1987. Metropolitan Chicago public high schools: Race, poverty, and educational opportunity. Chicago: Metropolitan Opportunity Project. Working paper no. 5, University of Chicago, June.

Garrett, Mary Margaret, Metropolitan [North Suburban] SDA Director. 1987. Interview with author, 4 March.

Geewax, Marilyn. 1988. A laid-back aggressive business style. In *The Atlanta Journal and Constitution* reprint, *The Shaping of America,* 33–36.

Georgia Department of Education. 1987. *1986–87 Student assessment test re-sults: Summary.* June. Atlanta, GA.

——. 1988. *Student assessment program: State summary, 1987–88.* June. Atlanta, GA.

Georgia Department of Human Resources. 1987. Comprehensive adolescent health. December.

Georgia Department of Labor. 1986, 1988, and 1989. Unpublished tables of employment statistics.

Georgia Governor's Commission on Postsecondary Education. 1982. *New directions for student aid in Georgia.* Atlanta: Governor's Commission.

Georgia JTPA Program Status Summary.

Georgia Job Training Program. 1 July 1985–30 June 1986.

Glazer, Nathan. 1975. *Affirmative discrimination.* New York: Basic Books.

Gold, N. N. 1972. *Mismatch of jobs and low-income people in metropolitan areas and its implications for the central city poor: Population, distribution, and policy,* edited by S. M. Mazie. Commission Research Reports. U.S. Commission on Population Growth and the American Future. Washington: Government Printing Office.

Grissom, James B., and Lorrie A. Shepard. 1989. Repeating and dropping out of school. In Shepard and Smith 1989, 34–63.

Hadden, Susan G., et al. 1979. *Consensus in politics in Atlanta: School board decision-making, 1974–1978.* Atlanta: Southern Center for Studies in Public Policy.

Hansen, Jane O., et al. 1987. *Divided we stand: The resegregation of our public schools.* Seven-part series in *Atlanta Journal and Constitution.* 27 September–3 October 1987.

Harris, J. Jerome. 1988. Address to leadership. Speech given in Atlanta, 10 January.

Hawley, Willis D., ed. 1981. *Effective school desegregation.* Beverly Hills: Sage Publications.

Hirsch, James S., and Suzanne Alexander. 1990. Reverse exodus, middle-class blacks quit Northern cities and settle in the South. *Wall Street Journal,* 22 May.

Holmes, C. T. 1989. Grade level retention effects: A meta-analysis of research studies. In Shepard and Smith 1989, 16–33.

Hutcheson, John, Director of Center for Public and Urban Research. 1987. Interview by author at Georgia State University, 2 July.

Isherwood, Aaron. 1987. Integrating Atlanta's public schools. Unpublished senior paper, University of Chicago Political Science Department.

Jackson, Audraine. 1990. Real estate: New opportunities, old obstacles for Atlanta's blacks. *Atlanta Tribune,* 17–18 April.

Jackson, Barbara L. 1981. Urban school desegregation from a black perspective. In *Race and schooling in the city,* edited by Adam Yarmolinsky, Lance Liebman, and Corrine Schelling, 204–16. Cambridge: Harvard University Press.

Jakubs, John F. 1986. Recent racial segregation in U.S. SMSAs. *Urban Geography* 7, no. 2: 146–63.

Jaynes, Gerald David, and Robin M. Williams, eds. 1989. *A common destiny: Blacks and American society*. Washington: National Academy Press.

Joint Center for Political Studies. 1988. *Metropolitan Area Fact Book: A Statistical Portrait of Blacks and Whites in Metropolitan America*, edited by Katherine McFate. Washington, D.C.

Jonas, Edward D., Jr. 1985. *Evaluation of Project Alert (Atlantans learning employment responsibilities together)*. Atlanta: Summer Youth Employment Program. Atlanta Public Schools, October 1985, Report no. 20–1.

Kahn, Tom. 1966. The economics of equality. In *Poverty in America*, edited by Louis Ferman, Joyce Kornbluh, and Alan Haber, pp. 158–69. Ann Arbor: University of Michigan Press.

Kain, John F. 1968. Housing segregation, Negro employment, and metropolitan decentralization. *Quarterly Journal of Economics* 82, no. 2 (May): 175–97.

———. 1985. Black suburbanization in the eighties: A new beginning or a false hope? In *American domestic priorities: An economic appraisal*, edited by John M. Quigley and Daniel L. Rubin, 253–84. Berkeley: University of California Press.

———, ed. 1969. *Race and poverty: The economics of discrimination*. Englewood Cliffs, NJ: Prentice Hall.

———, and John M. Quigley. 1972. Housing market discrimination, home ownership, and savings behavior. *American Economic Review* 62: 263–77.

Kasarda, John. 1985. Urban change and minority opportunities. In *The new urban reality*, edited by Paul E. Peterson, 33–67. Washington: Brookings Institution.

———. 1987. People and jobs on the move: America's new spatial dynamics. Paper presented at the conference on America's New Economic Geography. Washington, D.C., April.

Kerner Commission. 1968. U.S. National Advisory Commission on Civil Disorders. *Report of the National Advisory Commission on Civil Disorders*. New York: Bantam Books.

King, Martin Luther, Jr. 1968. *Where do we go from here: Chaos or community?* New York: Bantam Books.

Koretz, Daniel. 1986. *Trends in educational achievement*. Washington: Congressional Budget Office.

———. 1987. *Educational achievement: Explanations and implications of recent trends*. Washington: Congressional Budget Office.

Kusmik, Gloria, DeKalb SDA Director. 1987. Interview with author, 5 March.

Levitan, Sar A., and Benjamin Johnston. 1975. *The Job Corps: A social experiment that works*. Baltimore, MD: Johns Hopkins University Press.

Lieberson, Stanley. 1980. *A piece of the pie: Black and white immigrants since 1880*. Berkeley: University of California Press.

Lightfoot, Sara Lawrence. 1983. *The good high school: Portraits of character and culture*. New York: Basic Books.

Listokin, David, and Stephen Casey. 1980. *Mortgage lending and race: Conceptual and analytical perspectives on the urban financing problem*. New Brunswick, NJ: Rutgers Center for Urban Policy Research.

McCluskey, Ed. 1987. Georgia State Department of Education, interview with author, 28 May.

McCoy, Frank. 1990. Black power in City Hall. *Black Enterprise* (August): 149–52.

McDaniel, Augustine. 1987. The effects of non-promotion on social adjustment in elementary schools. Paper presented at Annual Meeting of American Educational Research Association. Washington, D.C., April.

McKinney, Scott, and Ann B. Schnare. 1986. *Trends in residential segregation by race.* Project Report 3627. Washington: Urban Institute.

Maclachlan, Gretchen E. 1978a. First report to the National Council on Employment Policy on the implementation of the Youth Employment and Demonstration Projects Act of 1977 (YEDPA). Four Georgia Prime Sponsors. 19 January. Atlanta, GA: Southern Center for Policy Studies at Clark University.

————. 1978b. Second interim report. May.

————. 1978c. Third interim report. November.

————. 1978d. Making CETA–PSE work: A case study of public service employment under Atlanta's CETA program. Atlanta: Southern Center for Studies in Public Policy.

————. 1980. Youth and the local employment agenda Georgia case study: City of Atlanta, Cobb County, DeKalb County, and Northeast balance of state. Unpublished paper. Georgia, January.

————. 1987. Job training in Georgia: State and local perspectives. Paper delivered at the Annual Meeting of the American Political Science Association. Chicago, September.

Magnum, Garth L., and John Walsh. 1978. *A decade of manpower development and training.* Salt Lake City, UT: Olympus Publishing Co.

Mallar, Charles, et al. 1978. *Evaluation of the economic impact of the Job Corps Program: First follow-up report.* Princeton, NJ: Mathematica Policy Research, Inc.

Masotti, Louis, and J. K. Madden, eds. 1973. *The urbanization of the suburbs.* Beverly Hills, CA: Sage Publications.

Massey, Douglas S., and Nancy A. Denton. 1987. Trends in the residential segregation of blacks, Hispanics, and Asians: 1970–1980. *American Sociological Review* 52 (December): 802–25.

Metro Fair Housing Services. 1989. The Atlanta study. March. Atlanta, GA.

Montgomery, Wynn, Atlanta SDA Director. 1987a. Interview with author, 5 March.

————. 1987b. Personal letter to author, 30 June.

Mooney, Brenda. 1981. City schools win parent support. In reprint of "Black and poor in Atlanta" in *Atlanta Constitution*, 18–27 October.

Mooney, Joseph. 1969. Housing segregation, Negro employment, and metropolitan decentralization: An alternative perspective. *Quarterly Journal of Economics* 83: 299–311.

Moore, Donald R., and Suzanne Davenport. 1989. *The new improved sorting machine.* Report to National Center on Effective Secondary Schools. School of Education, University of Wisconsin-Madison. Grant # G008690007. Chicago: Designs for Change.

Murray, Charles. 1984. *Losing ground: American social policy 1950–1980*. New York: Basic Books.

National Alliance of Business. 1988. *Building a quality workforce*. Washington, D.C.: National Alliance of Business.

National Assessment of Educational Progress. 1985. *The reading report card: Progress toward excellence in our schools*. Princeton, NJ: Educational Testing Service.

Nelson, Jack. 1974. *The impact of corporate suburban relocations on minority employment opportunities*. Report to the U.S. Equal Employment Opportunities Commission. Contract # EEO–73022. Washington: Government Printing Office.

Niemi, Albert. 1974. The impact of recent Civil Rights laws *American Journal of Economics and Sociology* 33 (no. 2): 137–44.

O'Neill, Jinx. 1987. Interview with author at the Georgia State JTPA Office, 4 March.

Orfield, Gary. 1983. *Public school desegregation in the United States, 1968–1980*. Washington: Joint Center for Political Studies.

————, Howard Mitzel, et al. 1984. *The Chicago study of access and choice in higher education*. Chicago: University of Chicago Commission on Public Policy Studies.

————, and Franklin Monfort. 1988. *Racial change and desegregation in large school districts: Trends through the 1986–1987 school year*. Alexandria, VA: National School Boards Association.

————, Franklin Monfort, and Melissa Aaron. 1989. *Status of school desegregation, 1968–1986*. Alexandria, VA: National School Boards Association.

————, Franklin Monfort, and Rosemary George. 1987. *School segregation in the 1980s: Trends in the United States and metropolitan areas*. Report to the Joint Center for Political Studies, July. Washington, D.C.

————, and Faith Paul. 1988. Declines in minority access: A tale of five cities. *Educational Record* (Fall 1987–Winter 1988): 57–62.

————, Helene Slessarev, et al. 1986. *Job training under the New Federalism: JTPA in the industrial heartland*. Chicago: Unemployment and Job Training Research Project, University of Chicago.

Palen, J. John, and Bruce London. 1989. *Gentrification, displacement and neighborhood revitalization*. Albany: State University of New York Press.

Palmer, John L., and Isabel V. Sawhill, eds. 1984. *The Reagan record*. Cambridge: Ballinger Publishing Co.

Parks, Dee, Marriott Marquis Director of Human Resources. 1987. Interview with author, 26 May.

Patton, June O. 1988. Black men: Missing in higher education. Chicago: Metropolitan Opportunity Project. Working paper no. 10, University of Chicago, March.

Paul, Faith. 1987. Declining minority access to college in metropolitan Atlanta, 1975–1986. Chicago: Metropolitan Opportunity Project. Working paper no. 11, University of Chicago, March.

Pearce, Diana. 1980. *Breaking down barriers: New evidence on the impact of metropolitan desegregation on housing patterns.* Report to National Institute of Education, Washington, D.C.

Peskin, Lawrence. 1987. Attrition, enrollment shifts, and race in metropolitan Atlanta public high schools. Chicago: Metropolitan Opportunity Project. Working paper no. 7, University of Chicago, July.

————. 1988. Race, income, and metropolitan Atlanta high schools. Chicago: Metropolitan Opportunity Project. Working paper no. 15. University of Chicago.

Peterson, Paul E., ed. 1985. *The new urban reality.* Washington: Brookings Institution.

PIC Perspective. 1989. *PIC Perspective* (Private Industry Council of Atlanta, Inc., newsletter) 4, no. 2 (Spring).

Plank, David N., and Marcia Turner. 1987. Changing patterns in black school politics: Atlanta, 1872–1973. *American Journal of Education* 95 (August): 584–608.

Roistacher, Elizabeth A. R., and John L. Goodman, Jr. 1976. Race and home-ownership: Is discrimination disappearing? *Economic Inquiry* 14: 59–70.

Rosenbaum, James E. 1986. School experiences of low-income black children in white suburbs. Paper prepared for National Conference on School Desegregation Research (September). Chicago.

Rabinowitz, Howard N. 1980. *Race relations in the urban South, 1865–1890.* Urbana: University of Illinois Press.

Rubinowitz, Leonard S. 1974. *Low-income housing: Suburban strategies.* Cambridge, MA: Ballinger.

Schmidt, William E. 1987. Racial roadblock seen in Atlanta transit system. *New York Times,* 19 July.

Schnare, Ann B. 1977. *Residential segregation by race in U.S. metropolitan areas: An analysis across cities and over time.* Washington: Urban Institute, Contract no. 246–2 (February).

Schneider, Jeffrey M. 1982. Memo to Gary Orfield, 6 May. NIE approved but unfunded desegregation research. National Institute of Education.

Scofield, Janet Ward. 1988. *Review of research on school desegregation's impact on elementary and secondary school students.* Report to Connecticut State Department of Education. 8 December.

Shepard, L. A. 1989. A review of research in kindergarten retention in one school district. In Shepard and Smith 1989, 64–78.

Shepard, Lorrie, and Mary Lee Smith. 1989. *Flunking grades: Research and policies on retention.* Philadelphia: Falmer Press.

Shlay, Anne B. 1987. Credit on color—segregation, racial transition, and housing credit flows. In *Fair housing in metropolitan Chicago: Perspectives after two decades,* edited by Gary Orfield, 109–88. Chicago: Chicago Area Fair Housing Alliance.

————. 1988. JTPA as a mobility program in metropolitan Atlanta. *Evaluation Forum,* n.s. 2: 20–22.

Slessarev, Helene. 1987. *Economic growth, job training, and racial inequality in metropolitan Atlanta.* Chicago: Metropolitan Opportunity Project. Working paper no. 2, University of Chicago, July.

Smith, David M. 1985. Social aspects of urban problems: Inequality in the American city: The case of Altanta, Georgia, 1960–1980. *Geographia Polonica* 51: 65–83.

Smith, Robert C. 1990. Recent elections and black politics: The maturation or death of black politics? *PS: Political Science and Politics* 23 (June): 160–62.

Snow, Rob, Associate Director of Center for Public and Urban Research. 1987. Interview by author, 2 July. Georgia State University.

Southern Regional Education Board. 1987. *A Progress report and recommendations on educational improvements in the SREB states.* Atlanta: SREB.

———. 1989. *Georgia: Annual tuition and fee comparison to SREB medians, 1988–1989.* Atlanta: SREB.

Stone, Clarence N. 1076. *Economic growth and neighborhood discontent: System bias in the urban renewal program of Atlanta.* Chapel Hill: University of North Carolina Press.

———. 1989. *Regime politics: Governing Atlanta, 1946–1988.* Lawrence, KS: University of Kansas Press.

Struyk, Raymond J., Neil Mayer, and John A. Tucillo. 1983. *Federal housing policy at President Reagan's midterm.* Washington: Urban Institute Press.

Sweat, Dan. 1989. Speech given at the Georgia Housing Coalition in Atlanta, Georgia, on 25 January.

Taeuber, Karl. 1983. Racial residential segregation, 1980. In *Citizens' Commission on Civil Rights. A decent home,* appendix. Washington: Citizens Commission on Civil Rights.

Taeuber, Karl E., and Alma F. Taeuber. 1969. *Negroes in cities: Residential segregation and neighborhood change.* New York: Atheneum Press.

Testa, Mark, Nan Marie Astone, Marilyn Krogh, and Kathryn M. Neckerman. 1989. Employment and marriage among inner-city fathers. *Annals* 501 (January): 79–91.

Thomas, Robert H. 1984. Black suburbanization and housing quality in Atlanta. *Journal of Urban Affairs* 6, no. 1 (Winter): 17–28.

Tobin, Gary, ed. 1987. Divided neighbors. Beverly Hills: Sage Publications.

U.S. Bureau of the Census. 1981. *Statistical Abstract of the United States, 1981.* Washington, D.C.: GPO.

———. 1987. *Educational attainment in the United States: March 1982 to 1985.* Current Population Reports, Series P-20, no. 415, Washington.

———. 1988. *Money income and poverty status in the United States, 1987.* Current Population Reports, series P-60, no. 161, Washington.

U.S. Bureau of Labor Statistics. 1989. Atlanta Regional Office. Unpublished printouts of labor force, employment, and unemployment statistics for metropolitan Atlanta.

U.S. Commission on Civil Rights. 1983. *A growing crisis: Disadvantaged women and their children.* May. Washington, D.C.: GPO.

———. 1986. *Economic progress of black men in America.* Washington, D.C.: GPO.

U.S. Congressional Budget Office. 1988. *Current housing problems and possible federal responses.* December.

U.S. Congressional Research Service. 1985. *Children in poverty.* Washington: Government Printing Office.

U.S. Department of Education, Center for Education Statistics. 1988. *Trends in minority enrollment in higher education, Fall 1976–Fall 1986.* Survey Report (April).

U.S. General Accounting Office. 1982. Letter Report to Senator Jake Garn, Committee on Appropriations. No. B–206027 (8 January).

———. 1989. *Job Training Partnership Act: Services and outcomes for participants with differing needs.* GAO/HRD 89–52.

U.S. House of Representatives, Committee on Ways and Means. 1989. *Background material and data on programs within the jurisdiction of the Committee on Ways and Means.* 100th Cong., 1st sess.

University System of Georgia, Board of Regents. 1983. *The Eighties and beyond: A commitment to excellence.* February. Atlanta.

von Furstenberg, George, Ann Horowitz, and Bennett Harrison, eds. 1974. *Patterns of racial discrimination.* Lexington, MA: Lexington Books.

Waymer, Bob. 1988. *J. Jerome Harris.* Atlanta, GA: Elloree Co.

Weissman, Hank, Georgia State JTPA Director. 1986. Interview with author, 30 August.

Wienk, Ronald E., Clifford E. Reid, John C. Cimonson, and Frederick J. Eggers. 1979. *Measuring racial discrimination in American housing markets: The housing market practices survey.* Washington: U.S. Department of Housing and Urban Development.

Wisenbaker, Joseph M. 1987. *Toward establishing equitable school-level student achievement expectations: A final report.* Report to Georgia State Department of Education. Contract # 960946. 30 April.

Wilson, Franklin. 1979. *Residential consumption, economic opportunity, and race.* New York: Academic Press.

Wilson, William Julius. 1987. *The truly disadvantaged: The inner city, the underclass, and public policy.* Chicago: University of Chicago Press.

———. 1990. Race-neutral programs and the Democratic coalition. *The American Prospect* 1 (Spring): 74–81.

Woolbright, Albert. 1986. Unpublished computer printouts of housing segregation data on several metropolitan areas. University of Chicago.

Yinger, John. 1979. Prejudice and discrimination in the urban housing market. In *Current issues in urban economics,* edited by Peter Mieszkowski and Mahon Straszheim, pp. 430–68. Baltimore, MD: Johns Hopkins Press.

———. 1986. Measuring racial discrimination with Fair Housing audits: Caught in the act. *American Economic Review* 76: 881–93.

Young, Andrew, Mayor of Atlanta. 1987. Interview by author, 2 October.

Index